AF425441

Memoir Moments

Memoir Moments

From Cornfields and Carhopping
To Jackie Kennedy and the Pope

And never being Jam-Proof

Mary Kuykendall

atmosphere press

© 2023 Mary Kuykendall

Published by Atmosphere Press

Cover design by Kevin Stone

No part of this book may be reproduced without permission from the author except in brief quotations and in reviews.

Atmospherepress.com

Table of Contents

Jim Tot

There were probably twenty of us, ages ten through fifteen, working for old man Jim Tot. He ran Mr. James Stump's sugar corn packing operation along the South Branch of the Potomac River in the Eastern Panhandle of West Virginia. In his eighties, he had been retired from the harder field work to keep us in line. A warning sign that we were not doing the job the way he wanted it done would come when the short and stout, feisty old Scotsman stroked his handlebar mustache. Most of us were girls, along with the younger boys, working under his watchful eye. Our older brothers were sent to the fields to learn how to work with the men pulling ears of corn by hand. They would toss them into long, narrow sleds pulled through the narrow cornrows by mules.

The sound of an approaching sled meant we had about five minutes to bag up the corn pile we were working on before the pickers dumped another load for us to bag. We played a game of trying to get all the corn bagged before another sled got there. If so, Jim Tot let us take a quick dip in the river which was just a ballfield run away from our packing site under the sycamore trees. As usual, when we lost, Jim Tot would egg us on. "We'll beat de next one in, see de pile is smaller den de last one ye wuz workin' on when dey came in." If we complained, he would tell us we had it better than our older brothers and the men. "Dey's out dere in de hot sun with no chance fer a break whilst ye young'uns are unda des nice trees thinkin' 'bout swimmin'."

Then he would explain sugar corn didn't wait on anybody to ripen; that it was important to get it to market as fast as you could and as early in the season as you could. "Dere's a bunch of kids south of here dat started baggin' corn two weeks early den ye young'uns," he would add. "But de price is still good dis early in de season. Ye kin rest more when we pick de fields over de third time; then it takes longer to git and de price hain't so good. We does a good job now and Mr. James, he become mighty relaxed."

I can still hear Jim Tot laugh when we heard the approaching men telling the younger ones how to pick corn—he knew they were repeating his talk to them when we started at sunup: "Look at the corn tassels. See if they are dry. Make sure the hair coming out of the ear has turned brown. Snap the ear straight down. It won't pull right from the side. If you see worms, leave it for the hog corn pickers."

My older cousin in the field would tell me later that they mostly yelled those instructions when they knew that Jim Tot could hear. They wanted this venerable old man's approval just as we did. Occasionally, when he was still the picking leader, they would pretend to do something wrong just to see him signal his ire by stroking his bushy mustache. At our noontime lunch, he kept it healthy and sturdy by buttering it up to eat corn. He told us it was more sanitary than using our hands and more efficient in spreading the butter. Our parents, upon hearing this, were glad we were not old enough to grow beards. They merely winced when we proclaimed that he never spit out loose hairs as he twirled the cob through his buttered mustache.

Lunchtime, of course, was looked forward to constantly as a time to eat, rest, and hear stories from Jim Tot. He would take out his pocket watch with the long silver chain twisted around his suspenders to announce the time. In fact, at the end of the day, trucks of all sizes would come lumbering down the mountainside road and through the fields to pick up the corn.

Mr. James not only rounded up farmers' kids and paid us $1 a day to bag corn, but he also paid our parents to rent their cattle or pulpwood trucks when the corn came on. We would cheer when we saw the trucks coming because it would be a sure chance to cool off and rest. To keep the corn cool on the way to area markets as well as three-hour trips to Pittsburgh and Washington, the men would scatter ice chunks among the burlap bags full of corn, with a layer on the top of the load.

It was when we sat down to eat our peanut butter and jelly sandwiches at noon and get an ear of corn from the pot Jim Tot had boiling that he would tell us about the old days. On a particularly hot day, he would repeat how they used to saw the ice out of the river in the winter in a heavily insulated shed by the river. The ice was buried deep in a pit of sawdust. More than half of it would survive until corn-picking season. When the Rural Electrification Act brought in electricity in the 40s, Mr. James began buying huge ice blocks from the new icehouse in town. But it—like the river ice had been—was still buried in sawdust for daily use. When the ice shed was opened, we were allowed to run in for a quick romp in the damp sawdust as the men dug out the blocks for chipping.

The men would use sledgehammers to break the blocks, aiming for the white streaks caused by air pockets. This would produce quicker, cleaner breaks with fewer fast-melting chips. Then we would hang around and watch them load the trucks and pack the ice around the burlap bags we had filled that morning. By following the trucks over the bumpy field road to the county road, we usually managed to get bits and pieces of ice as they fell through canvas openings or the truck rails. Jim Tot thought this was a better use of our energy than swimming, particularly when the ice was passed around for everyone. Mostly, the ice chips were used to soothe sunburns or gnat bites.

Years ago, Jim Tot had proposed the idea to Mr. James that we should store the unused burlap bags over the ice for further meltdown protection. Jim Tot had made hauling the bags in and out—and always having a jug of tea inside for storage—

part of our jobs. Then with chilled tea and cool burlaps to sit on, we would open our brown paper lunch bags and pull out apples and mostly peanut butter and jelly sandwiches. We had thirty minutes to eat and hear Jim Tot tell stories.

Everyone wanted to hear about the old boss man who owned all these fields, Mr. James A. Stump. None of us had been inside his big four-story brick house near town except for Jim Tot. He would tell us how Mr. James still had his daddy's confederate rifle over the fireplace mantel—the very one that his paw had used to try to keep the Yankees from stealing his horses and hay—and how Mr. James A. had been shot right off that haystack by them Yanks with the missus running out of the house to him and little Mr. James going right ahead of her. Mr. James did what his paw told him as he lay dying; he hid the gun in the spring house. His daddy was still cursing the Yanks while his ma tried to help him at the bottom of the stack. But little Mr. James did what his paw said, declared Jim Tot. He had hidden the rifle. The Yanks got the hay but they didn't find no gun.

Then Jim Tot would end by telling us slaves used to work pulling sugar corn in these same fields just as we were doing now...they called these lower fields "sugar bottom" and that was why he called sweet corn, sugar corn. Then he would tell us that we had it much better than slave children because we could not be sold and that our hard work could mean a better future.

Jim Tot really had our attention when he told us that when he was our age, he was putting in the railroad across the river. He had ridden the ties down the seven-mile mountain gorge of the South Branch of the Potomac River in high white water to get them to their positions for laying tracks. He had seen the railroad come and recently go in his eighty-eight years. He reckoned it was "whut dey call progress."

We knew we were in for a long explanation when he opened his tobacco pouch. He explained how railroads replaced horses and the C&O Canal, and how trucks replaced our railroad because they were faster and cheaper in getting produce directly to the markets. But he was quick to add he didn't agree with such progress. He would point to the mountains surrounding us and tell us how all those people could no longer go down to a train stop to sell their produce or even get a ride to town. "Dey movin' to town to make a livin' and it hain't much of one," he would conclude.

Then he would talk about how he had heard those big corporate farms in California could get three crops a year and how hard it was getting for the small farmer to compete with one growing season. "Dat new Jolly Green Giant dey got now hain't so amusin'," he would laugh. He did agree with Mr. James that trucks were better than the train since the faster corn got to the market, the better it was because heat not only made it hard but it lost its taste. "Dat's also why we ice it. Only thing wurse den two-day old sugar corn is week-old collards," he would declare as he chewed his plug and spit out tobacco juice. Then he would tell us how riding the ties over rough rapids could flatten you just like the train used to smash the Indian head on our pennies.

All too soon, the men would be back in the fields after prodding the mules away from the grassy bank along the river. As they went, my cousin would laugh as he and the others heard Jim Tot give us a running lecture on what to do: "Ye kids, don't ye forgit to feel fer dem worms...ye kin feel 'em with yer hands...no shuckin' it back...hit will rot...ye kin feel it if de ear is full...I wunt nothin' but good eatin' corn in des bags...dee rest ye throw over dere in dat pile...dat's fo hogs and lazy kids...an' one last thing afore ye start fillin' des bags...remember dat de harder and faster ye fill up des bags, de better de chance ye'll have to take a quick run in de river. Dos mules are getting' tired out dere...de sun's way high and it gonna git over a 100. Some of 'em are gonna get stubborn nough dey'll be hard to coax. So quit yer complainin' dat dere are too many men and mules and sleds. Ye can beat 'em. But ye got to be smart."

Then we would start on the count of one with no talking because he didn't want us to lose track of how many ears were going in the bags. Jim Tot and the other old men too old for the fields would hold the burlap bags up. One of us on each side would bend over and pick up four ears of corn and place them in the bag until the count of fifteen had been reached. This endless procedure resulted in hundreds of burlap bags of five-dozen ears each ready for market.

At the end of the day, the field boss would jostle with Jim Tot and ask him, "Are you getting them young'uns ready for real work in the field?" and Jim Tot would rub his huge white mustache and tobacco-stained whiskers and retort: "If ye all get any slower out dere, we're gonna start usin' de ice for a tea party here. Howse bout sendin' some corn in without de worms? I got nough bait here for de whole county to go fishin'." Then he would grin as he pointed to the discard pile.

Jim Tot was always ready with a feisty answer. The men said this was because he grew up with just coon dogs to bark orders to. He was known throughout the eastern panhandle for his skill at training beagles to hunt coons. Some said that was because the dogs associated with him. Word had it that he used a lot of the discarded corn to make moonshine. When that happened, some said he would get down on all fours like a dog and have them follow the scent he had planted. He was known to find a coon in a tree before his dogs did. He would bark at the base of the tree to complete his dog training, setting off a howl from the dogs you could hear for miles. Those who bought coon dogs from him said those beagles never forgot Jim Tot. If they got near his place, they made a run for it; they loved the old man, and that was why they always obeyed him.

Perhaps that was why we kids never disobeyed him either. If he saw we were underperforming for the other old men holding bags, he would move us over to fill his bag and invariably stroke his mustache. The instructions would be repeated and attitudes quickly corrected if the ears were thrown in haphazardly.

One day he noticed that my younger cousin, Jack, had a clever way of not being the first one to place four ears of corn in the bag. He would choose girl partners and proclaim, "Ladies before gentlemen." This resulted in Jack having one less bend per bag because it took just fifteen handfuls to make five dozen.

After partnering him up with another boy, Jim Tot watched to see what he would do and smiled when Jack would say, "Go 'head, you're younger," or "Old folks first." After that, Jack was told he was so polite he was giving him the honor of always being first to fill the corn bag.

Mr. James had thought it was funny but agreed with Jim Tot that Jack's parents ought to know about it so they could watch out for such tricky behavior—or as Jim Tot explained: "While Jack sure didn't fall off no turnip truck, it's best he not grows up and becomes one of dem robber barons."

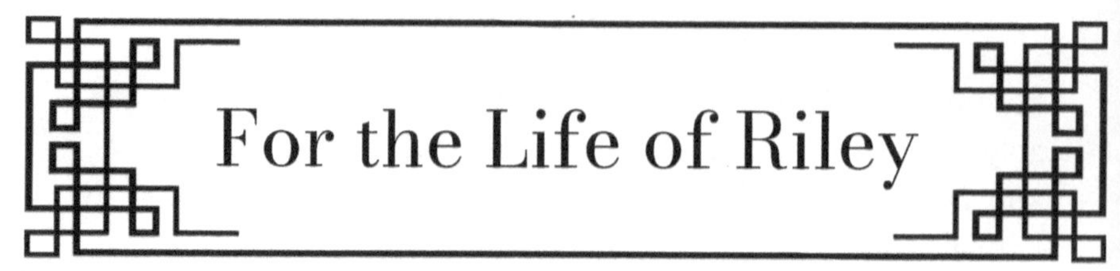

For the Life of Riley

A growing population, cultural changes, and access to disinformation on social media have certainly given educators today a major headache. I often look back on my early education and wonder if Mr. Riley would be able to cope with today's challenges.

I started out in a one-room school in the late 40s which became a two-room school in the 50s. This rural school covered first to eighth grade before we were bussed to a high school in town.

Fortunately for us, we had a teacher, Mr. Riley, who was able to deal with problems of the day back then—a lack of funding for schools.

New desks seldom had to be purchased because we had the wooden ones with cast iron legs that could be adjusted for a student's height. Some of them were double wide so if there were more new students coming in versus those going on to high school, we were teamed up to use the double-wide desks. I shared a desk with my cousin for four years.

He would combine eight grades into five or six judging on how he felt his students performed. Some jumped a grade and others stayed where they were. He also strategically placed students of each grade who needed help closer to the head of the classroom. There they could benefit by listening in on the class he had up front.

Often he would send a brighter student into the cloakroom with a younger student needing help—particularly if that bright student was bored and not behaving. His only help came once a month when the county sent out a writing instructor and health officer. Today, all of us have legible handwriting thanks to the county instructor who taught us the

Palmer script. The health officer dutifully filled out her opinions of our health which appeared on the back of our blue report cards. My mother saved those and often reminded me that I had been rated unsatisfactory for four of my eight years in grade school for not using my handkerchief. The only complaint our parents had about our school system back then was the time the county health officer dealt with a lice problem by cutting all our hair off. She protested it was the only thing she could do to prevent a bigger outbreak since she was there just once a month.

One would think that with so many students in one room, Mr. Riley would have had a discipline problem. But he had an answer for that. In the back of the classroom, he would place his largest student with the reward of not having to do chores if he kept everyone quiet.

There were plenty of chores. The dust tracked in from the dirt road was kept down by sprinkling water on the floors during recess. Heat in the winter was provided by a Morning Glory stove which burned coal. Those students who did not do their homework were assigned to bring in buckets of coal from a bin near the outdoor john.

Other assignments included bringing in water from the well to fill the water jug. We brought packed lunches to school, but Mr. Riley made sure we got a good meal by using some of the water to make vegetable soup on top of the Morning Glory stove. When homework was ignored more than once, keeping the outdoor john clean soon cured most slackers of this duty.

With all these chores, one might think we had no time for playing games at recess. Softball was our favorite game. We had a two-by-two-inch board for a bat with one end carved to fit our hands. Our bases were flat rocks. The river was far enough away that we never had to retrieve a ball from it. However, a good hit would have all of us searching for the ball in the bushes lining the river.

"Handy-Over" was also a popular recess activity that involved throwing a ball over the school roof. The goal was to catch the ball and get to the other side of the building without being tagged. Tagged people were eliminated. I still remember the punishment Roscoe Dean—who went on to become a football coach—and I got for the longest tagging time anyone could remember. He was short and fast and I was tall. When he came around the school corner after me, I ran down the valley trying to avoid being tagged. About the time he would catch up to me, I would head for a drainage ditch in a farmer's field that was too wide for him to jump across. We went several miles before he finally tagged me. We missed three class periods by the time we got back. For the next month, our assignment was to bring in the coal. When we came in blackened from a fight in the coal bin, another month was added.

We also had an outdoor john. At the beginning of the school year, everyone was needed to dig a huge hole. Our parents had even made sure the john they built for us had long handles on it. We not only dug a new hole when needed, but we were able to line up and carry the john to the new hole.

Because we ranged from first- to eighth-grade size, Mr. Riley placed a Coca-Cola box and apple crate in the john for the shorter students to stand on. And yes, those Montgomery and Sears catalogs came in handy.

Some of us who lived farther away rode our bikes to school while others walked. Mr. Riley was tolerant of us clattering in with motorcycle-style noise created by attaching cards to the spokes. We learned to share our bikes with those who didn't have them. If we didn't, added chores were assigned.

One of the students had a pet deer that followed him to school. The deer shied away from all of us at recess. But when it was rutting season, this became a problem getting to the john alone, so Mr. Riley rewarded the larger boys with "no chores" if they accompanied those of us who were chased by the deer.

Obviously, education has come a long way today in providing proper facilities. However, looking back, I wonder what Mr. Riley would have done to solve today's problems. I do know one thing he would do I heard about recently. A fourth-grade teacher I know, Danny, was having a problem with a bully kid who threatened to have his parents sue Danny if he touched the kid. So Danny lifted him in his chair and took him to the principal's office. In the process, the kid lost his bullying power because the rest of the class laughed.

Goodbye Dolly

I poured myself an eggnog on Christmas day, sat down at the computer, and told myself to go back to the first Christmas I remembered.

It was a quick memory search. I could still vividly see a hoe with a big red bow being handed to me. I can laugh now—and even be grateful for what it meant—but it was no laughing matter for my mother at the time.

She had spent a lot of time redressing my sister Edith's doll in a pinafore just like the one she had made for me. When my father went to the Southern States feed store to buy cottonseed which he spread over silage to add what he declared was probably a pound a day on cattle he was fattening for the market, my mother went with him to pick out the cotton bags the seed came in. The sturdy muslin bags came in all colors and in many different patterns. I liked the many-colored polka dots which seemed to jump out of the white muslin. I was wearing one of my pinafores made of this when I opened Santa's present.

But it was not the polka dot pinafore that got my attention. It was recognizing the doll that Edith had gotten new the year before. She was now holding another new doll and lost no time in needling me that maybe I could have it next year. We were just two years apart and it was bad enough that she was bigger. I had just started the second grade and she seemed to take delight in handing down her schoolbooks, telling me to study what she had underlined if I wanted to be as smart as her. So when I saw it was her doll and heard her condescending laugh, I threw it against the wall, breaking its porcelain face into pieces.

While my mother was picking up the pieces, I could hear the door to the basement below slam as my father left. My older sister, Decker, who was eight years older, had quickly outgrown dolls when she discovered she loved math in the first grade. She had immersed herself in a book of puzzles Santa had bought her. But she never failed to defend me. When my mother, tearful but determined that I should be punished, said that I would be spending the rest of the day in my room, Decker protested, pointing out I had overreacted to Edith's putdown and that we both should apologize.

About this time my father came back with the hoe, picked up the ribbon from the box, and tied it on the hoe handle. "If you don't like being a little girl, I have something for you to do in the fields." From then on, I became not only an outdoor kid with chores, but one that was soon working the field and, to his delight, loving every minute of it. I preferred it to washing dishes and scrubbing the floors like my sisters were doing. I was assigned a ten-acre cornfield and kept it clean of weeds for at least eight summers before I was old enough to work with other kids in the produce fields. Sweet corn, bird's eye beans, tomatoes, melons, and other perishable crops thrived in the rich, fertile soil of the South Branch of the Potomac River valley. Such crops had to be picked fast which meant we had to have the stamina to work from sunup to sundown to get them ready to be trucked to markets.

Today, I am grateful for that memorable gift. I became an outdoor kid and escaped household chores. I loved outdoing my father's expectations. If he said it would take me a week to get all the weeds out of fifty rows, I did it in five days. Then he would dare me that I could not do it in less than five and I would get up at sunup and do it in four. I grew up taking up his dares to the point of being ridiculous. We were taught never to leave anything on our plates and to eat everything. When he noticed I avoided beets, he put them on my plate and dared me to eat them. By this time, I was on to him and returned his dares. In this case, we had seen a dead chicken covered by white maggots when we came in from the field. We were also having rice, which reminded me of the maggots. I dared him to eat a bowl of rice while we watched the maggots devour the chicken. He did it and invited me to join him, which I did, much to my mother's disgust.

Needless to say, my mother had given up on me after the doll demolition. I had become the farmhand my father wanted. Decker had my father's attention at night working on math problems and I had his attention during the day. While my father grew up when the only school you could walk to was a county grade school, he was amazing at math. When the A&P grocery came to town, people would follow him in to see him add the totals up quicker than the cash registers they had, no matter how full the carts were. I can still see him those early years when he and Decker worked out her math assignments by the kerosene lamp. Even when she went to college and graduated cum laude in physics and chemistry, he kept up with her studies when she came home on weekends.

So my mother devoted herself to Edith. She saved her egg and butter money to buy her piano and dance lessons. My mother's ancestors had been well-off before the civil war and, while she deplored slavery, she also knew that their wealth had largely been a result of it. Her lessons in culture resulted in my middle sister marrying very well to the point where she never had to work and could devote herself to social events. She also considered herself a culinary expert.

Our differences became quite apparent during a threshing season one summer when ten men were staying in the barn. In those days before combines, this crew came with a threshing machine to make the rounds of all the farms to thresh grains, primarily wheat. They would be housed by each farmer, staying with them until every shock of grains had been threshed. The farmer's wives would go to great lengths to pack lunches for them to take to the fields after a good breakfast. It was the evening meal that most farmers' wives concentrated on to make sure it was hearty.

When the doctor declared our mother was too sick to get out of bed on the last day they were there, it was up to Edith and me to get the last evening meal because Decker was away at college. Edith promptly ordered me to make what my mother always made and said she would make a special salad which she was sure would be a special treat. Since I would rather peel a bushel of potatoes to mash by myself than put up with her snide comments, I did not object. I also fried steaks for everyone, opened five cans of green beans and corn, and used the juice from the steak to make gravy. Each end of the table had a huge bowl of green beans, corn, mashed potatoes, gravy bowls, and a platter of steaks. My father had come up with this arrangement, noting that time should not be wasted passing food.

The men were just coming in from the field when Edith started arranging her special salad. It consisted of a ring of pineapple nested on a huge lettuce leaf with a banana stuck end-up in the hole of the pineapple ring. On top of the banana was a cherry. She announced it was a candlestick salad.

It was then the difference between myself and Edith became quite apparent to all. When I noticed that the men were wolfing down the basics, I saw they were avoiding the candlestick salad. Normally we would eat after the men left, but I pulled up a chair and helped myself to the salad by popping the cherry in my mouth and then grabbing the banana and eating it monkey-style. The men, including my father, followed my example.

Edith left the room and told my ill mother that she did not think I could ever be civilized. My father helped with the dishes when the men left. He said he was really glad that I had turned out not to be such a doll baby.

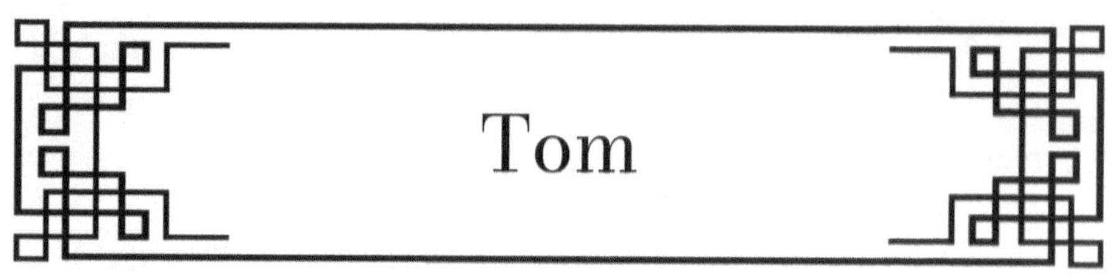

Tom

On my ninth birthday, I heard my mother yell for me to come to the kitchen window. She had been watching for my father to come down the road from the upper farm. He was late for supper. But this time it was not the irritation of having to warm up the food—it was her disgust when she saw a car had stopped long enough to throw out a cat.

Even though this was not unusual, she never failed to deplore the riffraff who would do this.

I was ordered out the door to get the animal so she could call the game warden and have it euthanized. Mercy killing, she called it, denouncing the driver for having no mercy. Sometimes the cats I gathered up were declawed—resulting in her condemning the ignorance of those who must not know or care that a declawed cat had no chance of surviving on its own. It would make her even madder when I returned with a female cat with sore nipples, often thin and wretched in spirit as well as nursing condition. My mother would calm down enough to hope the kittens had been given to someone who would care for them.

Her orders to retrieve the cat this time included the usual question she always answered herself. "Why do they always seem to throw the animals out at the deer crossing sign?" Then she would wonder if they actually thought people were stupid enough to think they were stopping for a deer crossing and not throwing out an animal.

By this time, I was on my way, running up the road to retrieve the cat. The reason I remember this particular birthday was because I met Tom. He was different from all the other black cats I had collected. My father had agreed we would keep them because they earned their keep by ridding the barn and granary of mice, rats, and even snakes.

This cat was half-grown and solid black except for his tail, which was solid white. His green eyes studied me with interest—not wariness or fear or anguish. His rib cage was protruding from his muddy, matted hair. He let me pick him up but he kept his eyes directly on me.

I could see that he was not castrated. I knew my mother would immediately send him to the game warden to have him euthanized. Because most people were economically challenged, she seldom chastised people for not neutering. She saved her ire for those that had spent the money having their cats declawed but not neutered.

I smoothed out the tangled hair on the young tom. I was trying to figure out how to get it into my barn collection. My father would get rid of all the tomcats when my cat collection grew to the point of vastly outnumbering their prey. I had also noticed that baby males born seemed to mysteriously disappear. My mother had assigned this "bag and river" duty to my father. She handled the road drop-offs of dogs as well as cats to the game warden.

As I was bonding with the green-eyed tom with the white tail next to the deer-crossing sign, my late-for-supper father came along in his truck. He stopped to pick me up. He, too, was intrigued by the white tail. Young Tom turned his green eyes on my father as we got into the truck to go to supper. He was purring loudly on my lap. When my father turned into the barnyard instead of parking in front of the house, I knew young Tom was going to become a barn cat—and that nothing would be said to my mother, now warming up supper, about his reproductive capabilities.

"Let's name him Tom because that is what his job will be," my father said. Pointing to the pure-bred Angus bull in the barnyard, he added, "He's going to be as busy as our bull has been. We'll see if he does as well in having offspring that looks like him."

He went on to explain that we could produce a breed of cats that were all black with white tips on their tails like Tom had. He told me I was old enough now to know that about selective breeding—that the offspring of those who did not have white tails would have to be shown painless mercy in the river.

"In five years or so, you should be an A student in genetics—and be the only one I know who has a barn full of black cats with white tails," he declared. Then he laughed to himself, adding that "with all that inbreeding they would become English aristocrats. Let's hope that unlike British royalty, they will still have the ability to earn their own keep."

The experiment worked. When I was fourteen, I had fully established myself as having something no one else had. I had been shunned by the other valley kids for being too tall and awkward for my age. It was pointed out to me there was no mistake I was his daughter if you looked at my foot size and height.

Tom's prowess as a tomcat to be contended with and admired had given me status. Moreover, Tom had not confined himself to our barnyard. His markings in the offspring of other cats up and down the valley did not go unnoticed. I was the proud owner of Tom.

But most of all I had a companion like no other. Tom not only reigned in the barn but also gave me his full attention. From that first meal of pot roast beef I sneaked out of the house to fill out his rib cage with, I was hooked just enjoying his pleasure as he ate whatever treat I had for him. He never failed to keep a green eye on me as he expressed his satisfaction with great purring.

Before school and after school, I looked in on Tom at the barn. He seemed to be asleep a lot in the mornings. My father, who had marveled at how few neighbors had actually seen Tom in their barns, said Tom was also a night prowler so I should not be surprised that he slept so much.

Then there were those times when Tom would disappear for two or three days, which really worried me. One day I decided to follow him to see where he went. We were probably over a mile back in the mountains when he spotted me. But I was totally lost and it had become dark. A search party had been formed and was about to head out again in the morning when I came out by the stream near our house with Tom. I had known to follow a stream out. To this day we still don't know what business he had back into the mountains. But he was good company that night and I was not afraid.

Today, as I look at the pictures I took with my Brownie box camera during my growing-up years, I have to laugh at how many there are of Tom. At least thirty pictures of Tom with his latest look-alikes in the barn, Tom eating, Tom sleeping, Tom on the porch swing, Tom waiting for his shot of milk when my father was milking the cow, Tom observing the Angus cattle, Tom looking out of the hay mow, Tom sitting on the tractor, and my favorite, Tom sitting in a snow throne chair I had built for him with a paper crown on his head. I even had one of Tom with a copper snake he had partially killed. He deposited it on our front porch, an act that caused my mother, who had started allowing me to bring him inside to play, to immediately rescind that grant.

We estimated Tom was about sixteen when he died, a long life for a cat. He had many scars from battles with other male cats in the valley trying to protect their domains. He had lost all but a few hairs on his head. It was badly scarred and scabby. My father said it was cancer because no matter how much we doused his head with sulfur, the running sores remained. My mother finally allowed him into the basement when he became too weak to gather food. He had lost his teeth. One of the saddest things I ever saw was the look in his green eyes when he caught a mouse and could not eat it. The mouse, no worse for the bath he got in Tom's mouth, simply jumped out at the first opportunity.

Tom had sired three generations of black look-alikes with white tails. One of his perfect sons was allowed to live and took over the job. When I went off to high school, my father stopped the successful genetics experiment, explaining it should not go on any longer. Such constant inbreeding and incest would result in physical as well as mental retardation. We often exchanged bulls to ensure our pure-bred line was healthy.

Today, I have to smile when I visit our valley and spot some black cats with white tails. Of course, I always stop by a stone marker under a pear tree near the barn for Tom. His name is carved on it along with a cutout of a white tail.

Being Sent to the Yardstick Library

When we had our 50th high school reunion, it was the first reunion for many of us who had left the area right after graduation, heading for college or jobs not available in the rural area.

Fortunately, everyone was issued a name tag. Too many years had gone by to depend on old yearbook pictures to recall classmates. But there was one person all of us remember as having the greatest impact on our lives and careers in later years.

That was the school librarian whom we fondly called "Old Yardstick."

She got that name because of the way she wielded the yardstick when we arrived at the library for one hour each day.

Back in those days, our high school was the only one in the county. Kids from the farthermost points spent three hours of their day on the bus getting to and from school. The school became so crowded in the 50s with baby boomers that work experience programs were introduced to relieve the congestion. The program involved students spending a couple of hours each school day working at shops, garages, and restaurants within walking distance of the school. Overcrowded classes were also relieved by requiring each student to go to the school library.

The school library was the largest single room in the main building. It was above the gymnasium. It was also well-stocked with books thanks to the town's smartest and richest man dying and leaving his collection to the school.

Six rows of stacks consumed half the area and were easily accessible from the six rows of tables at the other end. It was there that Old Yardstick ruled.

The grey-haired librarian always wore the same pleated skirt with a neatly ironed, fresh blouse each day. Wiry and wrinkled, she often came at you bent over, waving her yardstick back and forth. We judged she was only two feet taller than her three-foot yardstick. She moved fast and deliberately in her sturdy Oxford saddle shoes—always seeming to aim her yardstick at us. Yet no one could remember ever being hit by it.

When we filed in for study hall, she would use the yardstick to point to the seat we were to occupy at one of the tables. It only took her a day or two to separate troublemakers who tried to sit together. If we did not sit up straight or move fast enough for her, she would poke us with her yardstick. She would walk up and down the rows of tables, checking to see if we were studying. If a page was not turned enough to her satisfaction, she would use the edge of the yardstick to turn it for us.

It only took her about a week to find out from the teachers which of us were good students and which needed help. Jimmie, a senior, was accomplished in algebra and geometry. He was immediately prodded to the head of a table where he was told to pretend to be a teacher and help the younger students she seated there. She called all of the students except those at the head of the tables "knuckleheads."

Today Jimmie credits Old Yardstick for his not only getting through college in just three and a half years but also for his becoming a professor. He explained that math had become boring in class but Old Yardstick forced him to learn more by keeping a step ahead of some of the better knuckleheads.

Old Yardstick had labels for other subjects on her tables. Sally remembered being picked to head a table for those who needed help in history. Fred headed the table for English. Ann's interest in biology was soon discovered by Old Yardstick and

Johnny was known for always getting an A on geography tests.

The library became nearly as active as the gymnasium below us. Not only did it become a hub of learning, but it also served as a discipline center. Students acting up in class were no longer sent to the principal's office. When teachers found out how well their librarian was doing with their students, they were sent there.

Old Yardstick greeted them as she did the others with one exception. First, she dealt out punishment by having them sweep the library floors, empty the pencil sharpeners, and clean out wastebaskets. Their next job would be to go to the stacks and find books for those lined up in chairs along the walls who claimed they had finished their studying. Old Yardstick would ask them what interested them and the book covering that subject would be retrieved. Students soon learned not to make wisecracks answering her questions.

Sam remembered that once he told her he was interested in "everything." Old Yardstick had the kid that had acted up retrieve the Encyclopedia for him. A response of "nothing" resulted in that person joining the cleaning crew.

When the punishment chores were completed, Old Yardstick would ask what class they came from and then seat them at the appropriate table with all the other knuckleheads.

Harry noted that Old Yardstick was still there ruling the library in the early 70s. He recalled that to this day his younger brother remembered, after his cleaning chores, how he had loudly declared he was interested in "girls." He said his brother still had the newspaper Old Yardstick gave him announcing the discovery of Lucy, the hominid who lived over 3 million years ago and whose bones were found in Ethiopia. Harry added to our laughter when he noted his brother was now an orthopedic surgeon.

We chastised ourselves for maybe still being knuckleheads because we could not remember Old Yardstick's real name. One of the locals knew that she had died in the 1980s.

In our now-fond remembrance of Old Yardstick, our class of sixty decided it was time we show our appreciation to her for making a difference in our lives. We would form an "Old Yardstick Grant" to be awarded to the graduating student who measured up after being a knucklehead. Even if we did find out her real name, we figured she would not mind how we remembered her.

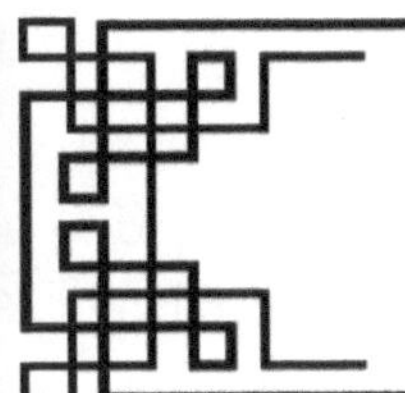
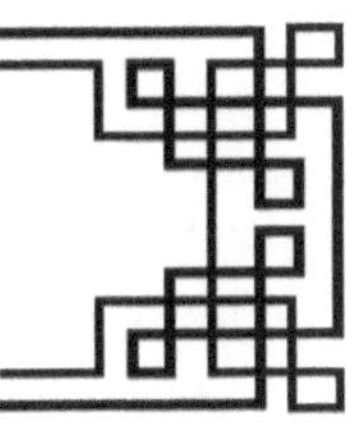

Peggy Sue

The job as a carhop at the fast food business seemed simple enough. I liked to roller skate. My concern was handling the money, but the owner told me that was why I would be wearing a money belt. Just click the metal lever on each attached cylinder to dispense pennies, nickels, dimes, and quarters, he said.

I was excited. It was a popular drive-in, not far from the state capitol building in Charleston. It had its own record-playing station and about 100 parking spots. The owner went over some of the rules with me. Some people, given the chance, would drive off without paying for their food. I was to get the money as soon as the food was delivered. It would also increase business because the driver could drive away and free up that space for another car. If change for a bill over $20 was required, not to worry said the owner, those customers would wait for their change.

When I took this summer job, I was in my freshman year in college. I had been anxious to get what was considered a real job—one dealing with the public. Since I was ten, I held summer jobs working on produce farms and orchards. This job meant I could live with my older sister in Charleston, West Virginia. I heard skating waitresses could make up to $100 a week in tips. The most I had ever made at the orchard was $45 a week which, at the time, I thought was great because it was $20 more than I made packing sweet corn. I would also be only working eight-hour days instead of twelve. My sister was excited because she felt between what she could loan me and what I made in tips would be enough to pay the tuition and room and board at the university that fall.

But I was most excited about wearing the sleek black and white uniform with flared cowboy-style pants and a fringed jacket. The matching hat had a logo of a Scottie dog on it with the name "Hodo's." The owner had named his business after his family dog.

Hodo's biggest competitor was a growing southern fast-food drive-in chain called Shoney's. Their cheerleader-style uniforms were bright red and, as the Hodo owner said, they not only looked like little girls but they acted like it in those silly getups. Their necklaces of pom-poms were constantly getting in their way when they were trying to skate with loaded trays. Our Hodo's western outfits included beaded string ties which were adjusted with a turquoise stone pendant. A cowhide leather belt featured a large, oval brass buckle that held in place the metal five-coin slot exchanger.

The boulevard along the state capitol in West Virginia was a busy place. As soon as you left the capitol building—built in 1865 and modeled after the national one—you immediately passed fashionable department stores and shopping plazas. Hodo's and Shoney's were tucked in between these buildings, some of which were ten stories high, but none overshadowed the capitol building with its glorious walkways and gardens along the Kanawha River.

I was one of ten carhop girls on the third shift. Hodo's was open twenty-four hours and I began at midnight. Fortunately, the owner had designed the shifts so that the carhops could use buses to get to work. I would not have to bother my sister for rides to and from work. I got off work at 8 a.m. and found the buses bringing state and businesspeople to work were pretty much empty going back to the outer city. My sister lived above a garage to save money so she could pay back her college bill. She had a good job at Union Carbide. I was assigned to the back lot "because I was such a good skater," but I soon realized that all newcomers had to work their way up to the front lots where the tips were better.

I had enough experience from working in produce fields not to mind some of the comments I received from hormone-driven rowdies who frequented the back rows. I quickly learned from the other girls to refer them to the Shoney's cheerleaders down the boulevard. It took me longer to realize that very few of the carhops were college-bound and that most, in fact, were young unwed mothers struggling to pay the bills at home.

I was also shocked into reality one day when I was filling in for another girl at the front lot. These reserved spaces were frequented by many state senators and businessmen looking for a quick snack. I had just taken the order for a Hodo's milkshake when I recognized the state senator from my hometown. I was in high school with his daughter and was just about to say so when he asked where Ellie Mae was. He said that she had not shown up at his place after work, that she left a message saying she was sick—and that she owed him $20, and would I tell her that she had better show up the next night if she wanted to keep her "job"?

I had heard that some of the carhops had "special customers." I also knew that Ellie Mae had three small children to take care of and, in fact, was not sick but had to take one of them to the emergency room. The Hodo's manager had no problem firing the girls and if a customer reported bad service, it didn't take him long to do it. The manager only paid $1 a shift, well aware we could make ten times that much in tips, even in the back lot.

As a result of my concern for Ellie Mae, I could not allow myself to tell the senator off or even let him know I knew who he was. I did feel some satisfaction in the way I gave him back his change from the $5 bill he gave me for the 50-cent milkshake. Rather than return bills, I used my change dispenser and scattered $4.50 in nickels, dimes, and quarters across his serving tray, making it hard for him to pick them up. He laughed and left most of it, telling me that I was smarter than Ellie Mae, he could do a lot for me if I was interested, and he had lots of $20 bills. He even opened his wallet to riffle through $50 bills.

Containing my disgust, I said, "No thanks." I told him I would pass the tips on to Ellie Mae. I so wanted to let him know I knew who he was and even add that my family knew his family back home. But I decided I would discuss this with Ellie Mae—it might be useful information for her in her negotiations.

I had a favorite customer in the back lot who required favors I could easily extend. It was a lady driving a white DeSoto. She came in around 1 a.m. and asked for a Seven-Up setup and three records to be played by the disk jockey at the record player station on the lot. Each customer was to only get one song request and it had to be with an order over $2. The Seven-Up was just 15 cents. I knew that ordering a 7-7 in West Virginia was code for "I have the Seagrams, can you supply the Seven-Up?" Her tip was $10. I shared it with the disk jockey and everyone was happy. The lady enjoyed her nightcap and she never had to wait for fast service or her favorite records played. I always kept my eye out for the incoming white DeSoto. Her favorite record was mine; *Bye, Bye Love* by the Everly Brothers. Sometimes she would ask for it to be played twice.

However, the back lot could be trying. One day, seven drunk, young guys in a red Plymouth convertible came in and ordered everything on the menu. I checked the order with the manager and he suggested I go back and tell them how much the bill would be before they placed the order, and to ask for the money upfront. They produced enough money for hamburgers, fries, and milkshakes. When I went back with the food, one of them grabbed me in the crotch while another started emptying the coin exchanger on my money belt. I dumped the milkshakes all over the leopard covers on the front and back seats which distracted them enough for me to get away.

Unfortunately, one of the young men was the son of a

nearby department store manager. I was not surprised when I was called in by my manager to explain my actions, which I did. To my surprise, he did not fire me but asked me to finish my summer job by working with the short-order cooks in the basement. It would be less money but he said he could not take the chance that the kid would not tell his father and he did not want to have to deal with him. He told me I was doing a good job and he liked me...that if I decided not to go back to school he would put me back on skates this fall when that kid was away in college.

I was to discover that many of the cooks were thirteen and fourteen years old. I realized this was against state labor laws. But these kids needed the money so I wasn't going to say anything. And maybe because they didn't have to deal with the public, they seemed to be happier than the carhops. They certainly ate better because the manager gave up trying to find ways to charge them for food. He couldn't watch over them every minute.

A couple of young entrepreneurs even managed to supply leftover food to those at home. Several came to work by canoe up the Kanawha River. On the return trip, the canoe was often loaded with Hodo's "specials." I could aid and abet these trips by diverting the manager's attention with questions when we left our shift. Several times I even went with one of the kids who dropped me off near where my sister lived. I still have memories of paddling the Kanawha River early in the morning, watching the rising sun gleam off the golden leaves of the capitol dome.

Many years later, this Peggy Sue—who was never a prom queen and always kept her Hodo's outfit, including the belt with the metal money changer—went through life (*and yes, she got that college degree*) and realized that yes, there are many "haves" and "have-nots" in this world.

She wonders what her fellow carhoppers are doing later today and knows that life may still be hard for many. But this

Peggy Sue also knows that the "haves" have perhaps really not lived life to the fullest because they have not had the life lesson of starting out as a "have-not."

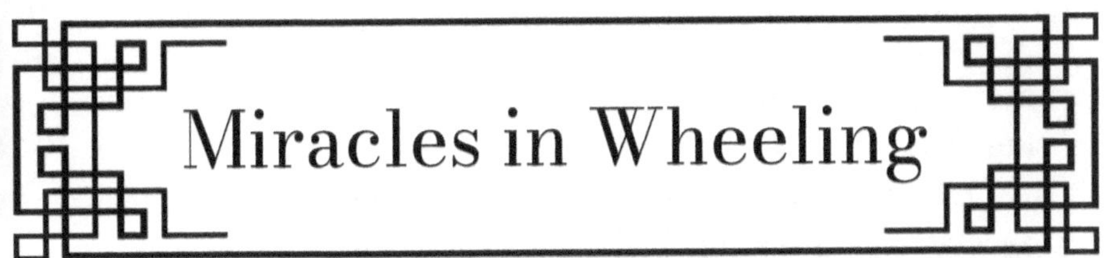

Miracles in Wheeling

"Don't take it the wrong way. You're an intern sent here for the summer from the university and the editor has a wicked sense of humor for academics. He wants to see if you can get an interview with a faith healer who is here for a week and hates the press."

With those not-so-consoling words from the lead reporter Al Molnar, who I had been assigned to as a mentor, we left in his company car to drop me off at the old Virginia Capitol theater which in its day was where you performed if you ever wanted to make it to the Grand Ole Opry in Nashville. The WVA radio station there at that time operated at 50,000 watts and not only boosted the careers of singers like Johnny Cash but also of the faith healer, Kathryn Kuhlman, whom I was about to meet. Kathryn was in the middle of a U.S. tour and had come down to Wheeling after her Pittsburgh, Pennsylvania sessions where she had been scorned by the *Pittsburgh Press*.

I was just nineteen and feeling very inept among a well-seasoned reporting staff that had welcomed me to the newspaper but seemed amused in doing so. *The News-Register* was an Odgen morning newspaper that was as sensational as the rest of the Hearst chain of papers. Molnar was well-known for his work in digging out corruption in local government as well as exposing a prostitution ring that even operated out of new government housing. Twenty-third Street in Wheeling was famous for its red-light district. Molnar had even interviewed a young girl who was born into the business and didn't know of any other life. He had brought tears, as well as disgust, from his readers when he noted that as a crib girl, she earned twice what the older ones brought in for their pimps. But as our editor with the wicked sense of humor said, the end result was more business than ever for the district from outsiders hearing about it.

It wasn't that I was naive. Summer jobs as a young teenager at corn packing sheds had exposed me to incest when a girl I packed corn with told me about what her father was doing to her.

So even though I felt I could handle any comments made to intimidate or embarrass me, I was feeling inadequate among the worldly adults in the newsroom. But I was determined to prove to the group that I could write and earn my way.

I even managed to laugh when Molnar pointed out the guy standing at the entrance to the Virginia Theater selling photos and said, "See that guy over there. When they come out of those healing sessions they are so hyped up with praising the Lord, they think they are buying real autographed pictures of Jesus Christ. He's driving a new car now."

I questioned the legality of it and Molnar just laughed and said, "Ask the faith healer inside" and drove off. I gave him back the finger he gave me when I turned in my first article to him to review covering a guy who had escaped from the Moundsville prison and raped a woman. He had rewritten part of it because I had struggled with the word "rape," calling it illegal intercourse. He had laughed at my temerity and wrote a headline for it that I will never forget: "Nut, Bolts and Screws" which the editor loved but would not allow to be printed.

I had walked by this theater several times on my way to cross the historic suspension bridge across Wheeling Island and the Ohio River. A huge crowd had already gathered under the marquee lights of the old vaudeville theater flashing Kathryn Kuhlman's healing powers in other cities. So I got in line to find somebody who could introduce me to Kathryn. By the time I got through the ornate lobby with its marble statues and glittering walls, I was feeling out of my element but felt better looking at the crowd which obviously had no more money than I had to spend on clothes. Then a tall, stocky, slick-haired guy with a single curl dangling down over his brow motioned me on when I asked to see Kathryn about a story for the *News-Register*. He just laughed and told me that she never let the press interview her because they told lies about her. "But you can go in if you want," he offered, probably doubting who I said I was.

Now feeling even more inadequate with this rejection, I mentally recharged myself with my ambition to prove myself. I would figure out a way to meet her so I stood as tall as I could to meet his amusing gaze and even thanked him.

I was again unsettled upon entering the theater. I had been told there were 3,000 seats and that Kathryn would be filling them up that day and was expected to do the same the next week. I believed it because it was already a crushing crowd a half-hour before her appearance. But it wasn't just the massive group of people looking for seats...it was the first time I had seen the pomp and glitter of the inside of those old Gilded Age theaters. It had what they called a proscenium arch over a large stage and lighting from huge fixtures in the fresco ceiling dotted with gold and silver leaves which would change to different rainbow colors. Two large statues of partially nude women, holding a globe, were embedded in the walls.

O.K., I said to myself, *just find a seat as close as you can to the stage and figure out what to do.* Coming on stage to set up things were several men in black suits which included the one at the door who had let me in. The microphone was tested and to my amazement the stage was bare with just a backdrop of moving clouds projected from the ceiling lights. When the various men lined up on the stage, there was a roar of "Praise the Lord" and I knew we would soon be seeing Kathryn.

I thought of Molnar speculating that maybe they would start up the old vaudeville organ which was used during silent films to illustrate screen actions. On the way here, he reminisced that as a kid, he always liked the sound of pounding hooves from the organ. "You should have seen Douglas

Fairbanks as Zorrow riding Tornado across the screen...you would have thought the horse was going to run over you. And there was Tom Mix, in the Rider of Death Valley." It was then he suggested they might use the sounds of thunder and lightning to announce the entrance of Kathryn.

When Kathryn did enter the stage, if there had been organ sounds to accompany her, you would never have heard them. The crowd was on their feet roaring with enthusiasm, some even going into the aisles with hands uplifted and others kneeling.

I must say I was on my feet too—and not just because everyone else was. Kathryn wore a flowing white gown, which was impressive in itself, but it was the brilliant red hair that caught my attention as well as her broad smile that she flashed right and left, taking in the whole crowd as they were taking her in. The only evangelistic preachers I had ever seen were stern-looking white men.

I was soon to find out that, unlike those who warned you would go to hell if you didn't behave, she did not put the fear of God into you. She was beaming with the joy of the Holy Spirit, she said, and wanted everyone to have the divine relations the Holy Spirit of God had given her. She did not speak in tongues or lecture, but walked back and forth on the stage declaring Jesus was there with them—and was there to help...that he not only died for our sins but also our diseases. Whenever she said, "I believe in his miracles," it seemed all 3,000 people filling the seats would respond with "hallelujahs" that echoed off the ceiling and walls.

Her presence on the stage was remarkable. Whenever she lifted her arms with wide flowing sleeves, she looked like an angel as she said that Jesus stands ready to hear your cry. He knows you better than you know yourself. Let him in. He will heal you if you believe in him. Let the Holy Spirit flow through you.

Unlike those self-proclaimed preachers who threatened hell, she was able to spread such joy in what she called the glory of God that people began to cry out that they could no longer feel pain. Several threw their crutches and braces into the aisles. Some even appeared to be in such a trance they fainted. That was when the twelve men in black suits who were called her disciples went into the audience to bring those on stage for Kathryn's blessing.

It was then I realized that if I coughed loudly as many had and appeared to be in distress by clearing my throat, maybe one of the men in black would take me up on stage and I could talk to her. It worked. But I was not prepared for what came next.

Once on stage, I looked back and had stage fright. I had not noticed the huge balcony. Looking back, I felt all 3,000 people were staring at me. When Kathryn put her hands on me and looked directly at me, I was mesmerized by her penetrating eyes and beautiful hair. I just turned red from feeling inadequate as well as thinking *"What have I done?"* It only took seconds for Kathryn to dismiss me as not having found the Holy Spirit. I didn't faint under her spell but squirmed with embarrassment under her steady gaze into my eyes. I was able to ask if I could meet her after the session to talk to her to explain. She agreed and signaled one of her disciples to take me to her office.

A couple of hours later, Kathryn came in and asked me if I really was a reporter. I gave her my full background, leaving nothing out—including my fear of losing my job if I failed to get an interview with her. After questioning me about what I thought of the session, I was honest about how she seemed to make everyone happy instead of afraid of going to hell and she laughed. She then said that I write a report right there of what I had seen, which I did, quoting exactly what she had said. I was glad that I had taken shorthand in high school and read every quote correctly. She then said, "If this appears in the *Wheeling News-Register* just as you have written it, then you are welcome to attend my other sessions this week."

When I got back to the office that night (*we were a morning newspaper*), I met with Molnar and the editor and told them everything that had happened. Molnar was right about the editor's wicked sense of humor and distrust. He just said, "Well, I'll be dammed. You did it." He told the news editor to get my story on the front page tomorrow and then to interview some medical and church pastors about what they thought of faith healing. "A little controversy will be good when they discount faith healing and we will just look at it as news."

I also told them there had been several people with cancer that felt cured. But when they were on stage with Kathryn, she also told them to continue to go to the doctor because the Holy Spirit could work through them, too. Hamm had just laughed and said one of those disciples must be a lawyer.

He was dismayed that Kathryn never allowed a photographer or even cameras in her sessions. But I had already thought of that and told him that Kathryn said that if the story ran as written she would allow me to sit just off-stage. I could signal her to get the name of the person healed so we could get a photo later...it would be up to them if they wanted their picture and story told. As cynical as the editor was, he said he had to hand it to her...it appeared that she actually was able to get people up there without it being a setup.

So when I arrived the next afternoon, Kathryn had already seen the paper and was good for her word. In fact, after the next edition, which featured several people healed, she had me set on stage with her disciples. She called me her little angel from the *Wheeling News-Register*. The editor was delighted with the publicity...not just from newspaper extra sales at the theater door, but many were subscribing thanks to Kathryn's promotion. When the photographer complained about trying to find some of those healed at their homes, I asked several of the more enthusiastic ones if they would go down to the newspaper office with me to meet the editor, tell their story, and have their photo run. Several did which absolutely stunned the editor, especially when one lady practically disrobed taking off all of her braces. Fortunately, Molnar had admonished the staff to act like nothing was unusual. I could tell, despite all of his bluster, he actually felt sorry for them and did not want anyone to make fun of them.

With newfound confidence, I no longer got stage fright and was quite busy deciding who would be a good interviewee for the paper and signaling Kathryn I wanted to interview them. By mid-week, she even made it easy for me to interview them by asking if they wanted to tell their story to "her angel." Then we would go backstage to one of the dressing rooms where our photographer was also allowed to take a photograph.

Even though I did not believe in faith healing and felt that when people felt cured, it was the trauma of the whole event—and a desire to be better—that caused people to believe in miracle healing. I did witness a healing I could not believe, though. I had gotten used to people with arthritis walking without canes and supporting braces and throwing away copper bracelets that were supposed to draw out the pain. But the time a young man cast his crutch aside and came up without shoes because his toes were so curled under with rheumatoid arthritis is an instance I still haven't gotten over. When Kathryn took him by the shoulders and touched his toes, then continued a chant ending with "May the Power of God flow straight through you," I could not believe what I was seeing. His toes actually uncurled. Kathryn noticed this too and spent even more time casting her spell. He was crying tears of joy and hallelujahs when he left the stage. I was so rattled that I forgot to signal for an interview.

When I told Molnar about it he decided it was a good thing Kathryn was leaving town the next day or I might be on the road with her. The editor had even taken to tease me about believing everything I quoted from Kathryn. I defended her when he asked how much money she was collecting and if she was quoting that part of the Bible that said you need to tithe ten percent. I pointed out that everyone got in free but that the disciples did pass around a collection plate which was quickly filled even though it was voluntary...that I never heard her say 10%. I added that I knew a Holy Roller preacher who came into our valley once with a truck and was stopped by my father when he tried to take 10% of the tenant's furniture from his house. He let up with teasing a bit.

Still, I noted a lot of money going into the collection boxes. The editor had a reporter check out where Kathryn and her disciples were staying to find out they were booked in the cheapest hotel in Wheeling and ate at diners. To his credit, this was published in a news story.

But looking back now, he was right. When Kathryn died in the late 70s, they found old master oil paintings worth millions in her home. All I can say is that at least she made people happy and, unlike some evangelists, she told them not to be afraid of Satan when they died because they had the Holy Spirit in them.

And today, I must admit I still remember seeing those toes straighten out. I am also reminded of that time in the summer of 1959 when it was a win-win situation for all of us because of Kathryn...me as a reporter, the newspaper gaining circulation, and the suffering feeling healed. When James Buckingham wrote the book *Daughter of Destiny*, he reported that she had "attracted 18,000 in one week and pictures of those healed appeared daily on the first page of the *Wheeling News-Register*."

An Interview with Jackie Kennedy

At the time I did not think of the interview as anything special. I was a newspaper intern between my junior and senior year of college and the School of Journalism had placed me on the *Wheeling News-Register* in West Virginia. It was a Hearst newspaper that lived up to its early muckraking reputation.

However, I loved the paper for its combativeness. I was thrilled to be assigned to one of their prize reporters, Al Molnar. He was nearly a one-man show in cleaning up local politics. Word used to go around the newsroom that Al was falling down on his job if he didn't get a prominent politician fired every six months for violating the public trust. Al was not only a mentor but also very kind to me, despite his bravado. When I first started, I did not realize I would only be paid every two weeks, not once a week. When Al realized I was not eating the last three days because I had run out of money, he invited me to a free meal which involved my going into a huge family reunion at Oglebay Park and pretend to be a relative – that no one would recognize as a new reporter. He was especially happy when I returned with a plateful of goodies for him, too. It had amused him I had found it cheaper to move out of the YWCA to find an apartment with three other girls for only $20 a month. It was the ballroom of an old abandoned hotel and we put up dividers to make four bedrooms. We shared a bathroom with other tenants. One of my roommates, Betty, worked at the WVA Radio station where she met a lot of struggling country music singers needing a cheap place to stay. Fortunately, I worked nights so when she bought one home my bed was used. The building was beside the Ohio River and thanks to Al, who had a friend with a motorboat, I learned to water ski when I got out of work in the early morning hours.

It was in this atmosphere I did an interview that today I look back on as my most notable encounter. Al was to interview Senator Jack Kennedy, who was doing battle with Hubert Humphrey in the Democratic primary race. Jack was coming in at the St. Clairsville airport across the river and would be speaking at the Eagles Club. Jack's choosing of West Virginia as a kickoff primary had national attention because it would test whether a Catholic could win in a state with a less-than-2% Catholic population. As a political and cynical observer, Al had thought it a brilliant strategy. He figured Jack's father also reckoned the other 98% was made up of racists and hillbillies who probably thought Catholics just had better tents than all the other evangelists roaming the area. When I told him my father from our small valley district of thirty Democrat voters had received $150 for campaign expenses and had just divided the money among them, Al just laughed and said, "Good to hear your father didn't take it all."

As Al was getting ready to leave to interview Jack, the mayor's office called to say they were just told Jackie Kennedy was now coming in at Wheeling Airport. The mayor had enlisted his wife and her bowling league team to form a car cavalcade to escort Jackie to the Eagles Club to meet up with Jack. When he was told a *Life Magazine* photographer was with Jackie, he called a major campaign contributor, the owner of the Imperial Glass Company which was en route, to give Jackie a tour.

Al briefed me as best as he could, telling me about the Kennedy clan, including personal information such as the number of children Ethel had and, unfortunately, the fact that Jackie had been named one of the ten best-dressed women in the world. I immediately felt I wasn't up to the job...certainly not in an outfit I'd had since high school. I was conscious of the large safety pin I had used to replace the button which held up my A-line skirt. I had not taken the time to sew it back on because you couldn't see it under my long pullover.

When he dropped me off, it hit me that I did not have a way to follow Jackie. We only had one press car. But Al was already giving me a $5 bill to buy the mayor's wife a beer at the airport as we waited for Jackie. "That will get you in the front car with her," he said. Then he admonished me not to forget my assignment. I was to try to get Jackie to announce that Jack was going to decide to run for president. This would end national speculation and be a scoop for the *Wheeling News-Register*.

When I met the mayor's wife and her bowling team, I felt better about my appearance. The group was lining their cars and exchanging bowling shoes for heels. They were in a raucous mood and knew even less about Jackie Kennedy than I did, thanks to Al. I reiterated what he had told me.

As it turns out, all our hurrying had been for naught as Jackie's plane was late. I had about 50 cents left of the $5 bill when it came in and we all rushed out to greet her. The cars were lined up in place and the mayor's wife had agreed I was to ride in the front convertible with her along with Jackie. It was a sweltering hot day.

When Jackie stepped off the plane, she did indeed look like the best-dressed woman in the world. And the mayor's wife, who had thanked me for the extra beer, said so. Then she added, forgetting it was Ethel with the big family, that Jackie "sure looked good having all them children." However, Jackie never flinched—even though years later we would learn she had had a recent miscarriage. She was totally gracious. When she was led to the convertible, which I had gotten to first, I opened the back door for her. It soon became apparent the mayor's wife had been most generous in offering everyone a ride in her convertible as several more struggled to get in.

It was then I spotted an opportunity. I asked Jackie if she would be more comfortable in the hardtop car behind us. She, too, might have been wondering what was going to happen to her pillbox hat when we got on the highway. She immediately followed me out of the back seat and into the car behind me.

She did express surprise that I was a reporter at the age of nineteen but smiled when I told her I was just a summer intern. She told me she started out as a reporter and took her own pictures. I began the interview by asking her how she liked Washington, D.C., and noting how exciting it must be there with all the social life. Years later I would learn her social life was not all that good with the wandering Jack. But she answered everything with a smile and I became completely enchanted with her as she made me feel comfortable by thanking me for getting her into the hardtop car and encouraging me in my journalism career.

As we were heading down Rt. 40, a double-lane highway into Wheeling, a car pulled up beside us with several women dressed in their bowling clothes with their team's name on their T-shirts. The one in back yelled out her window to ask if we had gotten rid of Jackie yet...that they were holding up the tournament for the team from the mayor's office. The woman in the front tried to shush her by pointing to Jackie in the back beside me. But Jackie heard it, and just as quietly asked me about the bowling game as the car passed us. I gave her the details and even added an apology, explaining that no one expected her to be in this old hardtop car and that it was my fault.

When we got to the Imperial Glass Company, Jackie asked the tour to be cut in half because she had been late and asked, "Would it be possible just to see the glassblower section?" She had already impressed the plant manager with her knowledge of what they produced, but even more so when she went over to some glassblowers and asked several technical questions about how the glass was made. She revealed a genuine knowledge of glass, commenting on several pieces that were not only equal to but better than some she had seen in Venice.

The owner, well aware of the famous Venetian glassblowers, immediately insisted she take one of the pieces she was admiring. He had been embarrassed when the mayor's wife, at the gift shop, had gathered up a colorful breakfast setting "for all those kids you have." Jackie graciously accepted both gifts and tried to pay for the expensive blower's Fostoria gift. When told absolutely not, she asked for an order form that she wanted to pass on to others in her family as well as those in the Senate and White House "interested in fine crystal." *(Years later, she did order china for the White House from Imperial.)*

As I told Al later, I had no doubt that everyone at Imperial, including me, was going to vote for Jackie even though he reminded me I was not old enough.

When we got to the Eagles Club, Jackie graciously thanked the mayor's wife and her committee for the ride and stop at the Imperial plant. She told them she was sure I could get her inside the club without any trouble. She then wished them a winning tournament and off we went into the club.

Jack was in the middle of his talk, so Jackie asked that we sit in the back rather than disrupt things by going to the front where she was supposed to be seated. The room temperature was nearly as sweltering as it was outside. I asked Jackie if she would care for a drink. About halfway up the side of the room was a barrel containing Iron City beer from Pittsburgh on ice plus a table with iced tea. Those around us were having the beer. To my surprise, she requested the beer, which I promptly returned with, including one for myself. I proudly opened both cans by producing from my purse my beer opener which we called a church key in those days. During the talk, I kept reminding myself of my mission from Al: "Get her to say that Jack is going to run for president."

She was indeed relaxed during the talk and at one point had said, "Really, Jack," and "How are you going to do that?" when he promised that one day West Virginians would own the mines they worked in. This line and many others had gotten heavy applause. It was then I commented on how much everyone seemed to like him and asked if she was going to go on the presidential campaign trail with him and she said "yes." That was our headline in the newspaper the next day, proclaiming that Jack was running for president and we were the first ones to announce it.

Al Molnar wrote the lead for me on the story even though I got the byline. He said I deserved it and introduced me to the word "carpe diem." I was thrilled he was so proud. He even stood up to the editor who had found out that the *Saturday Evening Post* magazine photographer, who had been following Jack Kennedy, had taken a picture of just Jackie and me. The photographer had laughed about the green reporter from the "hick newspaper." Our editor had been furious when the *Post* called our WVU all-American basketballer, Jerry West, "the hick from Cabin Creek." He didn't want the newspaper branded with the same disdain. He called higher Hearst officials to squash the photo.

But now fifty years later, I am proud to say that Mark Shaw of *Life Magazine*, who was also following Jackie during the primary, did take a photo that shows me with the mayor's wife and her group. It was taken in the gift shop and it is on page 54 of a book showing a collection of Shaw's photographs of the Kennedys entitled "The John F. Kennedys."

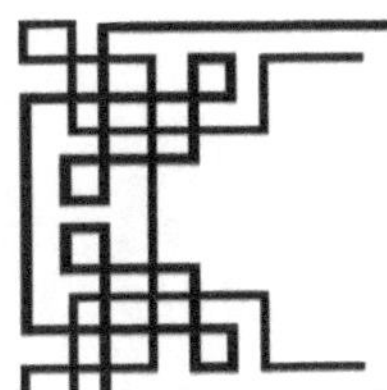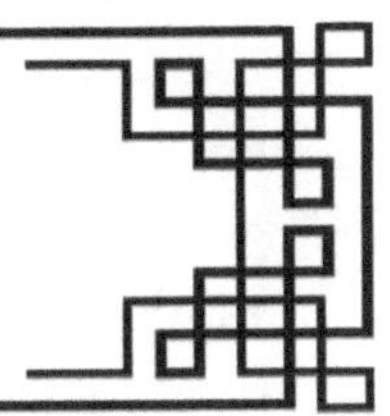

College Jobs

When I look back at my college experience, I realize my best memories are of the jobs I had on campus to pay for my tuition, room, and board.

I was able to get some of my tuition paid for by Viceroy and Marlborough by passing out their free four-pack cigarettes to other students. I cut my room and board by a third by working in the kitchen of the women's dormitory, which housed and fed over 300 women. I particularly enjoyed this job because it meant I did not have to sit in the dining room with the dean of women. No one was allowed to leave before she did. I was not interested in her style of becoming a lady. I preferred my job of using a boat paddle to stir the lima beans and mashed potatoes.

But I did lose both jobs and had to look for others. When the cigarette companies found out I was smoking a lot of their inventory, I lost that job my junior year. A friendly battle with the well-dressed waiters—fraternity men to satisfy the formality requirements of our dean of women—resulted in me losing that job. Little did I know when I was making snowballs out of some leftover mashed potatoes that one of them would open the double doors to the dining room when I heaved it at another waiter. The Dean of Women's table was near that door.

My roommates in my dormitory wing also regretted the firing because I had been making good use of a small crate-size elevator that ran down to the kitchen from the outside of the building. It was used by the local suppliers to deliver groceries. We were particularly fond of the chocolate candy cakes they delivered. One of my jobs was to slice the cakes.

Because there were so many, I could easily end up with a couple of extra cakes by being judicious in my slicing technique. I would send these back up the elevator to some of my waiting roommates.

We justified this behavior because it had not taken us long to realize we were the poor wing of this great dormitory. The Dean of Women felt that either we would be intimidated by roommates with money or the moneyed roommates would not care to associate with us. Whatever the case, we soon found out that most of our parents either worked in the coal mines or on a farm. It did not make us feel any better when we had to go to mass meetings to hear the society girls exclaim their joy at being picked at one or more sororities for acceptance. Everyone knew belonging to a sorority or fraternity cost more than the entire college education.

I had already earned the disgust of the both the Dean who had urge me to take a modern dance course to become more cultured as well as the instructor when I didn't buy a sash to flash in exercises and used my sock instead. So when our class was chosen for a campus-wide performance at Christmas, she decided I should be the Christmas tree her good dancers could deftly chop down. All I had to do was stand tall but she didn't count on me to knock myself out when I fell over.

One of my roommates was a chemistry major. She contributed to our dessert-eating ventures by taking her tubing and vials to the rich wing where we emptied some of the soda machines. In those days, the bottles slid along rails in a cold tank and were released one at a time with a dime in the coin slot. We were able to pop the tops off as they were loosely set on the rails. We would suck the soda out through the tubes to fill the vials, leaving the empty bottles for the "rich" wing.

But my best-paying job was putting up the mail in the dormitory. This required getting up at 5 a.m. I would sort the mail and put it in boxes for the 300 women, which would take an hour or two. The big money came when I was able to make a copy of the key used by the postal worker. It was the only door without an alarm. So my customers for a $50 key were the rich wing girls who wanted to stay out past curfew. The first was a gal from Chestnut Hill in Philadelphia who was very worldly and generous. She also set me up for other sales. She thought sororities were silly, so she was in the dorm for four years. Her father was a doctor and she had her own car. We became friends and I often became her driver which gave her an excuse to pay for my beers.

All women had to be in the dormitory by 7 a.m. However, if you were a straight-A student you could stay out until 9 a.m. I did achieve this for several semesters, but, according to the dean of women, I also managed to graduate with the most restrictions to your room. Part of her program to make ladies out of us included restrictions for not handling your silverware right in the dining room. This did not bother me in the kitchen but the ones about always having your bed made or leaving clothing or an empty coke bottle in the room or coming in late after curfew did help earn me 132 nights of being confined to the dorm in four years.

She would remind me that my sister Decker had just one restriction in four years and was well respected not only for being a straight-A student but also for having good manners. I totally agreed with her and asked if she knew the restriction was her senior year when she came in late after a job interview with Union Carbide—which thankfully she got and might not have had she cut the interview short. I was well aware of how wonderful my sister was. We had mortgaged the farm to get her to college and she had taken twenty-one credit hours each semester to get out in three and a half years. She was not only paying back the mortgage but had signed a note at the bank to loan me money for college.

This only earned me a "then you ought to be grateful and be more like her" comment. Unfortunately, I wasn't and today I know I wasted a lot of time wasting time. Anyhow, she acknowledged that I was obviously a knowledgeable student of the restriction policy. I had shown her that when she came in for a room check and I refused to stand up. The rule was two nights of restrictions if you did not get up when she entered your room. I chose to sit on two coke bottles on my unmade bed rather than get up and reveal them, which would have resulted in three restrictions. I saved myself one night of restriction. This, undoubtedly, was a great offense to her. After that, I was often room-checked by her.

Yet, she did become my friend on one occasion. She even gave me the paid job of being a proctor to maintain order in my wing that year. It occurred during one of those infamous panty raids led by fraternity men. They would use a pole to break down the dormitory entrance and rush in to raid the drawers of the women to see who could collect the most panties. My roommate and I, achieving A's the year before, had earned a room over the dormitory entrance. The city police had been ignoring the dean's call for help under the premise of "boys will be boys" and "nobody is getting hurt." When the frat boys came in one night with their large pole to knock down the door, I was ready for them. I had been dating an ROTC student who had given me some M-80s they used in training. I had not realized how powerful they were. So when I launched some of them down on the frat rats, there was lots of yelling and screaming as they dropped the pole. One was moving around on the ground and moaning when the police arrived. In the meantime, the dean used the PA system to summon all of us to the dining room. She announced that the police were coming in to search the rooms for dynamite. She looked directly at me as she dismissed us. I immediately got back to my room and tore the rest of the M-80s apart and flushed them down the drain.

Later, after the police had left, the dean was back on the PA announcing that they had found nothing and she expressed her disgust at the police thinking the ladies at Arnold Hall would ever have such potentially harmful material in their possession. When she gave me the proctor job for my wing, she added that part of my job was to make sure no one had firecrackers.

Another one of my college jobs was sorting and stacking all of the newspapers from around the U.S. that came into the Journalism School library. This resulted in me being corralled once to take pictures of a football game. The sports photographer called in sick minutes before the game was to start. I was the only J student in the building at the time. So the professor told me, knowing that I had taken the course in photography, to take the photographer's pass and speed graphic down to the stadium and get a photo for our student newspaper, the *Athenaeum*.

When I got to the sidelines, the game was already underway. I had just taken an action shot when the wide receiver, followed by several players, hit the ground, taking me and the camera with them.

I decided being near the action was not safe. So I went to the other end of the field. Down there, I found West Virginia's Mountaineer mascot dressed in buckskins with his musket. I persuaded him to pretend to climb the wooden goalpost for a photo. Then all hell broke loose when an interception was made at the other end. It seemed like everyone arrived at the same time, scaring the mascot—who was heavy for the goalpost—and bringing him down with it. So my picture had a pile of players, the mascot, and a broken goalpost in it. The professor loved it because it was the first time the Associated Press had ever asked for a copy of a photo from the Journalism School.

While we had student passes to all the games, only the fraternity- and sorority-affiliated students could set on the 50-yard line. The only way a non-affiliated student could get a good seat was to join the marching band. I had a roommate one year who played the French horn and was in the band.

When she was sick once, I donned her uniform and horn and was doing fine the first half until everyone got up for halftime to perform. I panicked, not knowing the march formations, but the French horn player next to me just said do everything I do and you will be O.K. She was not affiliated either. So that was my second time being on the field.

But it was the favored treatment given to affiliated students that bugged many of us, including the journalism professor who had sent me to the game. Even the student yearbook was published by a fraternity instead of the School of Journalism. Naturally, it was filled with pictures of affiliated students. Only affiliated students could run for student office.

The professor, realizing most of his students were independent, decided we should change things. The first thing he did was have us do a sit-in on the president's law to force him to open up the elections and allow independents to run. We independents had them outnumbered four to one. But because it was a land-grant university, most of the independents were in the School of Agriculture or Engineering and they could care less. But there was a group coming back from the Korean War on the GI Bill who were motivated. They were particularly helpful when we decided to run our own float in the Homecoming Parade which led to the football field where we occupied the 50-yard seats. The float featured a moonshine still without a queen and king enveloped in crepe paper decorations. We demanded and got equal rights in stadium seating.

There was one journalism student who was affiliated with the biggest fraternity on campus, the one that published the yearbook. He was secretly a Catholic and they didn't know it. He first got in trouble with them by inviting me as an independent to one of their dances. I used some of my mail key money to buy a gown and went. I will never forget the sorority women who would not even speak to me in the ladies' room. He was investigated by the fraternity and they found out he was a Catholic. He was thrown out but he didn't go quietly.

He contacted the national organization and they closed the West Virginia chapter for an entire year. After that they hung signs around campus saying he was "queer." But by this time he had joined us, referred to as the "GD independents," and he just laughed.

As the professor in charge of the student newspaper said, we had the ink and we needed to use it to change things. I had a cousin whose family could afford to get her into the Tri-Delta sorority. She knew that I needed money. Soon a letter arrived offering me money not to run for the Student Legislature. This was quickly published in our student newspaper. I received another letter declaring I was banned forever from joining a sorority and we published that, too.

By the middle of my senior year, we independents had broken the grip of the affiliated. My last act of defiance was when I heard a fraternity was inviting independent women to a party but they were billing it as a "pig party." I rounded up about thirty independent women. We even arrived ready and fulfilled our intention of drinking and eating them out of house and home. That was the last time they had such a party.

One would think I would remember taking some classes at the university which I have to remind myself I did. One of them paid off. I was good in history and was paid to take the exam for a couple of football players. Another was a program in the Journalism School to have each of us take a class in another school to broaden our perspective. My choice of a course to be a "jack of all trades but an expert in none" was an astronomy course. Expecting to enjoy studying constellations, I soon found myself on top of the physics building trying to measure the distance between stars. I was on my way to flunking the course when the professor, noting that I was on the student newspaper and working summers on the *Wheeling News-Register*, said he was trying to raise money to purchase a portable planetarium he could take to high schools. I began writing news releases for newspapers in the state, resulting in him getting some contributions and me getting a C in the course. In fact, he was so grateful that he once let me have the key to the university planetarium where I hosted J School students for a "Thank God It's Friday" session under the revolving stars.

So in looking back at my college experience, I am grateful I could find jobs that only left me with a bill of $1,200 instead of $200,000. I am also grateful because those jobs prepared me for real-world challenges, too.

Fending

When my father died, leaving my mother to rent the farm, there were some people in the valley—the ones she called "riffraff"—who underestimated her ability to fend for herself.

They found this out when they decided the farm could now be used for jacking deer at night.

It was accepted that the valley was overrun with deer. My father, like others in the valley, had permits to kill them because of crop damage. That was fine with my mother, who understood the need to protect the cornfields by downsizing the deer population. But it had to be done legally. It was against the law to shoot from a car and to use a spotlight at night to stun the deer, making it easy to shoot them.

When crop damage was especially severe, most farmers would look the other way when the spotlighters came. But not my mother. She would be cranking up the phone to ring Central to get the game warden on the line.

We had a rural phone system everyone shared. Each farmer was assigned a number of rings. In our case, it was two longs and two shorts. The central operator's number of rings was one long. Everyone in the valley could listen in on this shared party line and often did, sometimes resulting in an entire church-covered dish supper being planned.

It didn't take long for my mother to realize the night hunters would quickly disappear when she rang up the operator. So she started asking Central to connect her to her aunt who was also a law-abiding citizen. She would invite her to a fake event, a signal for her to use another phone system to call the game warden.

We just had one road in and out of the valley. It only took

two game wardens to catch them. After one of the spotlighters killed a big steer in the field, mistaking it for a deer, my mother took great delight in putting up a poster picture of a cow along the road, labeled "COW." She even convinced the game wardens to put up a plastic deer in the field near a well-known deer crossing from the mountain to the valley. It had been shot so many times it eventually collapsed—but not before several spotlighters were arrested. Despite getting hate mail from the illegal hunters, particularly on Valentine's Day, saluting her as their favorite witch, she never let up for the next twenty-five years.

Even a new generation of spotlighters would have to learn she would not be intimidated though she lived by herself. Once when I came home from college, I found I had lost the nerve I thought I had inherited from her. We were watching TV when a spotlight streaked through the big picture window of our living room.

"Today's riffraff is even worse," she said as she jumped up to the window to see where the light was coming from. "Of all the nerve," she angrily declared, "they have driven off the road and down into the cornfield by the river."

Times had changed. Not only could she get them for illegal hunting but there were heavy fines for trespassing and carrying guns. The spotlighters had been known to hide their guns and pretend they were just looking around. Each illegal gun cost as much as $500.

Despite it being dark and well past midnight, she ordered me to sneak down through the cornfield and see where they hid their guns. She dialed the game warden directly without fear of discovery, proclaiming the new phone system was at least good for that despite having to dial all those numbers. As I was going out the back door, she went out the front to get the truck. She drove it to the head of the dirt road leading down to the cornfield and parked it sideways to block the exit from the dirt road to the field.

As I was trying to make my way in the dark through the cornfield, I remembered a large copperhead snake I had once encountered in that area. I calmed myself by knowing that I had full-length pants. I was also grateful for having grabbed a full-length jacket as the blades of the tall corn were sharp. I struggled blindly through the corn rows, hoping they would not hear or see me. I had gotten used to life in the city where people with guns shot other people, not deer. I asked myself, "What are you doing here in the middle of the night chasing down people with loaded guns? They could even be on drugs for all you know."

Still, I pushed on knowing that I had to be my mother's daughter. Even though I was trying to be quiet as I could, snaking my way down the two cornrows, I roused a deer that jumped up just ahead of me. It started thrashing its way through the cornfield. The sweep of the spotlight soon caught up with it. Several shots rang out. I hit the ground flat and stayed there for a while, renewing my question of "What on earth are you doing here?" and hoping there were no copperheads about.

It was then the deer jackers saw the lights coming up the valley road and figured my mother had gotten the game warden.

They ran for the bridge crossing the drainage ditch along the field. I was close enough to see them stack their guns tightly under it above the water line. They jumped in their car to flee, only to find themselves facing the side of the truck and my mother.

The game warden arrived about that time. He checked their car for guns as they protested that the night was so nice they thought they would just take a walk to the river. In the group was a distant cousin which made no difference to my mother. She just shook her finger at him and said, "Shame on you."

My mother yelled for me to come out of the cornfield, which I did, still shaking from the gunshots. I told her where the guns were. She led the game warden to the bridge where they had hidden their guns.

She slept soundly that night, but I didn't. I kept thinking about those loaded guns and the gunshots that landed near me when the deer jumped up. There are some things that are worse than copperhead snakes. But my mother feared neither.

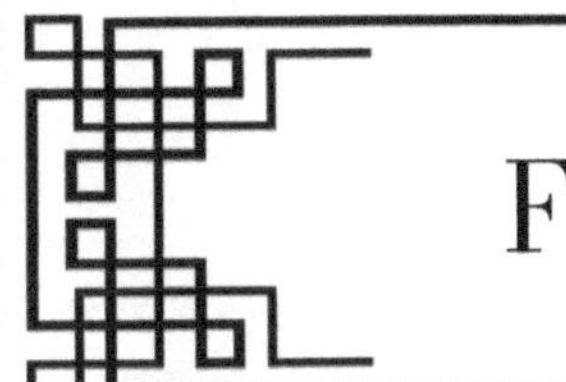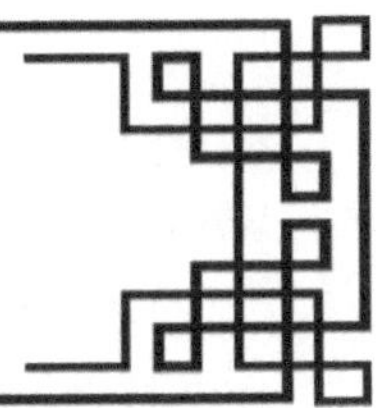

Farm Sentinel

Life not only changed for us when my father died, but the farm seemed to lose its will to live, too. The corn he had planted a month before was still trying to shoot its way up through the soil which he had thoroughly cultivated and pulverized. There had been plenty of rain although not the downpour on the day he died. He had gotten all of his sun-cured hay in the barn just before it hit. He was so attuned to nature that other farmers used to do as he did...they had only been an hour behind him in getting their hay in.

It was when my mother checked the barn to find out why he was late for supper that she found him beside the tractor. It was still running...something was wrong...he would never waste gas. She saw the new breeding bull he had gotten attached to; it had belonged to his cousin in the next county who had given up farming because he could no longer compete with the big corporate feedlots in the west. The big Hereford was nuzzling him gently, trying to get my father to move. My mother saw his face, peaceful but lifeless. She knew his weak heart was probably the cause.

She called for Mike, my brother. He was sharpening the blades on the mowing machine. My two sisters and I were called. I was at GE headquarters at the time and immediately left in shock for the all-night drive. The farm had given many of us our start in life.

When our ancestors settled the valley in the 1740s, there had been plenty of land to support the first three generations. But large families resulted in too many heirs and, thus, smaller farms. So the English rule had been adopted for the past three generations. The farm would go to the eldest son or, barring that, to the son that wanted to stay on the farm. The farm would educate the others so they could make a living.

This was certainly true when it was mortgaged to get my oldest sister through the state university. A generation ago, farming had been profitable enough to send my father's sisters through expensive finishing schools.

I was lucky that four years separated me from my oldest sister. She not only paid off the mortgage but managed to loan me the money to also go to the state university. My middle sister went to a nearby free nursing college.

Our mother had married our father when they were just eighteen, both graduating from the same high school class. Mike had been the only son so it was automatic that he would inherit the farm. At the time Daddy died, he was working part-time at the local machinery dealer to supplement the decreasing farm income. Because of the high cost of farm equipment, the valley farmers had begun sharing equipment such as combines. Mike's mechanical knowledge gained him the respect my father—knowing when it was going to rain—had.

When my mom and Mike phoned the horrible news that my father was dead, we couldn't believe it. On our last visit, we had walked the fields with them just to hear how things were going—a ritual that was good for all of us to connect with our past, as providers and beneficiaries. We were well aware of the risks and never-ending chores a farmer faced each day.

Still, we felt the farm, Daddy and Mom, and Mike had become indestructible...something we could always come home to. We went to the barn where my father had collapsed after his heart attack. I mostly remember the bull still tied to a nearby hay bin by Mike who had been nudging my father on the ground. The sounds of his grazing seemed soothing. Yet, he would pause to look over where my father had been with those huge, dark, unblinking eyes.

Over the next couple of months, the lawyer on my father's side of the family would be called upon to help. It turned out my father had not made social security payments for two hired hands. He had given both his and their contributions directly to them, figuring they would spend it more wisely than the government. Then it was discovered the farm, because it was so close to Washington, D.C., had tripled in value. It was being taxed on commercial value rather than farm income. The lawyer in our family as well as many others had been trying to get this rule changed which finally resulted in a Tax Reform Act. The act based a farm's value on the income it produced, not what it would be worth for commercial development. But it didn't go into effect until a year after my father died.

So it was too late for my brother, Mike. To keep the farm, the cattle herd and the farm equipment had to be sold to pay the taxes on a farm now valued at $500,000 instead of $25,000. Mike went to work as a tractor-trailer truck driver which paid better than working on farm equipment at the local dealer.

We went back to our jobs. Mom turned the farm over to our cousin, one of the few farmers still left with a herd and equipment, asking him only to pay the property taxes, knowing that was about all he could make on the land.

Then a near-tragedy struck again—just three months after our father's death. Mike had come home from driving the truck to repair the tractor. He got caught in the power takeoff. If he had not been wearing Daddy's old jacket, which ripped easily, he could have lost his arm or his life.

He and my mother had no sooner come back from the hospital that evening when two tractor-trailers loaded with lean cattle arrived—with a bill for $8,000. Daddy had cut back on developing his own small herd. He could make more money turning the pasture into corn fields and using the silage to fatten the lean cattle during the winter. Hillside farmers did not have this advantage. They eked out a living by selling their new heifers in the fall because they couldn't make enough hay to feed them. Daddy had not told my mother he had ordered this fall's shipment of lean cattle.

The driver helped Mom get them penned up in the barn-yard while Mike did what he could with one arm. They had just gotten the gates fastened when I arrived, having heard about Mike's accident earlier that day. We would have to work something out to fatten the cattle. The corn crop, though not good, had grown and maybe would produce enough silage to fatten them. Otherwise, it would be a huge financial loss as my brother simply could not, in his condition, handle that many cattle. Besides, he could not afford to lose his job. He was mar-ried and had one child with another on the way. A resale of the cattle as is would only bring half the value at most, a loss of $4,000.

While we were calming ourselves down at the kitchen table, trying to find a positive side, we could hear the restless cattle in the barnyard. This was not unusual. Strange cattle in a new place have to adjust to new surroundings. Mike had noticed several had what Daddy called "shipping fever." They were sweaty, frothing at the mouth, and hard to control. Mom had gotten the reluctant driver to herd the ailing ones inside the barn.

We had just managed to believe that, possibly, we could maybe even make a little money if our cousin and other rel-atives in the valley could feed the cattle until it was time to take them to the stock sale in February. The corn had not been harvested. But all of us could take whatever vacation we had now to cut the corn and fill the silo. We could take turns com-ing home on weekends and any other days we could get off to help our mother, cousin, and other relatives in the valley feed the cattle.

It was then we saw the spotlight from a car on the road sweep the fields. It was illegal to jack deer at night by stun-ning them with a spotlight. My mother ran to the phone to call the game warden. The deer were in the field just below the barn. The hunters were out of their cars, now shooting wildly. Mike was quickly on his feet as the sound of gunshots rang out. But it was too late. We both heard the nervous cattle stampeding. Not only did the sixty steers in the yard break through the gate, but the sick ones busted out of the side of the 100-year-old barn when a bullet went into it.

The cattle were running in circles in the twenty-five-acre pasture field. It was a night with just a quarter-moon. Mike and I ran to the field to corral them back in the barnyard, while Mom got in the truck to go to the neighbors for help.

I could barely see the darting, whirling white markings on the Herefords. Most of the cattle were black Angus. All I could make out were running shapes. The ground was shuddering as they thundered around the field. You could hear them breathing hard and loud, losing pounds. We had just been talking about adding fat to the cattle and knew that they were losing weight as they stampeded. We had to get them back into the barnyard where they could settle down and eat.

The deer jackers with spotlights had gone, perhaps realizing what they had done. Despite his injuries and arm in a sling, Mike was able to get up on the tractor. He drove it to the end of the field where he used its lights to backlight me so I could see where I was going. I tried driving the cattle to the gate they had broken through, but they simply would not quit running. Mike and I began mimicking my father's soothing sounds. I could hear Mike's voice crack as his broken ribs were no doubt hurting him. He had gotten off the tractor to stand guard at one end of the field opposite the broken gate to the barnyard. The slivered moon threw reflected light off the white bandages so I knew he would keep them from going in that direction.

As I darted back and forth to round them up, I could feel Mike's relief as the dark Angus shadows and white-faced Herefords headed toward the broken gate. We dared not speak as noise would spook them. Then another gunshot rang out farther down the valley. All I could feel was the ground shaking under me as the mass of black and white came thundering toward me. I couldn't speak, hear, or even move. They were coming straight at me. I just felt the earth, the movement of the cattle. They were pushing memories, all rushing through me. It seemed like my father was just ahead of them. He seemed to be there in the dark night, telling me to stand up.

Then I knew what he would do. If I fell, the stampeding herd would not see me. I would be crushed under their feet, pulverized, swallowed by the earth. I could smell and feel the heavy breath of the cattle as they came straight at me. Then I felt the farm, my father, the growing fields. I reached up just like withered corn does when raindrops begin to fall. I was being whiplashed by the cattle as they began to divide around me and close in behind me. But I didn't fall. It seemed to last a lifetime, but I stood tall—as tall as my father, I said to myself as I reached up even further. I could see the shadows of the tassels of the tall corn in the field next to me as the cattle thundered by. I was still motionless when I heard them behind me.

They were turning again but not toward me. Mike's white bandage was moving and I heard his pain as he struggled up behind them. He had seen that I was safe. The cattle were heading to the river side of the field next to the cornfield. Mike quickly signaled me to close in along the back side so they would follow the fence. The fence led to the broken gate. They followed it. They found the opening. Amazingly, they went through.

Mike and I were right behind them. I propped up the broken gate and Mike brought the tractor up against it to secure it. I looked at the moon just above the cornfield. Back then, corn was not planted by drilling it in rows to get more corn. Seeds were drop-planted in hills so they could be tilled and weeded from two directions. Thus, from every vantage point, you could see the corn standing tall, in perfect harmony, advancing up and down the field. The corn now seemed to be moving in lockstep like soldiers, marching, watching us. I felt my father was there with others before him.

We watched as the cattle settled down, now munching on our best timothy hay strewn around the barnyard by my mother who had arrived with help. Somehow I knew the farm would be there for the next generation. It was still alive. It had saved me. I hoped I could return the favor.

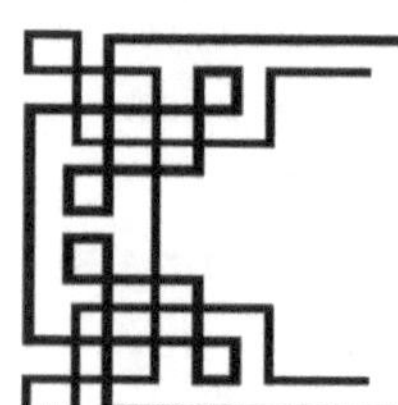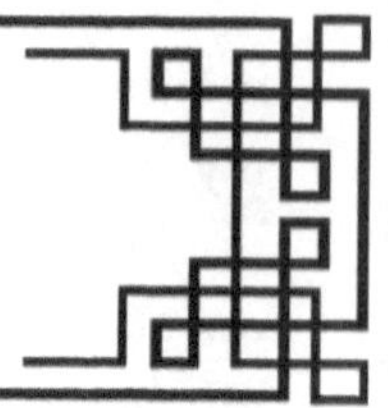

A Brother Who Spared a Dime

When you have to go to a funeral—especially for someone close to you—you ask yourself: How am I going to get through this without breaking down?

From the back of the room, you've seen it before: a son or daughter or mother or father simply can't concentrate on what the minister is saying. You see their shoulders heaving, handkerchiefs being passed, and your heart goes out to them in their grief.

I've had three and a half years to prepare for my younger brother's death. The Johns Hopkins surgeon could only get a third of the highly-metastasizing brain tumor out without making him a vegetable. As a farmer's son and later a truck driver, he had been intimidated by college people. When he came out of surgery, he joked these highly trained medical people were not so smart after all. They kept asking him the same simple questions over and over, such as "Where are you from again?" They never seemed to remember his answer. They even put an ice cube in his hand and ask how it felt. Haven't they ever done that themselves and know? he had questioned. When they asked him to move different parts of his body which had nothing to do with his head, he reminded them where the problem was.

After the surgery, my sisters, his daughters, and I took turns caring for him as he continued to battle the cancer. First it was to accompany him to the oncologist where he received an hour's worth of radiation every day for thirty days. He used to laugh about the specially-made helmet to direct the radiation. He said it was tighter than the bark on a tree. He joked about going to sleep in the MRI machine.

He was put on heavy medication to prevent seizures. He accepted the lethargic effects of those heavy dosages by claiming he had always wanted to sleep in late. We celebrated the results of MRI tests every three—and later six—months as the reports came in: The tumor is not growing.

The doctors were amazed. Even when we rushed him to the hospital because a clear fluid was coming out of his nose causing him to pass out, the doctors had good news. One of the fingers of the tumor, which they had described as a spider, had actually shrunk. It was one that went down near his right eye and into the sinus cavity. They quickly closed up the hole by taking fat from his abdomen to keep the spinal fluid from leaking out. He proclaimed this an easy way to lose weight. He even asked to watch the TV monitor as they checked the hole they had plugged. He apologized for being a snot-nosed kid as the camera recorded the canal passages on the way to the surgical area. His CB handle had been "laughing boy," a very apt moniker given to him by fellow drivers.

What we didn't know—and what the doctors had not told us because they had only expected him to live six months—was that the long-term effects of that much radiation would continue to eat at the brain cells and cause him to go blind. We found this out when his eyesight began to fail. At about this time, we learned the tumor was growing again. We were told further surgery would be of no use.

None of us could tell him what was going to happen. We decided to do everything possible to make his last days better. Farming as well as truck driving had been a tough, demanding profession, so he had never had a real vacation. I remembered an old geography book that had been passed down to him. It was among others my mother had kept in the bookcase for the next person. He had scribbled "I don't believe this" across a photo of the giant Sequoia tree with a car going through it. We decided to go to California. He got the last laugh on that, too, because that tree had fallen down. The U.S. Forest Service had forbidden desecration of such trees. Still, we were able to drive under one already down which had been partially cut to allow the road to go under it.

But time marched on and so did the radiation effects on his eyesight as well as the metastasizing tumor. He gave it a good fight. It would take all of his energy and set him back a couple of days, but we would canoe down parts of the South Branch of the Potomac River where he had never been. Or we would drive back into the mountains to sightsee...something he never had time for as a part-time farmer and truck driver. We talked about our early adventures as kids like the time we decided we should become hockey players. We cut branches to form hockey sticks and used a can as the putt. Each of us would take one side of the pond and race to the middle to see who got the putt first. It was a lot of fun and despite being warned about thin ice we figured our speed would save us. Because I was heavier, I was the first one to go in, which was not a problem since the pond was just four feet deep. But Mike got a laugh out of all the muddy bottom I brought out with me. We also had an angry milk cow that was stored by itself in a hillside area which we used to go in to be chased. We were both pretty good at sliding under the fence before the milk cow could get us.

Mike, like me, often got into trouble although in this case it was not his doing. He had made our father very proud when he won a tractor driving contest at the age of 14. But when a load of hay bales came loose under the traffic light in town, he was brought to the police station. At the time I was working there in a work experience program at our high school which found the program beneficial to relieve an over-crowded high school. I was able to convince the trooper to forgo the state fine. He had been aware that I did not have a driver's license when he once sent me up town to buy some supplies and used the other police car to pull me over. He was sympathetic but when our father came in to protest that Mike was a better driver than the town people, the fine went back on.

Sadly, our mother died before Mike on Mother's Day. He was able to go to the funeral and even laughed when he found out she forbade a hard-core evangelist from handling the service. He was a relative but she preferred her Presbyterian trained minister.

Mike and Mom had also become great friends when he came home to hopefully get well. They enjoyed driving down the valley road for eight miles to go to their favorite diner. When she had become unable to drive, she had not feared riding with him as he went blind. As a self-assured woman whom nobody ever questioned, she was able to give directions while he drove. Both were still upset with whomever it was that reported them being in town at the diner.

"He's a professional driver and my eyesight is perfect," she had protested as she described how they knew the road like the back of their hand. Mike had laughed and at her funeral said, "She's up there now giving somebody directions." All of us got through it with the decorum she would have advocated. She died just eight months before he did.

So when the time for his funeral came, I wondered if I could keep it together. His daughters had spent an emotionally exhausting last few weeks with him. Hospice administered morphine when the rapidly re-growing tumor had ruptured. They had grieved so much they didn't think there were any tears left. I knew I couldn't look at them during the funeral. They were so wonderful to him and he loved them so much.

My oldest sister, who inherited my father's drive and my mother's organization, had been with them every step of the way as they dealt with medical and legal problems, of which there were many. Time and time again she has always been there for Mike and me—solving problems with a compassion and generosity that seemed to have no limits. Fortunately for us, she always remained stoic while facing emergencies. I used to tell her that internalizing things is why she once had ulcers. I figured I would be the one that would break down. I had failed the test trying to look at my brother's baby and childhood pictures which his daughters had put in a photo album for the wake.

But it was one of the photos that saved me from my grief. One of Mike's grade school friends, Arley Shockey, came up to me after looking at a photo of Mike driving a tractor-trailer. Arley was the son of one of the many tenants who used to work the farms. He came from a family of sixteen and opportunities had been very limited. Many of his brothers had gone into the service to escape the poverty. One of them, Carl, and his wife had a son, also in the Army, who was to be married to a fashion designer from California. The designer was planning a huge wedding and she wanted them there. He and Donna had never been on a plane and probably not out of the state that much. They were worried about how her rich parents might feel about them; would they think they were hicks from West Virginia?

Mike had convinced them they had to go. This was when he was having seizures and scheduled for the Johns Hopkins operation. Some people were afraid to ride with him. Carl and his wife were like my mother. They knew Mike was a professional driver and they felt safe with him—that he would get them to Baltimore, Maryland, where they could catch the plane to California. That's when I got a call from Mike. I had experience at airports. He could get us there. All I had to do was make sure they got on the right plane. What was unsaid was that he knew I could take over the car if a seizure came on. We had gone over that before. Like my mother, I never wanted to take Mike's pride in driving away from him. The trip was a success with no difficulties on the road or at the airport. Donna was not hesitant about asking questions. Their layovers gave them plenty of time to find the right gates.

As Carl and Donna said to me before the funeral service:

"Mike was the greatest, the nicest person we have ever known. We wouldn't have gone to California without his help. Laughing Boy is up there somewhere helping somebody and giving directions." It was then I was able to deal with my emotions. Laughing Boy should be celebrated, not mourned.

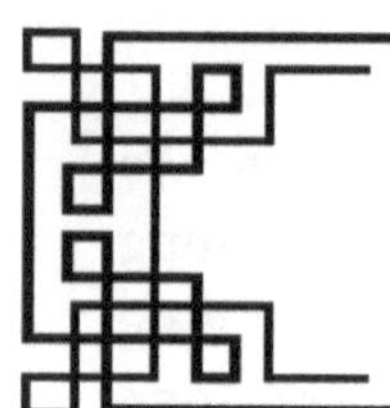

Nature's Cure

"If only everyone knew the simple joy of tasting cool, clear clean water." That was the answer my great uncle Henry had for everything going wrong—from world wars to genocide to divorce to just a bad day.

He would say this as he dipped his wooden ladle into the mountain stream running through his house. His great-great-grandfather Nicholas had settled in this Appalachian hollow 250 years ago. According to his note in the old family Bible, he chose this hillside because of its spring.

Now ninety-two, Uncle Henry is still living in the cabin Nicholas built directly below the mountain spring. Two wings were added over the years and his father had even added a garage. Uncle Henry had all the amenities plus some he said he didn't need such as the big plasma TV set his son had given him.

But even though there was infrastructure in his hollow now for all the houses and trailers lining the road and foothills, Uncle Henry never gave up his mountain stream for city water. He had saved enough land from what had been handed down to him from the original hillside farm to have a garden—as well shutter himself in with trees so he had no need for curtains.

Uncle Henry had even piped some of his mountain spring water down to the road so his neighbors could help themselves to his holistic solution to life's woes. In just thirty years, the sounds of whippoorwills and farm animals in the valley below had been replaced with lawnmowers and barking dogs. There were times when he wondered if there was some undiscovered plant that Mother Nature had wisely infused with birth control. It was needed now.

But Uncle Henry was not a recluse. He enjoyed the company of his neighbors, most of them relatives, including me. He would invite us up to share in his garden, particularly on rainy summer days. He would tell us to throw away our umbrellas, strip down, and enjoy the refreshing reminder of our place in nature and how peaceful the world can be. After recanting how his father used to look out over his corn fields and watch the parched corn blades pocketing out to receive the nourishing rain, he would point to his garden: "If you took the time," he would suggest, "you could see the green tops of buried carrots, radishes, and potatoes spring upward for the rain. Even now you can see the red tomatoes, green and yellow peppers, and even the spotted bird egg beans happily showing themselves off in the glistening rain."

Then he would cup his hands to gather the rain and declare, "Help yourself to my summer rain rainbow with its pots of gold."

My uncle also used the running water from the mountain spring to irrigate his garden when summer rains were scarce. He had never forgotten how his grandmother used to set out a couple of old washtubs to collect water for her flowers. He would help her punch tiny holes in used cans, fill them with water, and place them beside her flowers during dry periods so they could slowly drink their summer rain.

He would recall how his grandfather, rarely missing a forecast of rain, would scurry to gather the cut hay so it would not mold in the field. Afterward, he would relax and enjoy letting the summer rain wash off the heavy sweat he got hurrying the hay into the barn.

"And it wasn't like we kids didn't enjoy a good drenching, too, after working up a sweat," he would say when he knew he had our attention. "Our job was to get all the stray chickens back in the coop. Unlike ducks, they do not like rain and that's why ducks never smell like wet chickens. Another job we had at the coop was laying some boards across wet, loose ground which contained a lot of chicken manure. In a couple of days—especially when it got hot—worms and large night crawler worms would find their way up to refresh themselves under these cool, damp boards. When you pulled up a board you had to dart fast to grab them because they would quickly head down their tunnels to escape the heat of the sun. We not only used the worms for fishing but sold some of the larger night crawlers to fishermen along the river."

He would admonish us never to forget that even the worms knew the answer for having a good life: Cool, Clear, Clean Water.

Then Uncle Henry would urge us to drink from his ladle and dance and bathe in a summer rain as he did. He worried there was not enough fresh water in the world for the growing population. When he invited people to enjoy his pure mountain stream to relieve stress, he would declare: "You think the world has troubles now. Just know that all hell is going to break loose when there is no drinking water."

You see, of all of nature's wonders, Uncle Henry felt water was the most godly. Darwin's survival of the fittest was the rule in the animal world. But he deplored the fact mankind had gone a step further by developing the ability to kill without reason.

Then he would note plants were a close second to being godly. He would allow there was that pitcher feller the insects had to contend with. Uncle Henry could not think of an intentional non-benevolent act committed by water. Yes, there were downpours causing floods that could kill. Still, he reasoned, man could use his smarts to predict, control, and repair the damage of floods. Then he would admonish everyone: "Cool, clean, clear water from the earth is the nourishing life force of Mother Nature. Don't mess with it."

Over the years people just stopped complaining to Uncle Henry about government corruption, terrorism, crime, or greedy

Wall Street bankers and CEOs. They knew Uncle Henry would recommend a drink of his cool, clear, clean water or a summer rain bath to get rid of hate, jealousy, pride, avarice, and "all those wants of what other people have."

But now Uncle Henry is feeling the doom and gloom of world pressures. His cool, clear, clean water is being threatened. He was relieved his part of the Appalachians in the eastern panhandle of West Virginia was mostly limestone. But he had relatives in those Appalachian areas who had to move because mountaintops were being blasted off to get coal. The mountain hollows were filled with sludge, the streams polluted with acidic runoff, and many of their homes rendered worthless from dynamite damage. At least in the old days of underground mining, many had jobs. But it only took a few engineers to blow the tops off the mountains.

Uncle Henry understood the need for energy. He enjoyed his electric lights and had even grown fond of that huge, glaring plasma screen. But he also felt all that black-gold money the politicians liked could be spent on wind and solar power.

Uncle Henry ran his hand down the smooth handle of the cherry ladle, now burnishing a deep burgundy patina. He figured it had been made by Nicholas. He still had the stone trough in his kitchen which his ancestor had built to hold the piped running water—before it made its way to the garden. Uncle Henry said it still served as his best refrigerator. He still had a milk cow. Every morning he would fill his crocks and know that by suppertime, he could run his finger across the top and scoop up gobs of cream. Uncle Henry also raised rainbow trout in his spring-fed trough. He blessed them as they darted among his crocks when he fished one out for dinner. He did not like frozen fish.

Uncle Henry particularly enjoyed watching the piped water do its good work nourishing his garden below the house. He would channel the water into rows, taking pleasure in knowing the plants would soon enjoy it as much as he was.

But the news he had read earlier that day kept coming back into his thoughts. The energy companies were now buying leases for all the mountain land around him to drill for gas. He had read how they could easily drill more than a mile down into the earth and then go sideways using water and chemicals to explode the Marcellus shale to get gas. Reports were coming in from the northern panhandle of West Virginia of polluted aquifers. Mountains of coals were still being taken out of central and southern West Virginia, devastating the landscape as well as polluting creeks.

Now the companies were coming to his eastern panhandle. Uncle Henry felt his state was literally being blown up, above and now underground. He was tired of hearing how it helped his country to become more energy independent.

It was sad to see how sad Uncle Henry was becoming. He kept telling us, "Mother Nature has plenty of solar and wind power to give us. But don't mess with water. It is the priceless source of life."

When Uncle Henry heard the widespread fracking process in Pennsylvania had released so much methane that one lady had actually been able to set fire to the drinking water coming out of her well, he was devastated. Now he had to provide an answer to his own worry and concern which he said should concern the whole world.

He looked up at his mountain springhead. The sun was shining on it. The trees were swaying in the constant breeze. A summer rain began to fall. Uncle Henry stripped down, and with ladle in hand, he headed for his mountain spring where he could enjoy nature's bath and beverage.

We knew what he was going to say when he went up there. "If only everyone knew the simple joy of tasting cool, clear, clean water." Now he was adding: "Problems can be solved. Why can't everyone realize Mother Nature has the answer? It is blowing in the wind and shining on us."

Mistaken Identity

Spring in our river valley, fed by the Appalachians, means a devastating flood at least every twenty years. In the old days it was no problem because settlers built homes on high-ground sites used by Indians who were attuned to nature. Farmers did not worry about their homes, just their crops.

But as the population grew, townspeople wanted to enjoy the river too. As farming became less profitable, river lots were rented. Naturally, the townspeople did not want to make a big investment in a camp that could be flooded, so shacks were built and old rusty school buses moved in. When the federal government, through FEMA, allowed campers to recoup their losses from floods, trailer homes soon lined the river. When that expensive program ended, FEMA instituted flood plain rules requiring trailers to be taken out during the flood season. Today, camping has become so popular and farmers need extra income; huge trailer parks outline the river view.

I remember when these riverside edges were only lined with produce patches, particularly watermelons and cantaloupes, which liked the sandy soil. Farmers would plant these plots right after the spring flood season.

One year we had a flood in late summer. Lots of fruit and vegetables were seen bobbing down the river. My cousin and I got into an old long johnboat and skirted the edges of the rushing water to retrieve what we could. While loading melons, we spotted what looked like a human face down. My cousin became very frightened when he recognized his uncle's plaid shirt and overalls. Despite the heavy current, he jumped in to rescue him.

When he got to the body, he realized he had made a mistake. He forgot his aunt often used her husband's old clothes to dress the scarecrow they had in their tomato patch along the river.

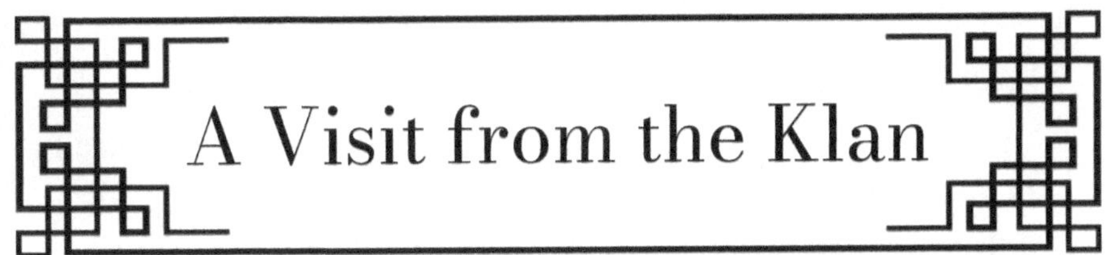

A Visit from the Klan

We were scanning the ads in our local county newspaper looking for a plumber when we saw an ad inviting all Americans who are patriots, believe in God and the Constitution, and are true sons of the Confederacy to a meeting. The ad, announcing a gathering at our county park, was between one from a sawmill and another from a housepainter looking for work.

My brother-in-law, George, who had just finished reading a biography of Robert Byrd, immediately said, "This sounds like the Ku Klux Klan."

My mother said that was impossible because, despite the valley having slaves over 150 years ago, there was no one, particularly our county leaders, who would allow such a meeting. She allowed as to how Byrd today would send such white trash packing before they unpacked.

George pointed out the first amendment protected freedom of speech and public parks had to be open to all groups, even hate groups. A closer reading of the ad extolling a belief in God noted that Catholics were not invited.

"That does it," George declared. "It has got to be the Klan."

Because I was already labeled as a Yankee having moved to New York state years ago, I was quick to tell George we ought to make sure it was them and then find a way to run them out of the valley. My sister, his wife, said it was best to ignore them and they would go away when they found out that no one was interested in joining them. Normally George would agree with her but maybe because he had grown up in Pennsylvania, it took no prodding from me for us to check it out.

We went in his car because it had West Virginia plates. When we pulled into Hampshire County Park along the South

Branch of the Potomac River, we immediately saw another sign it was the Klan. A car and two pickup trucks were parked in front of a cabin they had rented. Draped across the railing on the front porch was a large Confederate flag. On the porch swing sat a beefy guy in a white T-shirt and another perched on the tailgate of one of the pickups. They carefully eyed us as we got out of the car. They didn't say a thing as we approached. There was only the sound of a belch coming from the guy on the porch as he got up, beer in hand. A couple of six-packs were beside him in the cooler. As we went up the steps of the porch, the guy from the pickup came in behind us.

We realized then we should have worn white T-shirts, preferably with a hole or two in them. They eyed us from top to bottom and cast a questioning look at our tennis shoes. However, we both had worn blue jeans because of the work we had been doing fixing the plumbing in my mother's house. We introduced ourselves as man and wife.

Only George was asked for identification, which was a relief because we had not thought about identifying ourselves and I had a New York driver's license.

Then the porch interview began. We were asked to name the street that went by our post office in Romney, how many traffic lights were in the town, what was the name of the diner beside the hardware store, and how many miles it was to the next county. Since we answered those quickly, they did not go further down the list. They knew we were local.

Then George was invited to go in the cabin and I was told to sit on the porch swing. I protested and then was shown the ad: it was the sons of the confederacy that could be members, not the daughters. I let out a curse word that it was not fair which elicited a grin from the beefy porch guy, who handed me a beer and again pointed to the porch swing.

By this time George had gone in knowing I could take care of myself. Since my porch interrogator was quite relaxed, now farting as well as belching, I decided that I might be able to get some proof of who they were if I asked the right questions.

So I asked him if they had a women's support group and told him I was a very good seamstress and was particularly good at making pointed hats. It took him a bit by surprise and he looked confused for a moment but as I maintained a serious composure, he thought about it. He allowed as to how they could use some good sewers, but that my husband would have to be accepted as a member first.

I asked more questions after that such as... "What do you think of the roast beef sandwiches at Shirley's diner?" and "Do you think the woman at the post office is nice?" His answers told me he was not local because he liked the sandwiches and there were no women working at the post office. I did not tell him that a mailman was the only one at the post office and Shirley said there was no reason to have roast beef on the menu with all the chicken that was produced around there.

About five minutes had passed with these inane conversations when a patrol car pulled up. Getting out of it was a guy I had gone to high school with. He had been an all-state tackle for three of his four years. I knew he had become the county sheriff. I hoped that after thirty years he would not recognize me. I quickly got my glasses out of my bag and pulled back my hair with a rubber band as he approached. I hung my head and looked through my purse to avoid eye contact. The sheriff ignored both of us and went inside the cabin, to my relief.

I immediately excused myself to the beefy guy on the porch, saying that I was going to the car to get my knitting yarn and needles, when shouts rang inside the cabin. George came out with the sheriff. While he could not arrest them for holding their meeting, he had told them he would be watching every move they made including the out-of-date inspection sticker on one of the pickups...that if they left now there would be no trouble.

It was enough for them. He told George and me to stay in our car as he watched them pack up and leave. When he came over to our car, he called me by name and asked me what in the hell I thought I was doing on that porch. I explained why we were there and how I tried to disguise myself so he would not know me. This time he laughed and quoted that old saying—you can take the girl out of the country but you can't take the country out of the girl.

Years later, George would have to do some explaining of himself, too. When he was up for promotion at Union Carbide as a section manager of corrosion engineering, he was called in to be told his name was on the membership list of the Ku Klux Klan. Fortunately, his black boss knew there had to be a reason for it and accepted the explanation. Both George and his boss went on to other promotions.

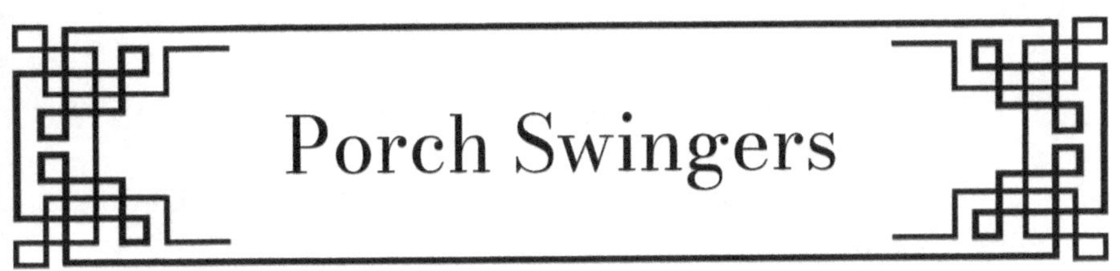

Porch Swingers

Some say making pot smoking legal would not only be a source of tax revenue but cut down on spending in the War on Drugs program. Those smoking it claim it is an intellectual stimulant as well as a medical aid for glaucoma. Then there were the hippies who said it was very recreational.

My mother was aghast during Labor Day weekend in 1971 when several thousand hippies descended on the South Branch Valley of the Potomac River. Word had spread that the Department of Agriculture had found cannabis (*known as hemp to the locals*) was an invasive and thriving plant along the river and fence row.

It was my mother's opinion that pot seekers and users were uncivilized. They came in droves, either by car or by canoe. They were mostly long-haired youths carrying gunny sacks and plastic bags, rushing through the fields and along the river without asking permission.

When she read the *Evening Star* newspaper we got from D.C. in the mail each day, she was even more upset. Our Uncle Garrett Kuykendall was featured on the front page examining marijuana growing wild on his farm.

The staff writer had come to Romney, West Virginia, to write about all the hippies converging on the farms, noting that "the grass that sells for up to a dollar a smoke in Washington grows wild and free in Hampshire County. There are bushels of it growing in the field along the shores of the South Branch of the Potomac. The farmers who work the rich bottom land hack wearily at the cannabis weed in the spring, but they can't keep it from reappearing each growing season, sprouting sometimes to the height of over 12 feet, and filling the warm dairy meadows with a spicy scent that seems to attract the grazing cattle."

Uncle Garrett commented that the cattle also liked it, which set my mother off, causing her not to speak to him for several months. Newspaper reports that began estimating the marijuana along the riverbanks in Hampshire, Hardy, and Grant was worth $60 to $70 million made her even more disgusted. Now there were sellers as well as users trespassing, much to her disdain.

What my mother did like was the arrival of the federal narcotics agents along with the state police and D.C. officials. They conducted what was said to be the biggest raid in West Virginia's history. She was not only quick to welcome them but also volunteered our barns as holding cells while they rounded up hundreds.

Most of the hippies had long hair which she declared had never seen a comb. The girls with rings in their ears didn't bother her but some of the men also had pierced ears. She had been even more astounded to see some even pierced their noses. She had already associated dragon tattoos with rednecks. Even though Uncle Garrett pointed out that most seemed to have doves, hearts, and flower tattoos, she still did not like the idea of puncturing the body with paint. She wondered how they would look when they gained weight and got old. "Those doves will look like turkeys and those hearts will look like tomatoes," she declared.

Because Labor Day weekend was very hot that year, many of these pot seekers had been apprehended in the river without their clothes. My mother had been shocked when she came out of the house with iced tea for the agents. She found her front porch swings loaded with naked hippies, swinging to and fro. She demanded they be put in the hay barn where they could cover themselves up until she could contact the Salvation Army or the Red Cross for clothing.

When the raid was finally over and the valley had been

cleared of several thousand hippies, my mother finally relaxed.

But removing the hemp from the valley had been costly for West Virginia officials. The agriculture commissioner asked and received legislation for a noxious weed law and a total of $72,275 for 1972 to be followed by similar expenditures for the next five years to "eradicate some 2500 acres of stands of wild marijuana."

It was pointed out the problem began when the U.S. army set up a rope factory in 1916 on the banks of the river above Moorefield. The seeds of the hemp plant they used floated into the river and infested the rich bottom lands. But the federal agents said the hemp had already been there because tanneries in the 1800s had used seed oil from the hemp plant to tan hides. So there were many arguments over who should pay for the removal of the hemp.

But my mother said it didn't matter what happened in the past. It was the Department of Agriculture that started it all. She had interviewed one of the fully dressed hippies who handed her an innocuous report from the department which had caused them to invade the valley.

"For heaven's sake," she wrote to the Department of Agriculture officials, "don't you people ever again mention our valley again as a place that needed a pesticide to eradicate heavy, uncontrollable growths of cannabis in Hampshire, Hardy, and Grant County."

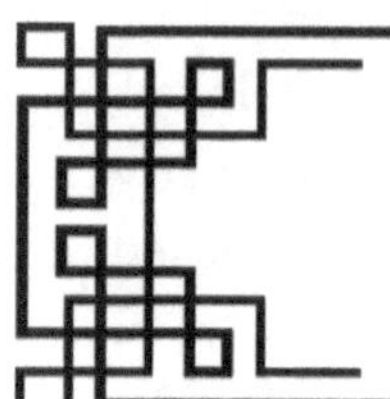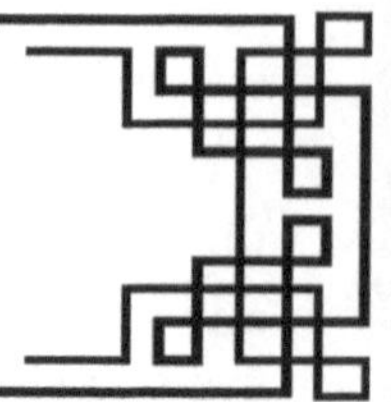

Decker and Her Connections

When my sister Decker and her husband, George, who both had good jobs at Union Carbide in Charleston, West Virginia, retired, they decided to move out of the city. Perhaps it was growing up on family farms that made them feel different in the fancy mountain estate overlooking the state capitol.

It always rankled them they had once been written up by the *Charleston Gazette* for not having a TV set. An enterprising reporter back in the 60s had noticed theirs was the only house in the high-end neighborhood without a TV antenna. He accompanied his story commenting they surely can afford one in that development along with a photo of their house. It wasn't just the neighbors that wondered about them. Rubbernecker began driving up to check out the odd couple.

What the writer would have known if he had gone inside was they preferred reading. There were as many filled bookcases as there were lamps. A closer inspection of their mailbox would have shown they got the local newspapers. Their radios were set on PBS.

So when they moved to what was once coal country, they bought a one-story house at the bottom of a hollow. It was quiet except for the lonesome sound of a nightly coal train coming from a mountain being blown up for black coal. Labor-intensive underground mining was too costly. Many of their neighbors were unemployed. Their rundown houses and trailers lined the hills around them. They fixed up the inside of the house, leaving the outside as is—they did not want to look ostentatious.

They cleared the brush and trash out of the rest of the

ravine and made it into a pasture. They had plenty of room for a garden. Along the road on the way to their house was a small church. This was fine with them because it gave each a chance to easily meet their neighbors. Because of their background, they were quick to make friends. Soon the excess in their garden was shared with everyone on the hillsides. The land included a large stand of trees. They bought a chainsaw and wood splitter. Neighbors would help them cut wood which was equally shared. Those who couldn't work also appreciated wood for their stoves.

Decker tutored some of their kids. Both she and George worked with Habitat for Humanity to help those who needed homes. Decker and George did not have kids but it can be said they certainly had a large extended family. Their savings and pensions allowed them to send some three or four kids a year to college or a trade school. My younger brother and I benefitted from this generosity. They sent him to a tractor-trailer driving school.

At the time, I was working on a peach orchard the summer after high school. My two cousins, Dave and Splinter, had a car and the pay was good. But it was an awful job. Those hot summer days resulted in rotten peaches on the ground surrounded by hungry, biting bees. Worse, the peaches in those days had a lot of fuzz on them causing us to itch. Fortunately, the orchard owner, was religious. He even had a small chapel in the orchard. When the heat and bees got really bad, Dave would let out a cuss word and we'd get a reprieve going into the chapel for a lecture. So when I met a stock car driver there, I saw a way out. He had forgiven me for wrecking his car in a ladies' power puff derby in Winchester. Today, I would not let a tough-talking woman run me off the first curve in a swamp. Fortunately for me, Decker, recently graduated from WVU, had other ideas. She handed me paperwork she had submitted to get me into West Virginia University. She signed a note with the bank so I could borrow the money.

When Decker and George paid school and college bills for others, they preferred to remain anonymous—not just to avoid attention but also to be treated normally. In tutoring, Decker always worked with the teachers to assure herself she was up-to-date on teaching techniques.

I remember a visit when I met one of her students. She was one of twelve people living in a trailer with the tacked-on porch. Along with the parents were one grandfather, two grandmothers, and seven children. Black lung had taken the life of one of the grandfathers. His son, the head of the household, had recently been diagnosed with it. The mine he worked for had been taken over by another company and they no longer received retirement or medical benefits. Four of the children went to school and two of them were pregnant, a fifteen-year-old and sixteen-year-old.

Decker had them on her tutoring list. It was the fifteen-year-old that got her attention the most. Decker knew how incredibly quick she was at learning and found out her IQ was actually 148. Her teacher, aware that Ivy League scholarships were available for poor Appalachian kids, pointed out this girl would certainly be a future candidate. But what about the pregnancy?

Decker deftly discussed abortion. But the girl's family's religion did not allow this. The family had been there for generations. Giving somebody up for adoption was also looked down upon. They were proud of their heritage and never missed a Memorial Day visit to the graveyard. It was filled with highly-engraved tombstones that probably cost them a month's pay when they had jobs.

Because they were on welfare now, a social worker was involved. It was obvious the children could be taken and sent to foster homes. At this time, foster parents were paid $750 to raise each child. But this social worker also understood the culture in the area. She was able to fill out the foster care forms to allow the grandparents to become foster parents. As a result, they were able to use the $1,500 to make a down payment on another trailer. Now there would be four in the new one and seven in the original one. The trailers are next to each other so the new mothers could easily visit their offspring.

Both the teacher and Decker, excited about what could be a great future for the fifteen-year-old, were anxious about her ability to cope socially because she was so timid. The sixteen-year-old got married and it looked like they both would live in the crowded trailer. The fifteen-year-old had just started her junior year in high school. Their backup plan involved sending her to a community college away from home to build up her self-confidence and then send her to university. It worked. She graduated with honors. All my sister had to do was pay anonymously for the room and board. Most importantly, she came back to West Virginia as a lawyer.

When George died, Decker found she was certainly not alone as she might have been overlooking the capitol. There was a huge crowd in the church at George's funeral. For me, it was a chance to learn more about both of them because all their Union Carbide friends were there. I will never forget one of Decker's research lab associates came up to me and said, "Do you know how smart your sister is? She made a lot of money for Union Carbide." I quickly said I did know. I told him we did not have electricity until the mid-forties and she would sit up with my father with a kerosene lamp going over her studies in math. I noted that she probably got those genes from him because he was known for being able to beat the cash register at the A&P grocery store—often attracting large crowds to watch him do it.

One of her first innovations as a chemist was developing the plastic that went into making skirts we wore in the 60s stand out. I was the beneficiary of one of her summer jobs when she was mixing up the ingredients for Channel No. 5. The French company had saved shipping money by giving the ingredients to Union Carbide. Then there was the time when she had made some acid to clean the hooves of Daddy's draft horses. She had put it in an old Halo shampoo bottle. I was living with her that summer and used it to wash my hair. When it did not lather, I realized there was a problem. It took several months for my straw-like hair to grow out. But never let it be said I am not only a huge admirer of her but also very grateful. I was about to run away from a job on the orchard after graduating from high school with a stock car driver when she notified me she had enrolled me at West Virginia University. But first I had to take a test to get in and if I didn't pass, I would go to a prep school. Unlike Decker, who was valedictorian, and Edith, who was salutatorian, I spent my high school years taking easy courses like typing and shorthand and was quick to sign up for a work experience program offered by our high school to alleviate overcrowding. I spent the entire afternoon my senior year working at the police station. However, my father was happy when the shop teacher allowed me in his class where I made some farm gates and a magazine rack for my mother. Anyhow, I was able to pass the exam even though I had to take some courses without credits. My gratitude doesn't stop there. Even though I got lots of college jobs, she still had to sign notes for me to borrow money. When I signed up for the Marines which would pay for my senior year (*and give me a car that I could drive around campus*) she wisely said no and got me out of it because I was underage.

About all I did for Decker was find us a ride with a dairy husbandry professor who was going to Texas to see his relatives and wanted other drivers to make the trip without stopping. Decker was engaged to George, who was at an air force base near his home. Because she was paying back her own college bill plus helping out our family, she had little money. So a free trip was appealing and after meeting and approving of him, we left. I will never forget the 1,000-mile drive across the state of Texas and they did not forget waking up to find out I had stopped to see "the world's biggest rattlesnakes." The sun was just coming up and the owner had left the door open to feed the snakes when I walked in. He was just as mad as they were. But it turned out to be a great trip. The professor liked Decker and George so he gave them more free time by inviting me to Carlsbad Caverns which was near where one of his relatives worked in a potash mine which we explored too. But making it even more exciting for me was a side trip I took to Juarez Mexico where I bought a keg of tequila. I had promised my J School buddies I would bring one back. When I got back to the border crossing with it, the agent said it was over the limit allowed. The place I bought it from wouldn't take it back so I drank enough of it to pass border requirements. Needless to say, my condition was noticed but, as usual, my wonderful sister tolerated me.

So back to her profit-making adventures for Union Carbide. Probably the most notable was developing an insecticide that sterilized the fruit flies. It is still in use today. She was well known for her portable chemical lab. If tank cars were polluted from previous chemicals, she would be called to the site to determine if they were ruined or could be made into another saleable chemical. Once she even went down with a crew to a sunken ship off the coast of Texas to determine the effect of a seawater leak into the chemicals.

The Union Carbide retiree noted George was admired for his smarts as well as integrity. He introduced me to an extremely well-dressed, stunning black woman. She had a deformed arm because her mother had taken a drug during her pregnancy called thalidomide. She had deftly worn a scarf the same color as her heels to detract from the deformity. She had worked for George as his secretary and was full of praise for him. She noted it was not just because he went against the norm then of not hiring black people, but because he was such a great, honest guy who treated everyone fairly and was quick to award people who showed merit.

George's death was quite a loss for all of us. He was especially good to our mother when our father died. He was not only an engineer but a jack of all trades when it came to plumbing and electrical work as well.

Over the years many animals benefited from Decker and George's generosity. Unwanted dogs and cats were often thrown out of cars. Many found their way to their house. Some they took to the animal shelter and others they kept. One was a mongrel they called "Boots," a brown, short-legged dog with white feet who required some extra training. He came back to their house once with half a stuffed turkey. It didn't take them long to figure out what happened. An older couple they often visited for coffee on their morning walks pointed out a run-down frame house farther up the hill. They did not have electricity. Boots probably got it off their porch where it had been placed to keep it cool for the next day. Boot's apology to them came in the form of gift certificates to a nearby restaurant.

If dogs could talk, I am sure one of them came near it as she seemed to understand every full sentence Decker said to her. It was a dog they called "Freckles." Freckles, like many of their dogs, was a throw-away. She was a small white dog with red spots and was pregnant. Her first medical treatment was an abortion. When she was first spotted in the field near their house, she would run off. But the lure of food left for her finally induced her to trust them. At first, she was wary of George, causing them to suspect her owner had been a male who mistreated her.

After George died, Freckles continued to be a constant companion for my sister—doing a two-mile walk each day to keep in shape. Freckles was "part hound and who knows what else," they used to say. She had an instinct for hunting. One day a bald eagle saw Freckles going after a small groundhog. For a while, it looked like Freckles might be the victim instead. But my sister was swift with the porch broom and the eagle lost.

Then there was the time Decker and Freckles were walking along the stream by her house. They discovered the makings of a meth lab. As a chemist, Decker quickly analyzed it and called the Hazmat officers. She had identified all the ingredients but one bottle of liquid. She was surprised to find out it was actual urine. It seemed the unemployed teens running the operation boiled it down to recover the Sudafed chemicals. But she did not have to fear retribution for getting rid of the operation. One of her neighbors quickly figured out who was responsible. He assured her that she was in no danger and never would be.

Freckles lived there for over sixteen years but Decker did not know how old she was when they found her. But what was always amazing to me was how she seemed to understand she had hit the jackpot with my sister. Decker could not touch a suitcase without Freckles immediately running to the car to make sure she was not left behind. If we were going somewhere, Decker would tell her to go to the bedroom, which she immediately did. But the minute she heard our car come back in the driveway she would be at the door, frantic until Decker told her she was fine.

Never one to go to the doctor, Decker often drove those who needed a ride to the doctor as well as to stores. We used to laugh that West Virginia was so hilly, the three dollar stores were everywhere because Walmart could not find enough flat land to build. Decker would also take people to meet a medical van that made the rounds in rural America because doctors were so scarce. It even had a C-scan in it. Those without insurance could also get checked out by a nurse practitioner. It would be the busiest day at the strip mall.

As for Decker, she used to say she was too busy to get sick. But she would add not having a job or future can make you sicker than most.

During my last conversation with her before she died, I asked what was new with the neighbors. She told me she had just gotten back from a two-minute wedding. Turns out the guy had just left her house after repairing her lawn mower and said, "Why don't you walk down to the church with me...I am getting married now." So she did. Turns out his wife was someone Decker had tutored in chemistry so she could pass the test to become a nurse. Her husband had died in the mines and it was a second marriage for her, too. "Really, just two minutes," I said. "Yes," she declared, "they did not want a formal ceremony so the minister just had them repeat 'I do's' and they kept the rings they had. But one of their kids made a cake and there was punch."

Then she declared: "Do you remember the days back home when punch was a bowl full of ginger ale with Neapolitan ice cream thrown in? Well, that is a delicious recipe that has stood the test of time. So I was among the last ones to leave."

Even though Decker outlived George by some fifteen years, she was never alone. One of their early benefactors, Danny, became a son to them. To me he is a combination of George and Decker with all their skills. He continues to be a good neighbor.

So there never really was a need for me to worry about Decker. As she once said, "I have lasting friendships you can't buy." Then I thought about Freckles. Now, she was a dog that would agree.

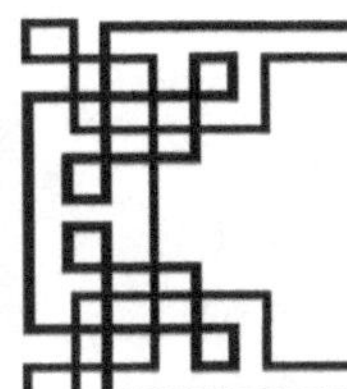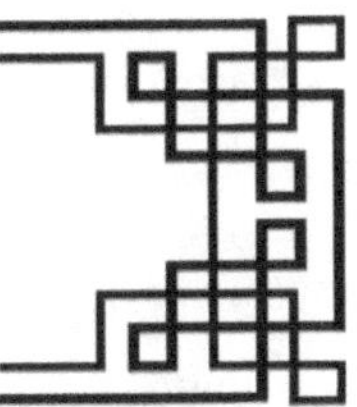

Make Something of Yourself

Farming was a tough business when we were growing up in the 40s and early 50s so we were often advised to "leave and make something of yourself." There were four of us, just two years apart from each other—my two sisters, Decker and Edith, and brother Mike. Getting out was not easy but fortunately the oldest—Decker—was brainy and mortgaging the farm to put her through West Virginia University turned out to be my good fortune, too. I was just four years younger and Decker, after majoring in physics and chemistry, got a job at Union Carbide. She not only began paying off her bill but she enrolled me in the University, too, foiling my plans to run off with a stock car driver. I ended up with General Electric.

The middle sister, Edith, groomed to be a socialite, received my mother's egg money for piano lessons. She was sent to live with well-to-do relatives in Winchester, Virginia, to become a nurse. She swore she would marry a doctor and it only took her a year out of training to do it. My young brother was expected to run the farm. But when my father died, the farm equipment had to be sold to pay the taxes. So my brother became a driver for McLean Trucking. My mother was able to stay in the farmhouse by renting it to neighbors.

Although all of us were very different, we got along fine and holidays were good times—except I had a problem with my brother-in-law, the doctor. Roland reminded me too much of some greedy CEO types I had worked for.

Over the years, it bothered me how he would do things like fill my mother's grocery cart with expensive items and then disappear at the checkout counter leaving the bill for my mother, Decker or me. My mother would never complain because she felt honored to have a doctor in the family.

For at least 15 Christmas holidays, Roland would needle me to get him a gallon of Vermont Maple syrup although he never gave a gift that was worth over two dollars. Each Christmas my mother would ask me to get it for him despite my protests of his being able to afford a Maple tree farm.

Then, one Christmas my husband was given a gallon of Vermont Maple syrup which cost about $60 at the time. It took us nearly a year to finish it. Now with an empty jug and another Christmas approaching, I decided it was time to fulfill the doctor's wishes. A trip to a high-volume grocery store resulted in a gallon of Aunt Jemina which cost me about $5 although I tried to find something cheaper to fill it up.

The only one I let in on about my secret gift was my brother Mike who I knew I could always count on for support. Like me, he did not feel the doctor added any great value to the family's reputation. Both of us felt Decker's husband, who was an engineer and quick to do any plumbing or electrical work needed for Mom, was not given the same royal consideration.

So when my mother made a huge stack of blueberry buckwheat pancakes for the esteemed doctor, Mike and I were waiting for him to try it out. Roland opened it with a flourish and a thank you to me for finally getting it after all these years. He poured a generous portion of it on his stack and, as usual, did not offer to share it and again thanked me for finally making his wish come true with a big smug smile.

I was afraid my brother would give away my secret. As Roland swished his fork around the syrup on top of the pancakes as he ate it, he declared it to be worth the wait. Despite my brother's probing with comments of "wow, that must really be good...I bet it came from the best Maple trees in Vermont... have you ever tasted anything so good?" and even asking if it was better than Aunt Jemina's, Roland continued eating with glee. The pleased doctor declared it to be delicious and sarcastically said it was too bad he had not been able to enjoy it years ago. He wolfed down the rest of the pancakes swimming in the syrup and passed his plate for another heap of pancakes which he doused with the syrup.

While my brother and I thoroughly enjoyed that Christmas breakfast, I could not tell my mother what I did. She would have said it was hateful and she was very disappointed with me. My only disappointment to this day, however, is that the revered doctor does not know what I did. When my mother is gone, I told myself I would tell him. But then I remembered that my sister Edith would not appreciate it.

While Edith and I ended up as friends, we did have our difficulties. I probably deserved her greatest disgust with me back in 1964. She had recently met Roland when she became an operating room nurse at the Ford Hospital in Detroit. His last name was Crane and she wanted to check out the Cranes in New England, after having learned that the Cranes in Dalton, Massachusetts, produced fine stationary including the paper money was printed on—plus Crane was a big name in plumbing manufacturing. She found an address for the Cranes in Westchester County and had written them we were coming to the World's Fair there and would like to drop by to say hello.

I was driving the used TR-3 I had just bought then. We drove to the World's Fair for most of the day and were coming back across the Whitestone bridge when it began raining. I had already had problems snapping the top in place. The rain shrunk the top causing it to come off. Fortunately, it stopped raining and Edith was able to get her hair fixed at the service station. When we got to the address in Westchester, we found the huge house covered the whole block. I parked in the circular driveway and we were soon greeted at the door by Mrs. Crane in a hostess skirt. She invited us into the parlor where her husband was smoking a pipe and reading the newspaper. He was the head of the Crane Foundation. They were both very gracious but it became apparent to me they were trying to figure out who Roland was. Edith gave them enough information that they realized it was their third cousin's son who had been sent to a boy's academy. This did not seem to be disconcerting to Edith, anxious to make a good impression. She started talking about our southern heritage beginning in the 18th century and how one of our great aunts had gone to a finishing school. But when the conversation alluded to our family having a plantation, I got nervous—particularly when they mentioned it would be nice to visit. One would also have thought Decker was running Union Carbide and that I was head of all GE communications. When Mr. Crane asked Edith why she chose nursing with such an enterprising background, I felt there was a bit of condescension going on. I immediately pointed out that Edith had come in third on the national boards to become a nurse and was the top of her class, noting that passing the boards would be a challenge for some doctors I knew. But then, realizing a visit to our farm and not a plantation would be disastrous for everyone, I went on to point out that Daddy had been very proud of Edith's skills since she was a teenager. I recalled the time both of us came back from fishing at the river to discover one of our Hampshire hogs had been run over by a truck. Edith took the fishing line from her bamboo pole and while I pushed the guts back in the hog, she sewed it up. The hog survived although its white belt was crooked from the surgery. It brought the usual price when it was sold. Edith had even taught my father how to use a hypodermic needle to administer penicillin which greatly enhanced his reputation as the valley veterinarian. Needless to say, Edith did not speak to me as I drove her to the airport. When I got back to Schenectady, the phone rang with my mother telling me I had ruined my sister's life and hung up. The next call came from Decker who wanted to know what happened. Decker, always the mediator and pragmatist, resolved our differences by pointing out I had been rude in my explaining we did not have a plantation but that I had saved all of us from an embarrassing visit.

As it turned out Edith soon married Roland and as far as I know he never knew about our visit to his distant relatives. He probably never knew his wife had proven to be a good surgeon in her teenage years either.

The Way We Were

I was about to finish my scrambled eggs when he stepped up to the counter. I had noticed him staring. I knew that he was part of my past but I could not place the name. I figured he would put me on the spot because everyone in my hometown knew each other. When they encountered someone who had left the area, they seemed to enjoy making you guess who they were.

But instead of saying "Guess who I am," he said, "You may not recognize me from packing corn fifty years ago but I will give you a hint. There are only eleven of us left."

I immediately knew he was a Kesner. There were seventeen in that family. My mother, with just four children, had marveled at the fact that his mother, Irene, had spent nearly half of her life pregnant, with just two miscarriages and all of them born at home.

Determined to come up with his first name, I decided to narrow the field with a comment of my own. "I remember when you went in the service. You left us alone in that sweaty field filling each bag with five dozen ears of corn."

I knew that seven of the boys in that family went into the service, not just to get out of poverty—but as a way to get an education. The GI bill was well known to farm boys—even though they knew that if a war was going on they may not make it back for a free college education. Many called it the greatest government program since the WPA and CCC programs. I knew that two of them, Dick and Sam, had not made it back and I commented on their sacrifice.

He seemed pleased that I knew this. He told me that he had gone into the Air Force and ended up with a job at the nearby Allegheny Ballistics plant which was now building weaponry for the drone. "O.K.," I said to myself. "This is either Charlie or Bill who went into the Air Force." I silently thanked my mother who had kept me up to date with what was going on in the valley over all these years.

Next, I asked him if he remembered the festivals we used to have at the church. They were so well known for home-made ice cream, cakes, and pies that people came from other valleys to attend. He laughed and said, "Of course, my family won nearly every cakewalk because there were so many of us." We laughed about those cakewalks. The church organist could be heard playing a hymn while everyone walked around in circle formation. When the music stopped, a broom was low-ered by the deacon and whoever was facing it won the cake.

I knew then I had the first name of this Kesner. "That's right, Bill," I said. "My mother always admired how deft you were in figuring out when the hymn would end and the broom be lowered. You were quick in hurrying up or slowing down the line to be in position to win the cake. I assume this sense of position served you well as a pilot."

We both laughed as he sat down and ordered more coffee for the both of us. He then told me he heard I had "become a Yankee." He quickly added, "But a nice one not about to invade the south again." So we discussed what both of us had been doing the past fifty years. Yes, our starts in life had been very different. My grandmother owned the farm his grandfa-ther worked on.

My father's farm, like many others in the valley, was small. Most of the valley kids took summer jobs working in produce fields or peach, apple, or cherry orchards. In our case, it was mostly packing corn for a farmer who cultivated over 500 acres of prime valley land. Both of us had started at age ten. Because sweet corn was a perishable crop, it was not unusual for us to spend our entire summer days working from sunup to sundown. Yet my siblings and I knew that military service would not be our only option for higher education. Our parents could mortgage the farm to get us into college.

I was humbled by the fact Bill had been so successful in his military positions. It didn't take me long to find out he had helped two of his younger sisters through nursing school and one through the state university.

I was not surprised when he said he and his wife did not have children. It must have been tough being one of seventeen children. Now being relaxed with our past, I told him that I had lived up to my identification after the age of seventeen as being "Bill's daughter who never married." I finally got married when I was sixty-two. He simply laughed and said, "Looks like both of us didn't want to contribute to those long cakewalk circles."

Then we began on the subject of what kids are doing today. Yes, it was great there were child labor laws. Still, both of us felt early working experience had given us the drive and confidence to do more in life. Yet we both knew there were some kids working with us back then that should have been in school. They worked odd jobs year around for the produce farmer because their parents were so poor. They were hidden when the truant officers came by and did not get any education at all. We knew some of them were on welfare today.

Even though both of us were retired, we were still active, particularly in not-for-profit groups. We could afford to donate time. But this next generation might not have the opportunities we had. We worried about how staying in the middle class today meant both parents must work. Worse, the future did not look good as the rich become richer and the poor poorer. At this rate we could become a third-world nation with no middle class.

It was then the coffee started to taste bad. We were becoming depressed. It was even worse when we discussed politics. We decided to take a drive up our river valley. It was there we found hope again for the future. People in the cities wanted healthy food raised without growth hormones and antibiotics. Those with gardens expanded them for sales at the farmer's market. They also found a market for free-range chickens and hogs and beef not raised in feedlots.

We high-fived each other and ended our drive to the church at the end of the valley where we wished we had a cake to celebrate. But when we saw the peach tree in back was ripe, we decided to renew our migrant worker skills.

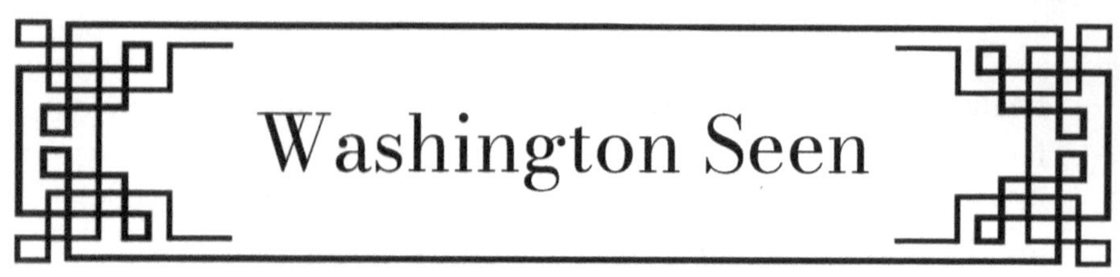

Washington Seen

We just stood there looking at each other in the store, trying to figure out who it was from the past. We knew we had shared something, something that was better left in the past. Yet it was not an unfriendly look we shared.

It had been some twenty years since I had been shopping in Cumberland, Maryland, where my mother used to bring me and my sisters for what was then big-city shopping to find a special dress. The independent store was still there, and still expensive despite competition from big mall stores like Macy's or Marshall's. As we continued to eye each other, we realized we were holding the same sweater at the cash register.

Then it struck us at the same time, both asking, "What are you doing here?" as we saw images of each other at the corn packing shed when we were twelve years old. I realized the question might be insulting to Helen and quickly mumbled that she must live here and it was me that was a stranger to the store as I had not been there since my mother bought me a high school graduation dress. Helen, knowing I would never have dreamed that she one day could afford to be shopping there, had replied yes, indeed, she lived only five blocks from the store, adding that she was indeed a frequent customer.

We hugged each other as we picked up where they had left off twenty years ago, two scared girls not knowing what life was about and anxious to find out. The fancy department store no longer had style shows, but it still had the corner showroom which was now a small café. There was a line so Helen and I put the sweaters on the counter, telling the clerk we would be back. When we sat down, we almost simultaneously said, "You are looking good." Then we laughed, knowing they would have never been so formal with each other back in the modern sugar corn packing shed.

Helen and I had been the only girls working in the shed that summer and happened to both be "going on sixteen." It had been our first real paying job with social security deductions and we had naturally lined up with each other as the foreman explained we would have to be at work at 6 a.m. every morning, we had thirty minutes for lunch, and we could go home at 8 p.m. There were about twenty boys our age plus several old men deemed too old to pick the corn in the hot fields. The shed had just been modernized with a refrigeration system to keep the corn fresh as it came in from the fields. The corn was dumped in the huge tank of cold water and a conveyer belt brought it up to the station where all the workers teamed up, one on each side of a crate, to pack in five dozen ears. In the old days, this job was performed right at the edge of the hot fields, so Helen and I soon learned not to complain about our hands getting cold and stiff as we packed corn. We also knew this job paid better than cleaning and cooking for the boss, so we quickly joined the others in commenting how nice it was to be working in a cool shed instead of outside in the hot sun like the adults were.

But despite our becoming fast friends that summer, both of us knew our lives were quite different and we would not likely meet again unless it was back at the corn shed for another summer. My parents were farmers. My dad had gotten pneumonia that year and money was hard to come by as he had to hire an extra man to do the work he couldn't. I worked at both the corn shed and at orchards after the corn season was over. Helen, on the other hand, came from a family which eked out a living following seasonal perishable crops in the south. Ever since she could remember, Helen had picked peaches, apples, beans, and even cotton. Unlike me, Helen had never been to school but had learned to read and write from her mother who had received some schooling before marrying Helen's father. He was working the fields now and I had not liked him when I met him. He looked at me with a look I didn't understand then. After that the foreman told me not to go near him.

During the lunch break, Helen and I would cook some of the corn to go with what people had brought in their lunch buckets. Helen would serve her father and I noticed she would become very timid when he came in at lunch and at the end of the day. While it was hard work and one could explain getting bruised if the conveyor built got too close or one of the heavy crates fell on you when the belts moved forward, I had noticed Helen had more than the usual cuts and sores from the thin, papery shucks over the corn ears and the sharp, stalky ends. But Helen would only look down if questioned and say that she was the one in the family that never seemed to do anything right and that her father was upset with her because of it.

It had not made a lot of sense to me and it still didn't when Helen and I decided to sneak on one of the big refrigerated tractor-trailers that came in to take the corn to Pittsburgh, Washington, Baltimore, and New York. Neither of us had ever been to a big city and we decided on Washington since that was where the Capitol was. Knowing my mother's dislike for the people who worked in the shed, I made up a story about staying with the foreman's family, which my mother approved of. I was with Helen when she told her father she was going to stay with me that night which seemed strange because he was not mad, just sounded so surprised. He had to know we were best friends even though I had stayed away from him.

When the Washington truck driver was overseeing the loading of the corn crates into his tractor-trailer that evening, we sneaked into the upper bed loft in the back of the cab. We figured that if we kept quiet by taking a nap, he would not discover us until it was too late for him to turn back. He was not much older than my brother and I had assured myself he would not be mad at us.

Our plan worked, especially since we were so tired from the day's work that we soon fell asleep in his upper bed loft. In fact, we didn't wake up until he was backing into the dock to unload the corn. Between the confusion of the teamsters at the dock on strike and the exasperation he felt just getting through the picket lines, he just sat there looking at us as he adjusted his rearview mirror to see what was going on in his upper loft.

After much explanation from us, he decided there was nothing he could do. He would hurry back and drop us off early the next morning at the corn shed when he left an empty trailer there to be loaded during the day. Still, he was upset and when he saw that he was going to have to unload the truck himself because the dockhands were teamsters, he told us we could earn our trip by helping him unload. In fact, he would even drive us by the Capitol Building on the way home so we could see it.

Hours later, the trailer was unloaded and we were giddy with laughter, mesmerized by the huge size of the distribution center. To me, it was larger than the valley I came from, and, unlike Helen, I had never seen so much produce in one place, but she had and described fields of melons that went for miles in the Carolinas. One of the managers who had been sent in to make sure the center was open even gave us a tour which included a sampling of apples, oranges, bananas, and strawberries. He even gave us an official sweater worn by the dockhands since the distribution center was also refrigerated.

The driver was as good as his word. He even let us sit up front with him in the high cab and we had a grand view of the lit-up Capitol at night. It looked just like the picture we had seen on the huge calendar pasted up on the big ammonia tank in the corn shed where the foreman checked off the days of work, noting who had been where.

On the way back the driver pulled over to take a quick nap and sent us to the overhead bunk to get some sleep, too. But we were too excited to get much sleep as we chattered continuously. It was when Helen rubbed one of her bruised arms and said that she had the best rest she ever had with me in the overhead bed that got the driver's attention. She mentioned that the driver had not come to bed with us. She wondered to me if he hit people after he played with them in bed.

The driver, who had been listening and teasing us to get some sleep, immediately changed his attitude—so much so that Helen and I felt we better not say anything more until we could figure it out if he was mad. He became very serious. His full attention was on Helen as he asked some very gentle questions. It was very confusing to both of us and Helen answered as best she could so he wouldn't be mad. He had been so good to us—driving by the Capitol and not bawling us out for hiding in his truck. We arrived back to the corn shed just as the sun was coming up and he made us swear no one would know that we had been in Washington with him. He even dropped us off about a mile below the sheds so no one would see us.

When the crew showed up for work, we came from behind a stack of empty crates, pretending that we had just arrived, too. Work resumed as usual and we were elated that we had seen the Capitol and sneaked off when we could to recount our adventure together. When the Washington driver picked up the tractor-trailer load of corn that evening, he made a point of coming over to Helen and me to assure himself no one knew about our trip. When my ride home came, he followed me to make me promise again never to say anything no matter what happened and said that everything was going to be alright no matter what anybody said. When I left, he was still talking to Helen.

The next morning was very confusing and scary to me. Helen's father had been found in the field badly beaten up and Helen had not shown up for work. The foreman was not that concerned since the sugar corn picking season was nearly over and, besides, who knew what Helen's father had done to get himself beaten up. The foreman had never liked him.

I worked at the refrigerated corn shed for two more summers after that and each time asked the workers if they knew Helen where she was. But none of them did. Several times I spotted the driver who had kept our secret about hiding on his truck. I would ask him if he ever saw Helen and he would just smile and told me not to worry about Helen, that he was sure she was fine and that she was a good girl.

Now, twenty years later, Helen and I were paying for our sweaters and laughing, wondering if that is what triggered our memories and how the cashmere sweaters we got on sale were very different from the heavy wool ones in the food distribution center in Washington.

My puzzlement about Helen had finally been cleared up. I found out the driver and his friend had taken Helen to a home for girls to get her away from her molesting father. The driver had checked on her for years and even helped her get a job. She was now a manager of a grocery store. She and her husband had two children.

Helen saved the best news for last as we chatted in that department store café. She said, "Why don't you come to dinner tonight? We're having an outdoor barbecue. You may recognize my husband. He owns several tractor-trailers now."

I was delighted. I got the address and, on the way there, I passed an open-air fruit market. I already had a bottle of wine for the celebration but it hit me that there was something much better to bring. I saw they had sweet corn and asked if they sold it by the crate. I laughed as I heaved the heavy crate of five dozen ears into my car.

When I got there, one of Helen's kids opened the door. I asked the kid to get her parents as I needed some help unloading the car. It broke the ice. We had a wonderful evening, full of laughs and catching up on all the good things that had happened since the summer of '55.

I left in happy tears when they toasted me for having introduced them. It had been my idea to hide on that truck and go to Washington.

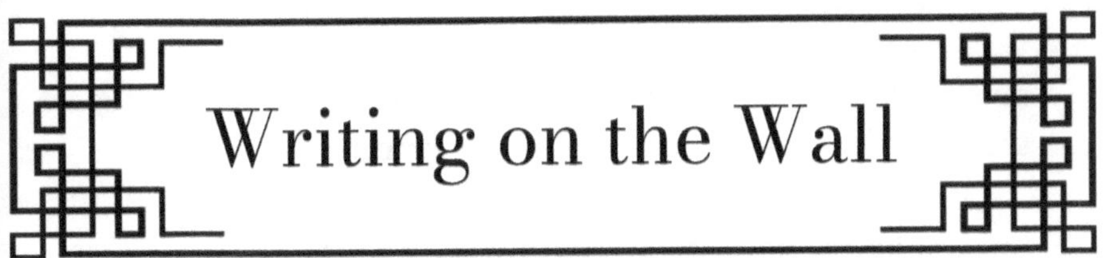

Writing on the Wall

My sister Edith used to say it is silly to keep a diary because if it is worth remembering, you will recall it.

But there are many times I have found you need a trigger to unleash some old memories.

One came rushing back to me when I was visiting our old birthplace. Our old fruit and nut trees had been replaced with hardwood trees. The lawn was still well-kept but now there were a variety of flowering shrubs around the house.

The new owner was trimming the azalea bushes along the west side of the house when I saw a faded inscription on the lower stone wall. I immediately recognized it as Mike's, my brother who was four years younger than me. While it would have been difficult for most people to read the faded crayon inscription, I knew it read "South Branch Valley."

When I burst out with a delighted laugh, the owner asked why it was so funny. I explained to the new owner the whole row of azaleas by the wall had once been the scene of a huge four- or five-foot-deep pit. It had been dug out by my brother to recreate our valley surrounded by mountains.

I pulled back the azalea she was trimming to see if there were more tell-tale signs of my brother's little valley by the wall. But fifty years had taken their toll and the azaleas looked like they had been flourishing with years of mulch.

I recalled he had dug the pit and used the soil to make higher mountains on each side which also prevented the rainwater from washing out his pit. On the east side he had carved out our mountain road which dropped down in our valley periodically but went back up the mountainside. Like our ancestors, he had also done what he could to preserve as much tillable flat land as possible. The west mountainside had the river below which came from the south and ran north.

He had carved small chips of wood into the shape of houses, barns, and sheds. Toothpicks were used for fencing which he carefully placed in saw-tooth fence fashion. Stone walls, some of which still existed from the early settlers, were replicated with pebbles. Those farmers that had ponds could quickly locate their farms because he used small mirrors to complete the picture. I remember my father laughing about that because he said it was a good thing there were only three ponds in the valley because his big sisters and mother had discovered the mirrors in their makeup compacts missing. He sliced and hued out corn stalks and lined them up to hold water in his river. My father called the pit his son's out-of-control terrarium.

Mike made room for himself in this busy farming valley by placing himself in our father's largest cornfield. Because he was just a toddler, one could walk by this pit and not know he was in there. He was usually clad in blue bib overalls. You might see that mop of blond hair on top. But you sure could hear him. His favorite item was a cast-iron truck he had gotten for Christmas. Our father was amazed at how well he could mimic the changing of gears. He would spend hours running it up and down the road on the east side of the pit. His only break in revving up his engine was when he chewed the candy cigarettes he liked.

His appetite for Cracker Jacks also became insatiable because he found a good use for all the miniature people and animals he found in each box. They were placed strategically along the road or in the fields where he would drive his truck to pick them up or load them in the back if they were animals. Socially, he was active as his miniature people often visited each other while the animals never failed to find themselves in a fresh pasture.

It was then that the new owner of the house started laughing. She told me how she had found many of these little plastic toys when she was planting her azaleas. She thought they were odd and had not known about Cracker Jacks. She had been curious and put them in a jar in the basement. Did I want them?

Yes, I certainly did.

Now I have a vivid reminder of a memory well worth maintaining. My brother is gone now. Today I wonder if it was that tiny truck that resulted in him becoming a cross-country tractor-trailer driver. I hoped he had found the same joy in a lot of other valleys across the country.

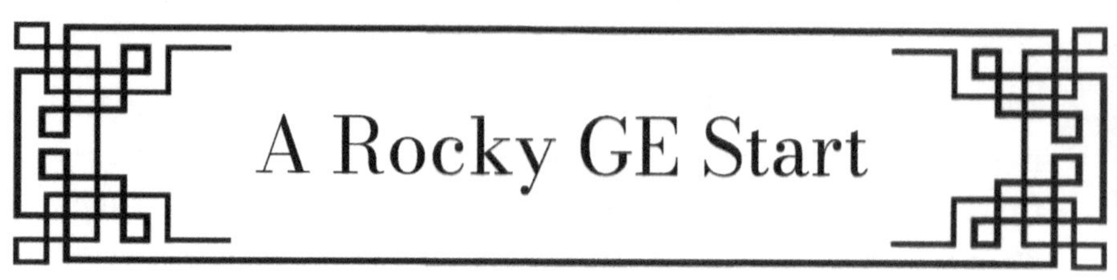

A Rocky GE Start

Looking back on a chaotic writing career at GE, I realize I could be my own worst enemy because of who I was.

I was due to go back to the *Wheeling News-Register* when I graduated to become a staff reporter at $70 a week. But this changed during several School of Journalism graduation parties *(we hated leaving each other)* when employment ads were read aloud. The one from GE was particularly intriguing because it promised opportunities unlimited in Schenectady, New York, the mothership of GE with 28,000 employees in the city that lights and hauls the world.

It was suggested by my J school pals it was time the Yanks up north knew I had style. We were tired of being labeled as hillbillies.

Even Norman Rockwell's *Saturday Evening Post* got into making fun of West Virginia when they offered to cover the homecoming game if the queen would be barefoot when crowned. They had already featured our basketball star, Jerry West, as the Hick from Cabin Creek, West Virginia. Despite our best efforts, we seem to lose even when winning games. When it was announced the games would be filmed in color, Coach Art Lewis had the West Virginia football field dyed green to show off the field. The dye proved to be color-fast on the uniforms with both sides turning green by halftime.

After much teasing our *Athenaeum* gang decided they should help me fill out an application for "unlimited opportunities" in Schenectady. We accomplished this at a party in the planetarium. To this day, I am amazed that I got a call from GE asking me to meet the editor of *GE News* in New York City. The letter went on about my unlimited capacity for adult refreshments *(I won the coveted School of J Bladder Award in 1959)* as well as my health, having been kicked off the soccer team because I sent both the sorority girl and the ball into the cage. But it was the health section that may have been the key to an interview. The professor, upset that I was not continuing his passion for the Fourth Estate at the *Wheeling News-Register*, noted that I was fairly good-looking and companies did not want to hire somebody who looked marriageable. He suggested I add that I had a hysterectomy.

When GE said it would pay my way to the big city, I set up another interview with a brokerage house looking for a communicator. But I never got to that interview scheduled three hours later. When I got off the Eastern Airlines plane at what was then Idlewild Airport (*JFK was still alive*) I met the editor, Al Denniston, who looked amazed when he saw me wearing a picture hat. My mother, who had always tried to make southern ladies out of her daughters, insisted I wear it. Considering the letter I had written about my "athletic" abilities, I decided it might be a good idea.

What I really had going for me, however, was a huge book of clippings from articles I had written for the *Wheeling News-Register* and those in our daily newspaper at the university, including being the editorial writer. He had been impressed.

When Denniston finished reading some of the articles in my huge book of *Athenaeum* and *Wheeling News-Register* clippings at the airport, he suggested that he show me New York City because I had never been there. I quickly agreed and put the book in a nearby locker.

After a visit to the Empire State Building, he suggested we have lunch at the Rainbow Room for another view of the city. It was here I began ordering drinks I had heard about but never had in a dry state where the only drinks were served in veteran's clubs. Even there you got your drink by ordering a Seven-Up and lifting the candle off the bottle top which contained Seagram's Seven and not shine if you were lucky. Perhaps it was this hard-core experience that enabled me to consume a Manhattan, then a Martini, a Singapore Sling, a Black Russian, a Stinger, and so on. I continued going down the list of drinks to Al's amazement. Fortunately, he had a train to meet to get back to Schenectady. He paid the cab driver to take me to the airport and rushed off. My problem began when the driver asked me which airport. I decided I couldn't have gotten that far away and told him the nearest one. When we got to LaGuardia, I found Eastern Airlines but my locker key to get my book of clippings would not work. The agents couldn't figure out why it wouldn't open either. It had the same number. So a maintenance person was called to blast it open at which time we found nothing.

It was then the agent asked to see my ticket with the discovery that I was at the wrong airport. Needless to say, I missed the flight. When I got to Washington, D.C., I missed the train from there to West Virginia. When I walked into our farmhouse a day later, my mother told me that GE had called and I had the job. They would pay me $20 more a week than what I had been offered by the *Wheeling News-Register*. Then she asked me where my hat was. I did not tell her how it had sailed off the top of the NBC building from the balcony of the Rainbow Room. Nor did I tell her I missed the other interview.

When I arrived by train in Schenectady (*as in most eastern industrialized U.S. cities, your first view is a junkyard*), I wondered what I had gotten myself into. But soon I was making my way to the local YWCA where I knew women could get a room. My experience in Wheeling had shown me that a single woman looking for a room was highly suspect of turning it into a red-light locale.

When I began the job, employment at the main plant was at 28,000. It was a city within a city. The newest building, the world's largest manufacturing building, covered over ten acres. It was number 273 because that was how many buildings had been built since Edison moved his dynamo plant out of New York City in 1891. The plant was vertically integrated.

Everything needed to build a turbine, motor, or generator was there. I will never forget the smell of cherry, walnut, and mahogany as patternmakers carved the shape of turbine parts into the wooden molds. I felt like I was in a Dante's *Inferno* scene in the iron and steel foundries where molten metal pours were made to make different castings of all the parts. Production and assembly were also supported by the wire mill, tool, and die shops, insulating materials and blueprint operations. Each product had its testing facility to assure it operated with the precision of a Swiss watch as advertised. In the product development and testing labs, the working environment of vulnerable turning parts such as turbine blades would be simulated to show the effect of being blasted by years of hot steam traveling thousands of miles an hour.

The AC and DC motor and generator business was just as impressive. In Building 60, huge hydro-generators the size of circus tents were being built to generate electricity from water dammed up in the Midwest.

Not everything was huge. The intricate, all-white, clean room in Building 169 where vacuum tubes were built was just as interesting.

The huge GE plant had its own power plant to provide electricity, its own railroad and plant bus system, a fire station, a couple of cafeterias, a medical clinic, an employee store with appliances, and a huge athletic facility with indoor and outdoor sports.

I was mesmerized by the huge plant and its history. Thomas Alva Edison and electrical pioneers like the brilliant mathematician Charles Proteus Steinmetz gave birth to the Electrical Age. They gave Schenectady the title of "the city that lights and hauls the world." Edison's two original buildings were still there. The world's first steam turbine—a 5,000-kilowatt vertical unit installed in 1903 at the Edison Fisk Street Station in Chicago—was now a monument in the plant—a salute to units that were now being built to produce over 1,000,000 kilowatts. Not far from it stood GE's first gas turbine which was built in 1949 for Oklahoma Gas and Electric. Plaques around the plant verified Schenectady as the birthplace of many consumer products such as the first practical hermetically-sealed home refrigerator developed by Christen Steenstrup. Many of those refrigerators—called the Monitor Top because the compressor looked like the gun turret of the Civil War Monitor—are still in operation as are many of the early steam and gas turbines. I thought it was fitting that one of Edison's original buildings was being used to develop robotic equipment.

I loved exploring every part of the plant with the *GE News* photographers. In addition to Denniston, there was an assistant editor. My job began as communication specialist. One of my first assignments was to solicit answers from employees on suggested questions that would make the company and employees more competitive. I immediately jumped into doing that feature since it got me into all the buildings.

My enthusiasm did take a dive, however, when I met Denniston's boss, Hal Reed, who obviously had acquired the stereotypical view of West Virginia. He lowered my salary by $10 a week noting it was $10 more a week than I had been offered at the *Wheeling News-Register*. He told me I should be grateful to have a man's job in big business. Naturally I was upset but at the same time I was determined to show him I was certainly capable of doing a man's job. Besides, it was too late to go back to Wheeling. That job was gone. I was down to my last dollar. I knew that my father was right. The only way to get ahead if you go into a man's world *(he didn't think I would make a good teacher or nurse)* would be to work through men. The best way to do this was to find a boss with a daughter like me who would help pave the way. It took me some time but I finally did and I lucked out because he was also a lawyer. I noticed the picture of his daughter on his desk. He would be the one who gave me the confidence to test the system.

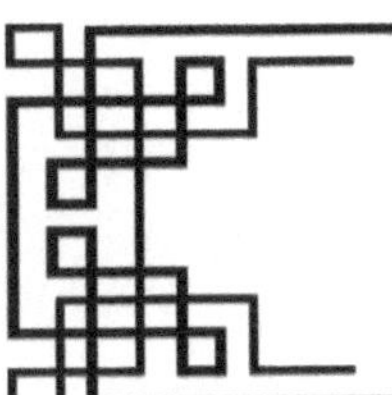

Those Early GE Years

My early years with *GE News* in the 60s were frustrating because I worked very hard to get recognized as a business writer which was considered a man's job. As an intern at the *Wheeling News-Register*, I was sent on assignments as if I was a general reporter. Yet my first job on the *GE News* was to write a column called "Something for the Girls," cover activities at the GE Athletic Association, put together the list of service awards of those with 50, 45, 40, 30, and 25 years which often took half a page, get photos arranged of new retirees with just one line of information because there were so many, and call the hospitals for a "get well" column or the funeral homes for the "sympathy" column as well as handling the free ad page for employees.

But I looked forward to meeting those long-service employees, particularly the fifty-year ones who had actually met Edison and Steinmetz. In those days, it was legal to hire teenagers and we had some seventy members of this group then. These contacts became very useful when GE Folkman, who did a Pensioners newsletter, retired. It was decided to incorporate the Pensioner's Page in the *GE News*. I quickly volunteered for that job. I was to discover the meaning of the phrase, "on the shoulders of giants," when doing stories on early electrical pioneers. I was thrilled to interview Dr. Coolidge, who invented the X-ray tube in 1918 at his 100th birthday party. I also interviewed Dr. Ernst Alexanderson who came up with an alternator in 1922 to broadcast radio and later TV (*I have a photo of him with his three-inch TV screen*). But it was some of the unsung heroes who touched me the most. One was a radio

pioneer, Rueben MacDonald, who had several patents involving radio transmission. In 1964, we found him at the age of
ninety-seven in a retirement home near Grant's Cottage
below Glens Falls, New York. He had no peers left at that age
and, as an orphan with no family, he was pleased to talk to
me and the photographer. He was born in Oklahoma and did
not know who his parents were. At the age of eight, he was
run over by a stagecoach which resulted in his lower legs having to be amputated. A rancher took him in and, as he put it,
a lady visiting from the east was appalled to see that he was
earning his keep by breaking horses. She brought him East,
sent him to school, and he ended up in Building 36 at GE
where the first TV broadcast was made to Proctor's Theater in
Schenectady. While some speculate that today's versions of a
hunchback Steinmetz or a near-deaf Edison might have to use
affirmative action today to get a job, I also think of Reuben
having a tough time getting a job today.

So editing the Pensioner's Page for me was interesting
and I did not mind the extra work. When the assistant editor left for another job, he was not replaced, so I added col-
umns of "Things in General" and "Around the Company" and
started an "Out of the Past" listing since I did not have enough
room on the Pensioners page. I also got the assistant's job of
rewriting articles from department newsletters which gave
me the chance to prove I could be a business writer. I would
visit the factories in that department for more information
which sometimes irritated the writers for those departments.
However, Denniston would explain it was in the GE family's
best interest to make sure everyone was aware of what was
going on.

Denniston was no longer interested in proving how adept
he was. He was still getting accolades for his interviews with
department heads on the state of their business. His favorite, however, was with Ronald Reagan when he came to the
company's annual meeting in 1958 in Schenectady. While celebrating his ninetieth birthday, he remembered how Reagan

confined his remarks to just thirty minutes because that was how long the contacts produced then could be worn without using drops.

Back then it was all about sales and jobs. I remember each year we would publish a companywide pie chart showing where our sales dollar went. It was always in the neighborhood of 46 cents for materials and supplies, 6 cents for taxes, 5 cents for profits, and 43 cents for employees.

Each week we would have a headline such as a picture of new equipment with the headline "Investments Like These Improve Productivity, Create Jobs" or a story about improved products being introduced such as "Demand for Large DC Custom 8000 Motors Results in 20 New Orders" or the typical announcement in the mid-60s by the Works Manager, A.C. Stevens, noting that "we expect to be able to get enough new business to keep employment levels at around 25,000 in the main plant."

There were another 7,000 working at the nearby Knolls Atomic Power Plant, the West Milton Test Site, the Malta Test Station, and the Research and Development Lab. There was so much business travel that an airport limousine service visited the plant every morning.

In those days, there were three shifts of factory workers maximizing the use of equipment. The parking lots were also always full including those at the GE Athletic Association. The GEAA offered twelve bowling alleys, a baseball field, a tennis court, a bocce area, and an archery and dart board area.

It was covering the bowling tournaments at the GEAA that I soon learned what was acceptable to be published and not published. There were over 100 teams from different product groups throughout the plant competing, including retired employees. One of these teams had a greater handicap than all the others because they were made up of employees who had been injured on the job. Some had the visible disability of the loss of a leg or an arm. I was so impressed at their esprit de corps and vigor that I put together a story with photos of that team. Needless to say, I was told to get rid of it when the proofs came back for approval because to others it looked like GE was mangling its workers.

Safety, of course, was something we were always pushing in the *GE News* *(obviously both the company and employees benefited from safe work practices)*. I had learned from day one never to let a factory employee not wear his safety glasses when a picture was being taken. But one got by me and I noticed it on the camera-ready proofs at the printing company. It was too late to drop the photo and rearrange the page, so I just took a pen and drew in some safety glasses for him. When the paper came out, despite my best efforts, you could tell the glasses had been added. However, the laughter at this did not result in a bad job review. Fortunately, the safety manager for that department said it was great because all the employees now knew what they would look like if they did not wear their safety glasses.

The popularity of the adlet page, in which employees could run free personal ads, was undeniable even though Denniston and I liked to think it was our news reporting. The adlet page was also time-consuming because ads were mailed in and had to be opened, collected, and typed under labels of "for sale, wanted, wanted to buy, for rent, wanted to rent," and "free." I resented the fact I was still supposed to handle all of this despite having absorbed the job of assistant editor.

I learned the hard way to check the phone numbers for ads like "free manure." Invariably it was a disgruntled employee using the phone number of his boss. Others would get more creative in the "wanted to buy" ads. There was the false ad seeking a condom, not a condo, under "wanted to rent," hoping it would get printed. But it was mostly the "wanted" ads that ranged from a case of beer to a night on the town and the "free" ads for various types of manure as well as for mothers-in-law which I quickly deleted.

One got by me that ended up in *Playboy* magazine. It brought huge laughs from employees (*glad we didn't have e-mails then*). It was a "for sale" ad sent in by a retired employee and he actually did have the items for sale. The items for sale were a comfortable bed and an upright organ. The fact the ad was real did not prevent me from being chewed out for not catching it. The editor of *Playboy* didn't help by noting that the assistant editor of the *GE News* in charge of the adlets was a woman.

However, it was after this they allowed me to farm out the typing of the adlets to the Typing Bureau. I grimaced when I saw the bill each week was close to what I was making each week.

While Denniston was all for giving me a raise, his boss Hal Reed pointed out that I was doing pretty well on overtime which I got because I was punching a clock. Even though so-called professional employees were not supposed to punch a clock, I had been told all the secretaries would be mad if I did not have to stand in line with them.

Denniston was not faring much better than I was under Reed's reign as the plantwide communication manager. Reed was one of those managers who felt employees should be so grateful working for him that they would want to help him at his home. Denniston was sometimes called on to tend to his horses on weekends when he was away with his family. I was told I could enjoy Saratoga Lake while I was babysitting his young son who he felt was not old enough to go on the boat with them. I soon found out the problem was not that he was too young—he was a spoiled brat. Worse, when he stomped a cat to death in front of me, I decided he needed a lesson and gave him a good pounding. Again, I considered myself as having lucked out because Reed decided the secretary in community relations could do a better job.

Today, I cannot believe how timid I was about not asking for more money and buying into the line that I should be grateful I had a man's job. But I was having a good time and I could get more money by working overtime. In those days, guys also paid for the date. My only problem on $5,200 a year boosted with overtime was budgeting enough money for food and rent and to buy clothes and shoes in addition to now paying the car bill and what I still owed my sister.

To this day I regret spending a week's salary on a mink collar to go to the University Club in Schenectady's Stockade where all the Ivy League trainees lived. All I attracted was an accountant from Connecticut who was a real bore and asked me where the rest of my coat was. I soon learned to spend any spare money on ski equipment and get on the bus which was filled with manufacturing and engineering trainees.

Still, I was having a lot of fun and I was enjoying being part of the business world learning how sales and jobs were created. However, in 1961 I came close to going back to Wheeling, and not by choice. A nationwide strike was called by the International Union of Electrical Workers. By this time, I had become familiar with who was big in management. One of my jobs was delivering the proofs of Friday's *GE News* to the plant lawyer, Emil Peters, for his approval. His office was near the area Vice President of Power Generation Bill Ginn, who was known for his flamboyant style and disregard for plant rules. Some wondered why he bothered working at GE since his wife was heir to the Colt fortune. He always seemed to be amused by everything.

I sure found this out one day when I strayed too close to his office entrance to see Mr. Peters. I had noticed a bronze grill in the floor at the entrance to his office but this time I stepped on it to avoid a delivery man. All of a sudden I felt bristles coming through my sandals. In my confusion, I yelled, thinking it was something alive. The delivery man was laughing and calming me down when Ginn came out of his office. He motioned the delivery man into his office and then amused himself demonstrating his automatic shoe-brushing machine to me.

He picked up on my West Virginia accent in the process

and from then on I was known as Miss West Virginia. He asked me why I was not wearing heels like the rest of the women. He had an even bigger laugh when I told him Hal Reed, my boss's boss, was short and did not like me towering over him so he said to wear some nice flats. Because I had a size eleven feet, I had to order them out of North Carolina and the pair had not arrived yet so I had on my summer sandals. I told him I was not complaining...that I was glad not to have to wear heels because they were not only expensive but it was difficult getting around the factories in them, particularly in the foundries which had dirt floors. This resulted in more laughter from him and an invitation into his office. When Ginn flipped a switch on his desk, a portion of the mahogany wall slid open to reveal a bar. The delivery man began restocking his supply. I was stunned and then told by Ginn that he assumed Miss West Virginia could keep her mouth shut to security. I assured him I could and solidified that promise by telling him that he shouldn't worry about the guards, that they often shared the beer with me that they took off the night shift employees trying to sneak it through the subway gate. He just laughed and told me to keep up the good work on the *GE News*.

So when the nationwide strike spread to Schenectady and everyone was locked out of the plant by picket lines, our communications group was busier than ever. All of us, including Bill Ginn, moved into the swank, elegant old Hotel Van Curler where I assumed he had the top floor which had a presidential suite. But I was to see him again. We were still able to publish the *GE News* outside the plant and find ways to have a bundle accidentally drop off a truck going by the plant entrances where thousands of electrical workers were circling to keep everyone out until their demands were met. We knew the *GE News* would be read because everyone liked the free adlet page. The city newspaper, losing business, had complained about it but to no avail. It was considered an employee benefit.

One of my jobs was to deliver news releases that were

practically written by lawyers instead of our editor and the press relations staff. The National Labor Relations Board was checking every word to assure themselves the company was not violating any policies to get people back to work. I also read instant news announcements to local radio stations. One of these was WSNY where I had developed a liking for Steve Fitz, a newsman there. He did not take the labor-management situation as seriously as many did. He was friendly and very popular in the community for being fair-minded. The pressure was on to support GE but he gave both the union and GE an equal amount of time to comment on the strike. He would take calls from both sides and replay them in an hour-long program. He knew that both the union and GE would be providing false "callers" to promote their position.

I had become known as the bowler's wife who wanted her husband to go back to work instead of bowling all day, noting things like the children were getting hungry and the company was making a fair offer. The union side answered with a bowler's wife who said he should be on the picket line instead of bowling, that there was not enough money for food and clothing for the kids. Fitz used to tease me about being such a good company girl and wondered how many factory workers had wives with southern accents.

But, unbeknown to me at the time, Fitz also had a live evening program where people called in on a certain topic. That evening, it involved a shopping trip the Schenectady Woman's Club was going to take to New York City. That was also where national negotiations were being held involving some 150 U.S. GE plants. When I called in, I did not realize it was a live show and Steve answered, asking me what I was going to do in New York. I immediately replied that Bill Ginn and I were going down there to settle the strike. It went live before Fitz could cut me off.

Before he could get back to me to tell me what happened, the door opened and in came my boss's boss, Reed. As bad luck would have it, our room had a TV set. I was watching Dick Clark's *Bandstand* show when he rushed in. He turned it off before I could get to it and fired me. Denniston came in and tried to save my job. But two more layers of bosses arrived all agreeing that it was best I leave.

Fortunately for me, Ginn's wife had planned on going on the shopping trip and asked her husband about it. By this time I had my coat on and was about to leave when the door opened and in came Ginn. I tried to apologize. But he just stood there with a big grin as others told him they had handled the situation and that I would be leaving the job. He just laughed and said: "Get back to work, Miss West Virginia, and try to keep your mouth shut. Don't tell the whole world we're going to New York."

Seeing the shocked looks, he told them somebody should show Miss West Virginia a good time in New York. And, looking at my short boss Reed, he added, "Tell her you have to wear heels down there."

A year later, when Ginn was tried for price fixing steam turbine prices with Westinghouse, no one was sadder than I was. Agents were all over the place and scanned every edition of the *GE News* to see if we were using it to let Westinghouse know what we were bidding. Even the head of union relations, Red Levy, who had become a close friend to Ginn, was upset over Ginn taking the fall. I had heard the whispers that Levy would never be promoted to the top corporate union relations post because he was Jewish. I liked him because he and his secretary, Judy Love, taught me how to play bridge at the noon hour. He treated everyone with respect, no matter their position in the company. Unlike one of the sanctimonious department plant relations managers, Carl Hudson, whom I had heard call the strikers "animals," Ginn regarded the union factory workers as very competent adversaries.

I will never forget the noon hour that a call came in to Levy from Ginn when he was in prison in Philadelphia and the press was reporting that a guy doing life for murder was in a cell next to him. Levy asked him how things were going. Ginn joked that he guessed Levy had heard that they were now accusing him of rigging the electric chair. While the charges stuck, I felt that a higher-up had to know what was going on. But it didn't surprise me that Ginn would plead guilty. It was another experience for him and he was, in the end, a company man to take the fall.

His replacement, Donald Craig, was a gentleman and a nice guy but not nearly as interesting as Ginn. I would find myself outside Craig's house one night wondering if I would get fired for trying to keep myself from being fired. If I thought I was working long hours then, I soon got a real test for my stamina when the company decided Schenectady needed to be more competitive. A major campaign was launched in late 1963 which drew nationwide attention because labor unions were perceived then as having too much control.

It was called the Make Schenectady Campaign which involved getting the union to go from piecework to daywork pay which would save millions for the company. Part of the deal involved keeping the motor division from moving. We were also being closely watched by the supposedly union-friendly NLRB.

Denniston had left and I was the editor even though my name was not listed "for fear the *GE News* would not be read by a woman editor." During this six-month campaign I had gotten used to spending Thursday evenings at the printers just making changes in a page or two of *MSC News*. But a special edition of the program had everybody on edge because of the sensitivity of laying out the whole final deal on four pages for the union to accept and to make this final offer within NLRB guidelines.

It was past midnight and I had been informed that if we did not have the approval by 3 a.m., it would be impossible to have 30,000 copies of the *GE News* printed and delivered in the plant on Friday morning. Another 2,500 copies needed to be in the mail for Saturday delivery to community leaders as well as the normal 10,000 retirees. Despite constantly reminding those approving the *GE News* as I sent cab after cab to their homes to get their approvals and then resent to show them changes had been made, each was making changes to each other's changes. Finally, at 2:30 a.m., I got the approvals.

A cheer rang out as several linotype operators, the pressroom foreman, and I started over to the nearby Tip Toe Inn to have a few drinks celebrating the overtime pay we would be getting. I had gotten used to it and began enjoying the toast they made to me to "keep up the bad job" because they liked the overtime. However, they knew from all the cab drivers that it was not me making the changes. They knew full well I would have been fired by then if I was that incompetent.

Just as we were about to leave, I got a call directly from the Vice President of the Motor businesses—Oscar Dunn. I knew it was him because I had covered different events in his division, mostly when he was giving out awards to try to motivate his day workers who received the same pay. He had gotten my number from his division newsletter editor and his message was simple. "Do not print that edition. I did not approve of it."

I was speechless. All I could do was just thank him and hang up. I immediately went into action—first it was a call to Denniston, then his boss, and then his boss and then the PR and Government Relations Manager and the lead lawyer who got proofs. None of them seemed to be home. I tried the bars at the Hotel Van Curler and Van Dyck but they were not there celebrating the final MSC offer. It was closing in on 3 a.m. If I did not get an O.K. by then it would mean there was not enough press time to get the *GE News* into the plant for distribution as usual.

Now the pressure was really on. *It was a Catch-22*, I said to myself. *Be fired if you do print it or if you don't print it.* I saw only one choice to keep both from happening. I knew that VP Craig had area responsibility and that if I got his O.K. I would be safe. I roared off in my TR 3 sports car (*overtime had allowed me to buy a used one*) to Craig's house telling the crew to go ahead to the Tip Toe Inn but to stay there until I got back in case there were changes. Craig's address was in the phone book and even though it was an elegant neighborhood, it was not that far away. I could get there in ten minutes. When I did arrive, the house was dark. But there was a car out front with two people in it. Even though they looked like they would rather not be disturbed, I knocked on the window. The girl turned out to be Craig's daughter. She could tell by the sound of my voice that it was imperative her father be gotten up which she did not want to do because she was past her curfew. She had planned on sneaking into the house. Since I said I was going in with her and she was saving me from being fired, she agreed and said goodbye to her boyfriend.

Craig, as sleepy as he was, was a perfect gentleman when I explained the phone call from Oscar Dunn. He just smiled and signed the proof I handed him saying it was O.K. to go to press.

I got back to the printing plant a minute or so before 3 a.m. to give the "go-ahead" again for printing and joined the gang at the Tip Toe Inn. Bill Mercer, the composing room foreman, had not one but two Rob Roys waiting for me containing his favorite scotch. We celebrated our amazing effort to get it out in time to be distributed to the first shift coming into the plant.

I also celebrated not having to go back to the plant to punch out the workday on the time clock at 3 a.m. I was still not considered a salaried professional employee in the mid-60s. I had to punch the clock like the secretaries, low-level office employees, and factory workers.

The linotype operators, tired of setting all that type about being more competitive on the job, suggested that they were going to make me more competitive by helping me save time. They gave me a rubber stamp with type on it that matched the type on the timecard machines. I could just whirl it to the time I was finished and would not have to drive back into the plant in the middle of the night to punch in my time on the job. So we always had a ceremony of stamping my timecard at the Tip Toe Inn. Looking back, I realize now that I should have built in the fifteen minutes it would have taken me to drive to the plant for the official time stamp.

And so it went with GE. Things fortunately changed when the Equal Employment and Opportunity Act passed in 1972. But that is in another book, *Rebuilding the GE House Jack Blew Down.*

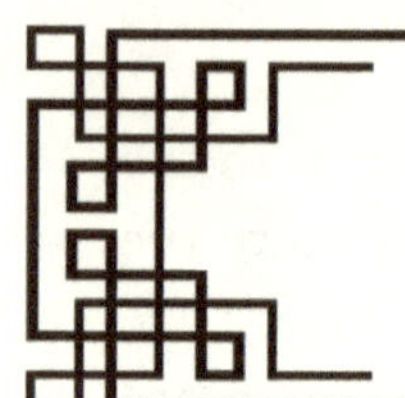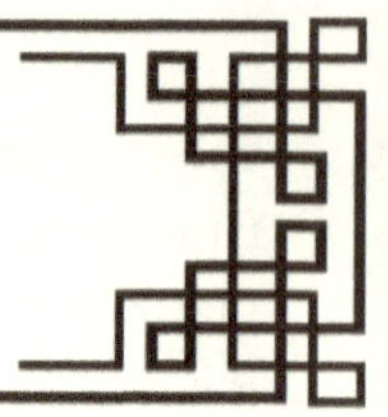

When in Rome

Ever go into your diary and wonder how you could have said that or not known the significance of the moment?

My revelation came from something I wrote on February 12, 1963. At that time, I was on a three-week ski trip to Europe. I should say that was my intention when I got on the chartered plane with about seventy-five others from the New York State Capital District Ski Association. It had been billed as a champagne flight at half the cost of a commercial one. Having not been out of college that long, where I had won a bladder award for my drinking skills, I was one of the first to sign up.

It had meant going a week without pay because GE just gave two weeks off with salary the first five years. I counted myself lucky being able to go because the friends I had made who skied were not able to get the extra time off. Like many of them, I was still paying back college loans, so I meant to make the most of the trip.

When I got on the plane, I noticed two men and two younger women were in the back already popping corks. So back I went to join them, passing skiers who were putting their luggage in the overhead carrier. I did recognize two of them but they were obviously more interested in each other than me. But as I rushed by, they did comment the flight was a long one and I better take it easy if I wanted to get in some of the greatest skiing in the world. They had been to Europe twice—exuding a worldly demeanor as they shunned the champagne and unpacked their goatskins with wine.

The foursome I joined in the back, after stowing my backpack, were obviously not skiers. I counted four heavy Samsonite overnight suitcases and several dress and suit bags in the overhead slots next to mine. The two girls, it turned out, as they passed the bottle to me, were sisters by the name of Ras, which I recognized as the name of a local furniture store. Yes, they said that was their family. They were going to Rome to see the country their grandparents had come from as well as to try to see the Pope.

The men were not traveling together. One was a young construction worker, Bruno, also on his first trip. He just wanted to party while the other man was more middle-aged. His name was Jim. He was a real estate agent who wanted to go to Italy. Later we were to find out he was going to Florence to buy gold bars. We were having a great time chatting and the flight organizer was very accommodating when he left the open cases of champagne in the rear of the plane.

By the time the plane was landing, we had become very congenial and had even stowed some of the free champagne in our bags. So when the foursome got up to leave I followed them with my backpack. It was not until we got into the baggage terminal and I was looking for my checked-in ski boots that I found this was the first of two stops for the plane. We were in Nice, France, and the plane was now on its way to Munich.

I had planned on renting skis so I wondered what would happen to my boots. Bruno probably laughed the hardest. Even though I was starting to sober up, I was able to see some humor in it. I had no idea where I was and I would obviously miss my reservations at an Alberg hotel in San Anton waiting for a commercial flight.

The Ras sisters were asking about train transportation to Rome. Jim overheard this and came to our rescue. He suggested it would be a lot cheaper if all of us came with him because he had a rental car reserved. He wouldn't even ask us to share the gas costs if we went on to Florence with him. He was going to buy some gold bars there and needed help getting them through customs. He could make sure I got a train from there to Munich. He suggested all of us could just have a good time touring Italy and, yes, even see the Pope. He had never done that before and that would make his mother very happy.

So we spent a night in Nice. They were having a celebration not that different from Mardi Gras in New Orleans, except the confetti was nearly knee-high in the streets. The Ras sisters and I joined a raucous group and took the advice of some to see the famous Russian ballet performance at the opera house there. My note in my diary was "How do those dancers skip with bent knees...we couldn't do it."

The next diary mention of "escaped through a window" reminded me of the close call we had when we went to a bar after the performance. I still knew enough French from college to overhear a bunch of sailors discussing their intentions in plying us with drinks. We were outnumbered. So I persuaded the sisters to go to the bathroom with me where we were able to escape through a window.

This was a sobering experience; when we got back to the inn we were glad to see Jim and Bruno. They knew we were even more naive when they had to show us how to operate the water closets in a cheap room next to theirs.

We were still giggling about pulling back the feather ticks, thinking they were blankets instead of mattresses, when we got into Jim's Alfa-Romeo. The sisters and I occupied the back seat while Bruno, discovering a champagne bottle he forgot in his dress bag, declared himself to be the navigator. When we reached the high cliffs around Genoa, the roads were so narrow it was difficult to get by an oncoming car. The Ras sisters decided that as a skier I must like heights. So I found myself looking out the right side of the car window. The only thing you could see was waves breaking on a rocky coast several thousand feet down. I persuaded myself this was good downhill training for the St. Anton peaks. I managed to continue enjoying what I had told my older sister would be an adventure of a lifetime when she loaned me some spending money for the trip.

We made it to Rome with a great appreciation for the little cafés on the way. We declared ourselves as exquisite wine connoisseurs with a preference for Chianti for everyday meals and Bordeaux for special occasions.

Despite several terrifying passings with other cars, there wasn't even a dent in the Alfa-Romeo when Jim turned it in. We were able to find the hotel where the Ras sisters had reservations. It was no trouble for Jim and Bruno to get a room and me to bunk with the sisters. That became our headquarters as we found that being in Rome in the middle of the winter was a great time to see everything. We would be the only ones on an English-speaking bus with the guide telling us that we were seeing at least five times as much as the summer tourists did. Still, after two days of cultural overload, Bruno suggested going to the Black Orchid where he heard they had some good nightlife activities.

My diary, with only five lines open for each day, took in some cryptic messages that week. Yes, I was fascinated with Rome, its fountains, and its history. But it was the entries noting that I danced with some guy who sang to the crowd and said he was Mario Lanza that jogged my memory the most. I remembered several boxes of chocolates that Bruno and Jim bought from the waitresses. They were not real chocolate but a quick trip to a back room. We got thrown out when the Ras sisters and I, who were so naive and appreciative of Bruno and Jim picking up so many tabs for us, decided to buy them more chocolates.

My "Mario Lanza" friend, who had been making his own offers, explained the "chocolates" to us when we left. But the owner was not taking chances on who we might be.

And yes, we did get to Florence where Jim bought his gold and we lived up to our agreement to each take a bar back to the States, again being naive when we went successfully went through customs.

But my other memory of Florence was admiring a four-story-high painted clock opposite a historic cathedral. I was stunned when I was told by the guide that the Medici family had so adored it they had blinded the painter to make sure there was none other like it. For years I wore the leather shoes I bought in Florence. Everyone had laughed when the clerk, noting my size eleven, had said "Grosso!" An oversize advertising pair on the second-floor window was retrieved and they fit me fine.

Other entries like our visit to Venice with the notation "I met Hitchcock's Birds" reminded me of the laugh everyone got when I bought a packet of cracked corn from a vendor to feed the pigeons in the middle of St. Mark's Square. Half-starved from lack of tourists in the winter, thousands of pigeons poured down from the skies to tear my paper bag apart, leaving me in near shreds, too.

The next day found us fishing Bruno out of a canal where he had made a less-than-sober leap into a gondola. However, the gondolier was very happy when we took him with us to enjoy Venetian refreshments for the rest of the afternoon as Bruno dried off.

And, yes, the Ras sisters finally got to visit some relatives the final week. Jim and Bruno did go on to Paris and I got on the train to Munich for an uneventful week of skiing at St. Anton—with the exception of having to sleep in the hallway the first night until I could make new reservations. I not only rented skis but boots, too.

But looking back today, it is the diary entry for Wednesday, Feb. 12, 1964, that occupies my mind the most. That was back in Rome. Jim announced he had managed to get us entry to the private prayer room where the Pope meets with the public. The Catholic Ras sisters were exuberant. "No standing below the Vatican balcony on a Saturday when the Pope blesses thousands of people at one time," Jim had announced. "We are going to personally meet the Pope at his Wednesday meeting."

The Ras sisters had their rosary beads with them when we

entered the room. Bruno and Jim led the way as white-robed attendants carried the Pope into the room. He was seated on a throne on top of what looked to me like a flying Persian carpet. Lots of people started blocking the view to get near him to have their beads blessed. I remember lots of jewels hanging from the golden canopy and a huge white cross behind his throne.

The grandeur and elegance of the Vatican, starting with a visit to see the Pieta, had already overwhelmed me. It made me feel like the plain Presbyterian farm girl from West Virginia that I knew I was. So when I saw a lone black woman, with her baby huddling into a far corner of the room, looking like she didn't belong there, I joined her.

I watched as my friends, the mesmerized Ras sisters, with Jim and Bruno made way for them as the crowd thronged forward to get near the pope. They reached up, like many others, to have their rosaries blessed.

Then, all of a sudden, the Pope lifted his eyes as a TV camera came out of a side room. His attendants began carrying the Pope to our corner of the room. I panicked but not as much as the black woman whom the Pope was eyeing with great intensity. He was reaching for her baby to bless, but she had been so overcome by his attention, I saw she was going to faint. As she was falling, I grabbed the baby and handed it to the Pope while a couple of his attendants helped the black woman get to her feet. She was from California. The Pope then blessed her as well as me.

The rest of the day the Ras sisters and even Jim and Bruno just stared at me saying that the Pope had not only touched me twice but he had also blessed me.

I look now at my diary and all that I have written on that Wednesday, Feb. 12 is: "Met the Pope today, passed him a baby to bless...am anxious to get skiing."

Today, I know that I met the great liberal Pope John, the 23rd, who was letting the world know that he was endorsing the coming passage of the 1964 Civil Rights Bill in the U.S.

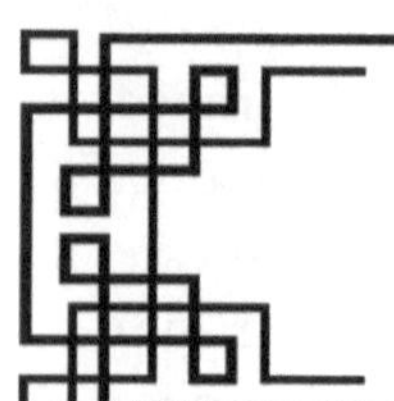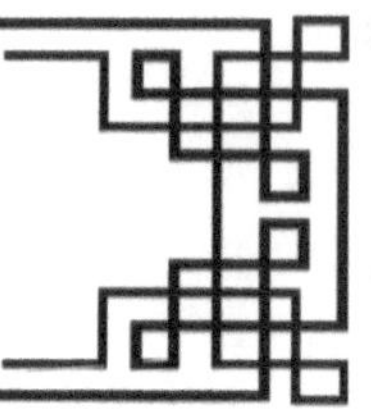

Those Reckless Times

Looking back now, I find it hard to remember some things I did that I wish I hadn't. Simply put, I acted like there was no tomorrow. That was the case after a day of ski racing.

I had just scored my first win over Paul. For several years he had managed to beat me, not just in seconds, but twice in over a minute. It had been humbling. He often teased me about my spirit being willing but my body not able. Paul's favorite expression was calling people a "candy ass" if they failed.

As usual, the entire team headed to a local bar to celebrate the day's event. My feelings of victory were soon released after a couple of ales. I toasted myself at his expense—even noting his new skis had not helped him.

Perhaps this is what caused him to over-imbibe at the bar, too. It only took an hour for him to challenge me to a car race. He declared my TR-3 was no match for his Mustang...that my car was all show and no action. It was then our mutual friend, Ev, declared he would be the starting gate for this race. So out the door we went followed by the rest of the team to watch us head down Union Street to see who could get to the Mohawk River Bridge first. It was a distance of over fifteen blocks.

When Ev lowered his ski poles for a go, off we went. But unknown to us, this bar had been a favorite of the local police when they needed to collect some fines. We were soon to find out an officer had been watching the event. He called in reinforcements to deal with us.

I first heard the sirens when I managed to overtake Paul by going up a handicap spot in a sidewalk to get in front while he was trying to get around a car in front of him. It was then

I saw the flashing lights coming up behind him. Then I saw another police car coming out of a side street ahead of us. I quickly turned off the sidewalk to a side street. I turned off my car lights, hoping he would not see me.

I lived above a garage several blocks away. I figured I could ease my way there in the dark with just the help of street-lights. The sounds of the sirens were all coming from Union Street as I made my way home. I was careful to weave my way through several street intersections until I got to the garage.

I was relieved when I came up to the dark alley leading to the garage. It looked like I had made it home without a problem. I started to jump out of the car to open the garage door when all of a sudden I was grabbed and slammed up against a brick wall. I could hardly breathe from the encounter. Rough hands were going up and down all over me when he said, "Jesus Christ, it's a girl." He had followed me without his lights on, too.

I could hear the sirens had stopped on lower Union Street. It was then he ordered me into his car. When we got to where the other police had Paul in handcuffs, they asked who I was. "She was the one driving the TR-3," he declared. He told them he had thought I was a g-dammed hippie at first because of my long hair. He had pinned me against the wall to check me out for weapons. In the tussle, I must have hit my chin, which was still bleeding, against the wall.

This was certainly not the time for Paul to turn gentle-man, but he did. He berated the officer for how he had treated me—which only got a laugh from them when he used the word "lady."

Maybe it was because I had been roughed up but they decided to just take Paul to jail. He was still in the gentle-man mood when he suggested they drive me home instead of walking there in the dark by myself. My officer just glared at him at this point but did do as Paul suggested, adding that he was sure I could take care of myself after what I had been doing.

No sooner had I gotten into the apartment when Ev arrived. He had heard the sirens. We discussed what we needed to do. First we called a lawyer I knew and then Paul's family to let them know the lawyer would be handling things. Fortunately this lawyer, a friend to both of us, knew it was a first offense. With his connections he was able to get Paul out of jail that same night. But there were heavy fines. Our lawyer reminded us we were lucky they had not taken a test for alcohol. We also got a needed lecture from the judge on how we both could have killed other people as well as ourselves.

I would like to confess we would have been better citizens in the late 60s protesting the Viet Nam war. But it is what it was. We both had regrets.

Paul continued to beat me in area races—even though I once tried to get him to purposely lose a race. It was during this time each GE plant would send teams from Vermont, Massachusetts, New Hampshire, Pennsylvania, Maine, and New York plants to compete. GE athletic associations in each plant would pay for the race events and trophies if their team won. Our problem was Schenectady management was doing away with the association because they feared it would lead to white-collar unions as a result of close association with unionized blue-collar workers. As team captain, I was informed they would not pay if we participated. We decided to go anyway. But realizing how expensive it would be if we won, I tried to persuade Paul to fall down on the course, which he refused to do, telling me to do it. Fortunately for both of us, another team member unintentionally did so

We also did a lot of canoe racing together. Paul was highly competitive. For years he had wanted to beat a couple, Sam and Sue Allison, who lived along the Hudson River at North Creek. They were white water experts. We had lost to them several times. So Paul was excited when he heard they had entered a flat water race on Long Lake which was not their specialty. We began training a couple months ahead and had gotten in sync to his satisfaction. I had even matched him in taking pounds off to lighten the boat. So on the day of the race, I was told we could even save more weight if we took our shoes off. He had already rigged up the boat with tubing so we could drink water without losing a stroke.

We were matching them stroke for stroke but not passing them. Then Paul saw an opportunity. He used his paddle as a rudder to force them to almost crash into a bank, causing Sue to drop her paddle. I reached over and handed it back to her. It took a long time for him to get over what would surely have been a win for us if I had not done that. So we came in second but in his mind it would have been first if I had paid attention to his last order.

I think I was a glutton for punishment because I also did the seventy-mile race from Cooperstown to Bainbridge with Paul—not just once but twice. This race is so grueling that the first time I passed out at the finish line but was revived with what I think was a salt intake. But we won our class.

The second time I had a supply of candy as Paul had suggested. But being mindful of my weight, I had gotten used to the sugar-free kind. So when Paul ran out of his, he started eating mine. Unbeknown to me, he had a condition which required sugar. This time it was him that was not feeling well and our pace got slower. When we finally finished, some twenty minutes behind our first time, he noticed the bag of candy I had with the label "sugar-free." That nearly ended our competitive canoe racing.

He had me make up for the infraction by helping him haul a canoe full of grinding stones from an old mill he found on the remote east side of Lake George. We could not get there by car but we were able to roll them down the mountainside. The trip across Lake George was much more precarious. We only had about a three-inch bow clearance on one trip when a motorboat went by. Paul was able to rudder us into position to handle the swell. We leaned left when it came and right when we were atop the wake to keep enough water out to prevent us from going down with the stones. Today these stones are still in the walkway to his house.

Paul used his garage to construct canoes as well as kayaks. He would clone them from the latest new ones and then sell them. He taught many of us how to handle the Class 3 and 4 rapids in the upper Hudson headwaters. He had a special two-seater fiberglass canoe which was dubbed "Rock Bait" because of its many patches hitting rocks. Over the years, he estimated it weighed thirty more pounds than its original weight because of all the repairs.

But never let it be said that Paul is not a gentleman. We signed up for a kayak race on the Dead River in Maine. It was an individual race and Paul had just made me a white water kayak which fit like a glove. (*Today I can't get in it*). When we got there it was not "ladies first." We were to go last and it was not only over fifteen miles long but there were two portages. Moreover, one had to dodge logs being sent down the river by a lumber company. The men's race started at noon and ours at 2 p.m. By the time I and a few other women got through the last portage, it was getting dark. In the meantime, Paul was berating the race organizer for having us run last. But we made it in before dark. And next year's race was a "ladies first."

Biking was another sport we always enjoyed. To this day, I will never forget when he got hit by a car. He was ahead of me and had signaled he was turning left into a bike path which the driver said he didn't see. I can still see Paul going through the air and hitting an iron pole at the entrance. The driver did stop. He called for help. Paul came to and, knowing that he had severe rib damage, even told the EMTs who arrived that if he passed out not to give him CPR.

He reminded me of the time at the ski lodge in Vermont when my TR-3 would not start. He decided he would tow me with his car to see if it would start. The road was icy and my tires were not good. I was swaying behind him when all of a sudden the car started. I surged ahead and pulled him into a ditch as I tried to gain control of the swerving car. Fortunately the only dents were in his car...not his ribs.

Still, he often came to my rescue. Our ski club rented a lodge from a maple tree farmer during the winter. All of us took turns being lodge chairmen which involved checking people in, collecting the money to pay the farmer, and cooking the meals. One weekend, a local judge I knew showed up. He was a known alcoholic and his wife had divorced him because of his infidelity. When he was sober, he was civilized. But word had it he was a disgusting drunk. Unfortunately, that weekend we also had a woman no one knew from the Albany area that came to ski. We were aware that the judge was doing his best to charm her by showing her medals he had gotten in Viet Nam and discussing his court cases. He invited her to dinner after skiing.

Because neither of them showed up for the lodge dinner, I began to worry. I stayed up while others went to bed looking forward to Sunday skiing because it was snowing. It was around 10 p.m. when I heard her run in, breathing heavily as she locked the door behind her. He had tried to rape her at the covered bridge near the lodge. She had gotten away from him and just had a torn shirt. She begged me not to tell anyone... that all she wanted to do was go to bed and leave early in the morning. I assured her that she had nothing to fear from him now that she was safe in the lodge. I would take care of the situation and I would not tell anyone. (*Today I would not agree to that.*)

So when he came in I told him he had to leave—that I did not care if he was a judge. Evidently, in his drunken state, he decided that since he had not scored with her, he would try with me. We had a center kitchen aisle. He started lunging at me as we went around it. There was a nearby board with hanging pots on it. I grabbed an iron skillet and hit him in the head with it. He went down with a thud and just lay there.

Again, Paul came to the rescue. I went upstairs where the guys slept and roused him and another guy, Lee Tomlinson. I knew Lee had first-aid training as a ski patrolman. They eased my anxiety by determining he was not dead...just dead drunk. We dragged him into the room where the owner stored his maple syrup. We avoided that room because the furniture was always sticky.

Anyhow, it was an anxious night for us wondering what he would do when he woke up. It turned out that people were right about him. He could get so drunk he couldn't remember anything. He began complaining about being stuck to the couch and asking what kind of ski club had such poor accommodations. Paul had placed his luggage and ski gear on the sticky floor beside him. We didn't even have to tell him to leave. He got up and left and said he was never coming back again. Paul echoed our relief and sentiments: "Good riddance."

While it seemed over the years Paul would be better off not knowing me, we always remained good friends. But there were times when he sarcastically questioned whether it was better to be competing against me or with me or should he just avoid me.

Three Black Clouds

There have been so many times in my life when, once something bad happens, it will occur two more times. I call it my three black clouds. I just grit my teeth until I get through the other two. But there was one time the pattern was slightly broken.

It happened during one of the many weekend trips to and from Schenectady and Fairfield, Connecticut, where I worked at GE headquarters from 1975 until 1980. I had never fit in there and had even considered my job there a three-cloud one. I was a token female professional employee. I had nothing in common with the executives I wrote speeches for—even the other people on the staff treated me as an anomaly. I was often the only female at internal GE meetings. I was still being questioned about my association with a modern dancer, Dan Wagoner, who broke into a NYC meeting we were having still in his skin- colored leotards to find me. He had just purchased one of our original stone houses built by Issac Kuykendall who several generations later was still practicing what brought the original one over to this country as an indentured stone mason for New York's Van Rennselaer. He bought it because it was isolated by a horseshow curve in the river and would be a good place for his company to do choreography. Even though he explained he had found out I was from West Virginia and was there to find out more about the house and valley, they still complained to the hotel management their disdain for letting him come into the meeting in his at-first-glance naked condition.

Anyhow, it was my Friday night enthusiasm in getting away from such people that caused me to get a speeding ticket about twenty miles from the Massachusetts line. I could ill afford it and now there were two more clouds to come. Still, I consoled myself with the thought I was going to have a great weekend including a Friday night party at the ski club. The trooper had not taken that long to write the ticket so I still had time to get there. I was also looking forward to showing and sharing with them my latest corporate perk. It was a case of Rhine wine that a VP had given me off his company plane when he saw me eyeing it. It was elegant-looking stuff in brown, long-necked bottles.

After the ticket, I concentrated on not going over the limit by more than ten miles per hour because experience had taught me that troopers give you that edge. I thought about who would be at the party. I thought about everything except the fact that I had not filled the gas tank the night before the trip.

It was when I was well on my way to the New York Thruway that I recognized the sluggishness of the fuel-injected Jeep. The sputtering engine told me this was going to be my second black cloud. Having been on this route nearly every weekend for five years, I knew the nearest gas station was about three or four miles behind me. I parked off the road and crossed the divider to hitch a ride to the station when I saw a McLean truck coming my way. I would prevent this third black cloud. I would ask him if he knew my teamster brother, Mike, who went by "Laughing Boy." He didn't, but had heard of the name and laughed. He even went off the exit and got back on just to keep me from having to walk the length of the ramp. The Sunoco station was right there.

When I walked in, I found two young boys, one about twelve and the other maybe fifteen. Their father had taken the tow truck out on a job and left them in charge. They did not know when he was coming back. I waited a little while and then it hit me: I would buy the gas can as well as the gas, hitchhike back, and get it in the tank. But the boys were reluctant having never sold a gas tank.

At the mention of a Jeep, the older boy excitedly asked if it was four-wheel drive. I suggested he hitchhike back to the car with me with enough gas to get back to the garage. I noted the top was also down. He was game for this and off we went.

As soon as we found a ride and got to the Jeep, my third cloud appeared very quickly. I realized the gas can's neck was too wide. It would not fit into the gas tank slot far enough to open the valve. Those were the days when you had to be careful about putting leaded gas into cars built for unleaded gas. They had made the nozzles different to prevent this.

We kept trying thinner and thinner sticks ahead of the gas can nozzle to keep the valve open. But there was not enough room and we were losing gas in the process. I had only myself to blame. I hadn't even thought of checking the gas can when we left to make sure the nozzle was the unleaded gas size. Now I had a kid with me in this mess and on top of that I was missing the party. Then it dawned on me that one of those slender, long-necked Rhine wine bottles would probably do the trick of holding the valve open. The kid thought it was a great idea, too. We tried one out and it went in deep.

The kid was as happy as I was. He offered to break it over the guardrails so we could use the neck as a funnel for the gas can. The kid broke it just fine except for one thing—a piece of glass had gone into his palm. So we spent some time bandaging that with an emergency kit my wonderful teamster brother had given me for Christmas. While we were funneling the gas into the tank, I realized that it was stupid to have broken the bottle. All I had to do was drink the wine and fill the empty bottle with gas. My second thought was it was not a good idea to do this in front of this kid. So maybe it was just as well we dumped it out.

Still, this third cloud was passing for me as we poured the gas from the can through the wine funnel. Even though the kid had a permit and wanted to drive us back, I thought better of this and compromised by saying he could drive it to the garage when we got off the Thruway. Obviously his father, who had returned, was upset when we drove in. When he saw the bandage, it took us some time to explain what had happened. His son assured him he was O.K. as I repeated that I was extremely grateful to his son for helping me. In addition to paying for the gas in the can plus a fill-up, I offered to pay for the kid's time, which he accepted. Still, I could tell the kid was going to get a heavy lecture about leaving the garage.

Back on the road again heading to Schenectady, I realized I had missed the party. I consoled myself by realizing I had gotten through my three black clouds. I was looking forward to having some fun on Saturday and Sunday before I had to go back to work. When I got off the Thruway, I noticed a trooper checking tires at one of the exit lanes. I swung over to go through that one, figuring it was time I got credit from a state trooper for doing something right. The tires on my Jeep were just three months old. I wanted to see how far his dime would go into the tread. I learned then never to inadvertently insult an officer who considers himself above doing humbling work. While he "inspected" my tires, he also noticed my inspection tag was out of date and gave me a ticket.

Since then I have learned just to deal with my three dark clouds and never tempt a fourth.

Hapless Harvey

I was in the middle of my water aerobic exercises in the abandoned Boy Scout swimming hole when I suddenly felt I was not alone in this once-pristine creek.

The swimming area had become a haven for many to escape the summer heat as well as a party site in the afternoon and evenings. While most visitors treated the creek with respect, that minority pushed aside the rock barriers so they could drive their ATVs and motorcycles into the secluded area, carrying coolers full of beer and food.

The fishermen gave up evening fishing. I changed my workouts to late morning, letting the fisherman have their best biting hours earlier. It seemed to be working well for all of us. The fishermen and I still had our solitude despite the fact we often had to pick up litter and beer cans left behind.

I had just finished my dog paddling workout and had gone into shallow water to do scissor exercises when I realized I was being watched. I was sure it was not a fisherman because it was just too hot for fish to be biting that late in the morning. I looked up to see a hefty guy, probably in his mid-forties. He was wearing a white T-shirt and khaki pants. No fishing gear in sight. He was drinking a beer and smoking a cigarette. If he was a hiker he would have had a water bottle and possibly a backpack.

He must have just walked in from the parking lot. I had not heard an ATV. I knew he was not a nature lover either. He had paid no heed to a killdeer that had announced its arrival as it sounded its way down the winding creek looking for minnows in pools of water. When it encountered us at the swimming hole, it had swooped up out of sight.

I did not like the way he was looking at me, staring down his nose with a twisted smile. He just stood there wide-legged with his arms resting on his hips. What looked like the tails of tattooed dragons came out of his T-shirt. He looked like he had not shaved for a week or so because his scraggy chin hair was about the length of his crew cut.

All of a sudden, he loudly declared, "I am really hot." He flipped his lit cigarette into the creek and tossed his beer can into the ferns. He then pulled his T-shirt over his head and dropped it along with his pants. He was stark naked. I was so surprised it didn't even occur to me then he did not wear shorts.

He obviously saw the fried egg look of surprise on my face. He strode into the water, unabashed with legs wide apart in an exaggerated manner. With arms stretched out, he pointed to his erect member, noting that he was sure I had seen a stiff one before and that its name was Happy Harvey.

He must have seen my fear as I backed away from him. With a wicked grin, he added that he had never met anyone that was afraid of Harvey and for me not to be. He pointed to what must have been a tattooed heart above Harvey before he acquired his beer belly. Now it looked more like a tomato someone had stepped on, but I withheld that comment.

I immediately tried to hide my fear. I avoided looking at him directly because I did not trust what my eyes would tell him. His tone was not menacing though his stance and certainly his conversation was. Still, I felt vulnerable. I had no experience dealing with such a situation and knew that screaming or telling him to get the hell out of there would be useless at this time of day.

I knew the swimming hole so well I did not need a quick look around for an escape because I knew there was none. To my right and left was a high bank. He was standing on the downstream dam. Going upstream would be hard because of all the rocks in the riffles leading to the swimming hole.

I rationalized that if he had meant any harm, it would have already happened. After all, he had been up there for a while watching me and could have caught me unawares.

I certainly did not want to show fear in case he was violent. When I turned in either direction to avoid looking at him directly, he would walk around so I would get a full frontal view.

I needed to buy some time to figure out if he was just having fun or if he was a rapist. So I swam out in the deep water and announced as calmly as I could that I was going to continue my water exercises. He started to wade forward and when he was in shoulder-deep, I realized he could not swim. He began blinking, his eyes widened, and his jaw dropped. You could see that he was afraid as he backed up to more shallow water.

When I told him the creek was over twelve feet deep and that is where I liked to exercise, he stepped back even further. Again, he tried to interest me by pointing out Harvey was ready. He began circling me in the shallow water.

Now that I had some control, as long as I stayed in deep water, I began nonchalantly dog paddling. I decided it was time to find out more about him so I could determine how to get out of this situation. I asked him what he did for a living. He replied he was in construction and added that he was on unemployment right now and stressed that he had lots of free time.

With as much concern and calmness as I could fake, I noted that a lot of people were not working these days. Then I stressed that while most people came to this swimming hole in the afternoon and evening, the high unemployment meant more people were coming during the late morning as well as later.

He looked around and observed how quiet it was. He pointed out that you could hear any cars that pulled into the lot and he hadn't heard any. I noted that the fishermen often cast lines along the entire creek area which now had three parking lots for their use and that they walked up and down the three-mile stream in their area to cast their lines.

He gave me a tight-lipped smile to let me know it did not concern him as he pointed out that Harvey was not only happy but fast. Even though Harvey had been in the cool water now for some ten minutes, his ardor had not diminished. Hoping that he was just an exhibitionist and not dangerous, I kept treading water furiously, waiting for an opening when I could get Harvey to lose interest in me if the cold water did not do it.

I had my chance when he asked why I exercised so much. Didn't I ever get tired and take a break? I told him that I guessed that I was just cheap...that I did not want to pay the swimming pool fees at the health spas...that I didn't even have to pay to exercise in the winter because skiing at the state areas was free if you were over seventy.

In a normal situation I would have been flattered when his jaw dropped with surprise. A sideways glance told me Harvey was also reacting to this news.

Now I knew what to do. I added that I used to bicycle for exercise but had given that up when I was diagnosed with rectal cancer.

That did it. He waded out and didn't even turn around. I waited until he retrieved his pants and shirt and headed down the path along the creek. I went out to the road where my car was and saw him pull out of the lower parking lot. I could not make out his license number but I made a mental note that he was driving an old blue PC Chrysler cruiser.

I told a local official about it and he said he knew the guy. He was notorious for bragging about all his conquests at the local bar. His name actually was Harvey. The official felt he was harmless. Still, he was going to visit the guy and tell him that there was a law against nudity. He laughed when I suggested that Harvey was probably at the bar now hoping no one realized he had tried to seduce an eighty-year-old with rectal cancer. I suggested that I might go there. After all, I had my bragging rights. I had turned him off.

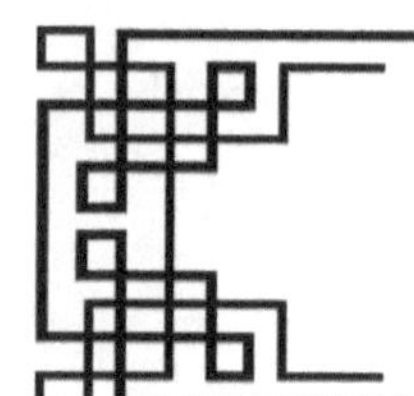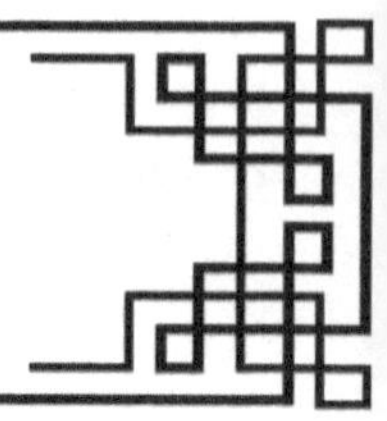

She Bagged
a Litterbug!

That's what they say about me at the gas station on the north end of the Farmington River State Forest a few miles before you get to the Massachusetts Turnpike.

Before entering the southern end of the "forever wild" protected forest along Route 8, a forty-mile road following the meandering twists and turns of the Farmington River, I went through a McDonald's drive-in at Winsted, Connecticut, to pick up a chocolate milkshake and burger.

In front of me was a family in a van with kids shouting out their orders to their dad, who often had to repeat the order as minds were changed and items added. Sure enough, there was confusion at the receiving counter as kids opened their bags claiming "that's not mine" or "where are the fries?" But it eventually got sorted out with the server checking the items against the order receipt and then ringing up a new bill for exchanged orders.

While irritated, I still was not as frustrated as some of those behind me, blowing horns. I was looking forward to the ride through the forest along the upper Farmington River which would be cool. I was in my open Jeep. I regretted not having the top up when I was on the interstate. I could feel my face flushing now with a sunburn about to show itself. But now I was going to have a cool ride.

The sun was directly overhead as I finally pulled out with my order. Just a burger and shake was simple and I had plenty of time to get the exact change ready for the cashier—much to the delight of the person behind me who quit honking his horn. I was right behind the van when to my dismay it entered the park. But regardless, I was ready for not only a refreshing breeze from the river in the park but I wondered if the rhododendron was in bloom. It was the right time of year. The park, with its variety of fir trees, always came alive with the big red rhododendron blossoms. During spring trips, I would take advantage of pull-over spots to find wildflowers of all kinds. I had been amazed to see the rare yellow lady slippers along the road as well as striped trilliums.

This time, my reverie was soon distracted by several burger wrappers flying out of the van. I could not believe it when one of the kids threw out a huge plastic soda container which must have still have had considerable ice and coke in it. It plopped in the creek some ten feet away—just as the kid had obviously aimed it to, judging by the cheer I heard.

I blew my horn, hoping the parents in the front seat would notice what was going out the back windows. To my astonishment, the driver threw out a Styrofoam container that had housed his Big Mac. Minutes later, I assumed it was the driver's wife who tossed out her coffee cup and several French fry containers which I had seen moving back and forth between the front and back seat.

I fumed. I tried to keep my eyes on the stream making its way through the boulders. But I just got madder as I regarded this affront to nature. When the driver threw out a lit cigarette, it was just too much for me.

I picked up the milkshake which was only half gone. I put it in the empty burger bag also near the gearshift. Did I have the nerve to do it?

"Yes, I do," I said to myself as I changed gears to pass the van. The man glanced at me as I came up alongside with a look of "What's that girl doing in a Jeep?" I had gotten these looks before from guys who felt women should stay in compacts. I planned my gear acceleration to get around him quickly.

When I threw the bagged milkshake into his open window, I knew I had made a direct hit when I heard the cursing behind me. But I did not have time to think about what he thought of the chocolate shake. He was accelerating very fast now. If I let him pass me, I was sure he would run me off the road.

It hit me that I had at least twenty miles to go before we left the park. There were no homes in there, not even a ranger station. There was a gas station about a mile outside the park. I was in trouble. My rearview mirror became my guide. Every time he swerved into the passing lane, I moved over in front of him. I was glad I had bought the Renegade Jeep with eight cylinders. However, its wheelbase was short and I had to be very careful on turns. But I had more horsepower than the bulky van he was driving and there were hills in the park where I could put some distance between them.

For the next half-hour, it was a roller coaster ride for me. I fully concentrated on using the full roadway to bank the curves without turning over, hoping there was no oncoming traffic. The horn behind me, along with his cussing, just kept my adrenaline going. Several times he came close enough to nearly ram into the back of my Jeep.

I had driven through this park for some ten years on my way to Massachusetts and knew what was ahead. I hoped he didn't. When we got to the bridge that crossed the stream and made a quick turn to the left, I thought he was not going to make it. I had been right. He did not know this road as well as I did. So I would brake unexpectedly to throw him off when I knew he could not pass and then use my gears to spurt ahead.

I knew the gas station was only about five miles from that bridge. My braking to confuse him and crisscrossing the road to keep him from passing was making him even madder. When he would try to ram me from behind, I would speed up immediately. Finally, I saw the back side of the sign welcoming motorists to the park and I knew I could make it to the service station.

I skidded into the lot and stopped right beside the door

to the inside of the garage, knowing I had to get help to deal with the man coming in right behind me.

I ran inside with him right behind me yelling, "You crazy bitch, you dirty bitch" at which point the station owner stepped between us asking what was going on.

I was out of breath but I relaxed when I saw the owner was bigger than my chaser. Amid the cursing and shouting, I explained why I had thrown the milkshake into the car...that I wanted to show them how it felt to have all that junk thrown out...that it was against the law to litter...that they should learn to respect nature...

About the time the garage owner got the man calmed down, one of the kids came in the door at which time I asked if they taught them at school not to litter. He said "yes" and while I should not have done it, I suggested he take his old man to school with him.

Now I had the garage owner as disgusted with me as he was the chaser. He ordered the man—now turning his road rage into a fist he was shaking at me—to leave because he was calling the police. Then he ordered me to stay there until they came because I would need an escort since I sure didn't have enough sense to shut up when I should.

I did as I was told and even filled up my gas tank.

Today, I always stop there for gas and the owner merely shakes his head and says, "I hope you are not bagging litter-bugs today."

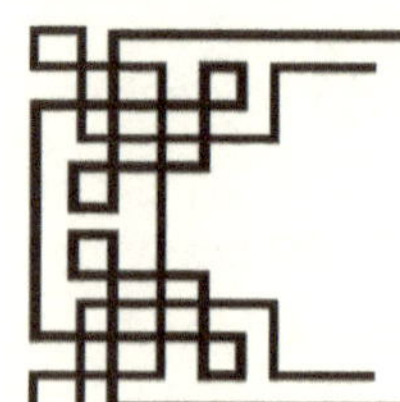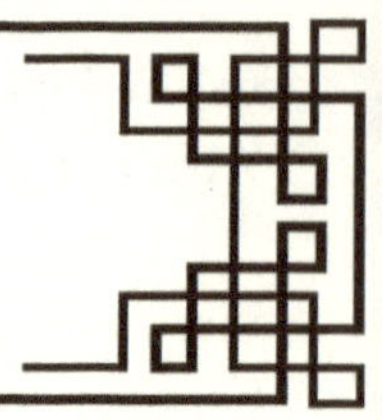

Deep Powder Adventures

It is not true you can't find deep powder skiing in the east. What is true is when you do, it can be much more than a thrilling day on the slopes. Getting to and from there has its challenges.

Unlike western skiing where over 100 inches of snow can be dumped in a twenty-four-hour period with huge rotary plows to clear the way for skiers to get there, the east has no reason to invest in such heavy snow removal equipment. A dump of four feet is very rare, occurring maybe once in ten years.

But this happened some years ago when a storm from the south comes up to meet one from the north. Sometimes the weathermen overdo it trying to prepare people for the worst. About eight inches had fallen, so I decided to make the two-hour drive to Bromley in Vermont. I would get there before it qualified as a western-style deep powder. I left barely able to see through the snow pouring down in our driveway to the highway. But the New York State plows had been out, so the going did not get tough until I got to the country roads in Vermont.

I felt confident my new four-wheel drive Jeep would get me through the first tracks I was making along the Battenkill Creek roads. It was heavy going. I was in the lowest gear on the hills. Fortunately, I knew the road well. I did not have much visibility—even with my windshield wipers on high. The problem was I knew I could not turn around on the narrow road to go back. I would be stuck for sure.

Finally I got to Arlington, where the Vermont State Road

plows had been earlier. I was again driving through a foot or so of snow. When I got to the mountain, I saw only a few cars in the parking lot. I congratulated myself on getting there—and being among those who would experience the joy of skiing in fresh deep powder. I knew the mountain well enough to make the first tracks on several of the trails. It kept snowing so hard, my tracks would be covered up before I could check to see if I had managed some good-looking turns. Still, I could feel the rhythm of what I call "dancing on the snow."

Skiing was so great, I did not even take the time to go in for lunch. If I had, I might have heard the report that the road up to the mountain was closing.

Exhausted, I managed to make the last ride on the lift before it closed. I found myself literally wading through the snow to the lodge. The cafeteria had closed. I got out of my boots, got my gear together, and headed for the parking lot. There, reality sunk in. There were only a couple of cars and they were completely covered with snow. I recognized my Jeep by the hump of the ski rack. The parking lot attendant told me the road was closed. My best bet would be to hike up to the Sun Lodge along the closed road beside the ski area—that there would be lots of room because no one had been able to get there for hours.

He was certainly right about that. In fact, I had to kick aside enough snow to get the door open. There was no one at the desk so I went to the bar. The bartender, after serving me a Black Russian, asked if I would watch over the place. He would check me in and then had to make dinner for the few guests there. The cook, maintenance man, and desk clerk had not been able to make it to work because of the closed road.

Cold and wet from wading through the snow to get there, I happily took over the bar, fixing myself more Black Russians and filling up on the mixed peanuts. When he came back, I thanked him as he thanked me. Off to my room I went with the key he gave me. I was sound asleep when all of a sudden

I woke up with water pouring down from the ceiling. Soon I heard the bartender's voice in the hallway yelling for everyone to go to the dining room lounge. There was no fire, but a frozen water pipe had broken. The lounge area was not affected so we could hang out there. There were plenty of couches to sleep on in case our beds had gotten too wet. Some of the guests went with me to the bar area which was not affected. Others used the couches in the lounge. The maintenance man showed up when the roads were cleared just before sunup.

My room faced the chairlift going up Bromley. I could see there were at least four feet of powder. Enough snow had been cleared to get the lift running, so I had another great day of powder—this time with great visibility in the sun. By the end of the day, the roads had been cleared all the way back to New York State.

My husband had been worried but understood why I was so excited about being able to ski powder in the east. He was the one that taught me to ski powder. I have never seen anyone do it better than him. He had been to the Bugaboos twice. But his favorite ski area, Alta, also became mine. It gets over 500 inches a year. It is known for its light, fluffy powder supposedly made so by the nearby Salt Lake basin area.

But it had not been easy teaching me. He was quite worried when I was following him through one of those huge Alta snowstorms. We were in the Wildcat glade area with its towering pine trees, which he and a Denver friend liked to sail through. I got too close to one of the trees, hit a buried branch, and found myself falling into what they call a tree well. The heavy fir-laded trees keep the snow from piling up immediately around their base. In this case, a fifteen-foot-deep pit had been formed around the tree trunk. On the way down, the branches took my skis and poles off near the top. I landed at the bottom, sticky little branches in my face. The snow was falling so fast that by the time my husband and his friend got back up on the lift, they had trouble finding me.

My tracks had been covered by the wind. It took me over an hour to break off branches until they could hold me so I could climb out. After pulling my skis and poles out of the branches, I got to the bottom where they were in line with a ski patrolman for another ride up to find me.

Even though my husband can no longer ski after too many repeat hip replacements, I still go to Alta hoping to find those great powder days. I am still embarrassed remembering the day some Alta ski patrolmen told me to take a lesson. They had good reason. I was lucky enough to be at the Alta lodge when seventy inches of snow came down over a twenty-four-hour period. An avalanche had closed the road up to the area, so there were few people, which would mean what my husband would call "perfect"—fresh tracks all day. I was up early and out the door the minute the guns had knocked down the possible avalanche danger and lockdown was over. Despite the snow being nearly over my head, I was able to ski down to the lift from the hillside lodge without turning because I was tunneling. The ski patrolmen at the lift sent me to the ski store there to get floaters on my skis in case I went under the snow so they could find me. The red balls on the end of the cords tied on the back of my skis would float up through the snow to indicate where I was if I fell. They even attached the floaters to my skis for me. Naturally, they were in a hurry to make their first tracks. When we got off the Wildcat lift and skied down to the Germania lift, they probably didn't realize that I had tunneled my way down there behind them. It was steep enough that I did not have to turn, so I arrived there at about the same time they did. I was amazed at how they seemed to immediately glide on top of all the snow and dance their way down.

When we got off that lift, I followed them on the traverse to an area called the Ballroom under Baldy Cliff. It is free of trees but divided into chute-like sections. I could see their heads bobbing in rhythm as they started down. I took a deep breath and decided I would try to make some rhythm turns, too. *I can do this*, I told myself. I still can't remember if I got one or two turns in before I went down under the seventy inches of new powder. Because the chute was so steep, I felt myself sliding fast in total darkness under the snow. I could feel my skis come off, but I held on to my poles. Finally I came to a rest under an even larger pile of snow I had brought down with me. I was able to use my ski poles to clear the snow enough above me to see blue sky. As I was thrashing around to get on my feet, a couple of the patrolmen arrived to help me up. Two of the others had gone on to the lift to pick up my skis buried near the top. They quickly recovered them because the floaters indicated where they were.

Naturally, I was embarrassed and even more so when they came down with my skis because I had difficulty putting them on in the deep snow. They nicely accompanied me to the lift to tell the operator to take me down to ski school at the bottom where I could get private powder lessons. So when I was back with an instructor, my embarrassment got worse. They had roped off the Ballroom area, which could be seen from both lifts to display the conditions. There were six beautifully synchronized chutes displaying perfect "S turns" on top of the snow to the bottom. Then there was my run, which they called the Mole Run. Like a mole in a garden, the snow was heaved up in a straight formation all the way down the chute.

In fact, I am amazed at how nice Alta patrolmen are considering what they have to put up with. The next time I saw them, the conditions were like the blue ice we often get in the east. I was cutting into the High Rustler from the Greeley side. Once you drop into this area from the tree-lined side, you can't get out. I knew the conditions were bad, but my husband always said when I left, "Ski one on the High Rustler for me." There was no one in there. I could see that even side slipping was a challenge. Then a ski patrolman dropped in behind me and asked me what I was doing there...did I not see the trail was closed? I told him about my commitment to my husband. It was then, pointing to the long stretch of ice moguls below us, he asked, "How well does your husband get along with you?"

It took about an hour but I made it down. At the end of the day, I bought the patrolman a couple of drinks for his patience. He said he had skied in the east and found that getting to the areas in New England was a pain because the road to get there in heavy snow was often closed.

It was then that I told him about my great experience in deep powder at Bromley in Vermont. He asked if any ski patrolmen knew me there.

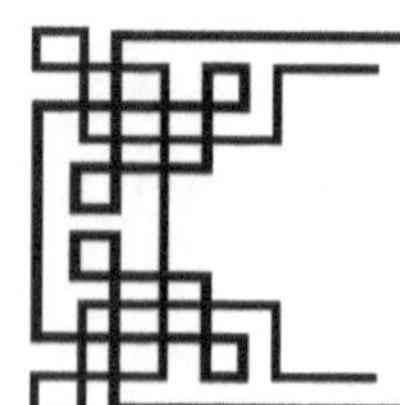

Miracle in Lake Placid

When the amateur U.S. hockey team beat the professional Russian team at the U.S. Olympics in Lake Placid in 1980, it was rightly called the "Miracle on Ice." To me, just being able to volunteer for the Alpine events was a miracle.

Fortunately for us in the Capital District area, my future husband Dick Weber was an FIS official. He had run ski races on the east coast, including several for those seeking to qualify for the Olympics. Therefore, through his contacts, about forty of us from the Capital District area were able to work in alpine events. To qualify, we also received training from working at two major events at Lake Placid before the Olympics—the Canada-American event in 1978 and a World Cup in 1979.

The head of the Alpine events was Serge Lussi. His father Gustav was an ice skater known for transforming skating techniques. Gustav was instrumental in getting the 1932 Olympics in Lake Placid. Serge and Dick had become close friends through the United States Eastern Ski Association. Serge owned the Holiday Inn in Saratoga where some of the competitors stayed and meals were served to some volunteers, including us.

All told, there were about 2,000 volunteers covering thirty-eight events in ten different disciplines—alpine skiing, biathlon, bobsleigh, cross-country skiing, figure skating, ice hockey, luge, Nordic combined, ski jumping, and speed skating.

We were given insulated blue and yellow suits, gloves, and a hat adorned with a raccoon mascot. The rings around its face represented goggles worn by the 1932 athletes. The raccoon was called Roni, which was the language of the Iroquoian native of the Adirondack. Schoolchildren came up with the name. Corporation donor names on clothing and equipment were usually discreetly displayed.

Serge managed to get Ford to donate vans for the Alpine volunteers which were greatly appreciated—even though they all were the same model and color, causing much confusion. Weary from long days, we often got into the wrong vehicle. Fortunately the keys were different.

We were also housed in a trailer park which caused some confusion because all of them were white and in block rows. As many as ten of us were crammed into each trailer. But we were so excited about just being there that we laughed it off—even when we found out the hot water had been hooked up to the toilet bowl instead of the wash basin.

The six Alpine Skiing events—men and women's downhill, slalom and giant slalom—lasted during the entire event from February 13 to February 24. Everyone had a label on their jacket sleeve naming their duty on the downhill trails. Most of our Capital District group was assigned to trail maintenance, a few to gate setting, and several to course control in which we worked with ski patrol on the course. I landed the great job with the label "controller" at the top of the men's downhill—thanks to Dick's recommendation. Still, some were probably right when they said it was because you could hear me without the radios we carried. Back then there were no such things as cell phones, and communication lines had to be installed up the mountain. Too often officials would tune in on the action which drained the batteries and made it hard to hear.

My job at the start was to announce each racer as they left the start gate to ski patrolmen with radios lined up along the course. If a skier fell or went off course, they would announce this information back and I would announce it to the TD and starter. If the skier was off the course, no action would be taken and the starter would do the countdown for the next racer. If trail maintenance was needed or someone was down the in-fall line, they would radio back when it was safe to send another racer.

Normally there was no problem except for the training runs in which the downhillers competed for position in the actual race. Unlike the World Cup race in 1979, Olympic competitors often did not have the skills of professional racers. Some were even from countries without a full team. Everyone had mused about a young girl from Lebanon in the women's downhill who snowplowed her way down the course on her first seeding run. But to her credit and much applause, she kept getting better and halved her time in the next training run.

Among those in the men's downhill was an eighteen-year-old, Leonhard Stock, from Austria. He garnered great public interest because he had been trained from the age of four by the Austrians. At the time, there was the theory that those identified with what was called a "fast twitch" would make a good slalom racer and those with a "slow twitch" would be better downhill competitors. The Austrians had designated the young Leonhard as a sure downhill winner. But without a record, he was way back in the seeding. His first training time was impressive despite deteriorating course conditions, causing him to attract much attention—particularly from the ABC TV people.

During the second training run, he was still halfway down the list of forty-seven racers. Conditions were still not the best during this warm period. One racer caught an edge in the soft snow and had taken out a gate that had to be repaired. The ABC crew was impatient and kept yelling at the start shack TD Lee Sossman to put more than one racer on the course to speed up the process. They wanted to film Stock and they didn't want to wait. To the starter's amazement, Sossman complied. At one point we had three racers on the course.

Things went well for several runs before ski patrolmen radioed with alarm that a racer was down on the course and in the fall line. This, of course, meant a pause at the start until they could check out his condition. I yelled "Stop the race," but the ABC crew just looked at the TD and he sent the next racer up. I yelled again but the starter obeyed the TD. All I could do was yell in my phone "Racer on course." The ski patrolmen let out a curse and did the only thing they could do; they ran out and quickly dragged the racer off the course, not knowing if he was O.K. As it turned out, the downed racer, who had been unconscious, came to and was later deemed not to have a concussion. But I agreed with the ski patrol that they should have had time to examine the racer. We filed a grievance but never got a response to the form.

While all of us admired the skill of the Austrians, their team of four did take first, second, seventh, and ninth place in the downhill of forty-eight. And yes, Leonhard Stock, now seeded ninth in the actual race, rightly amazed the world with his gold medal win—setting a sixty-two-seconds-faster record. Stock was clocked at going over 70 mph at one point on the course.

But dealing with some of the Austrian fans and officials had soured many of us. During the first training run, we had to station observers near the start line to prevent some of the Austrian fans from running across the course if they thought their racers did not get a good start. This would result in a restart. The Austrian team, unlike others, also had masseuses at the start to loosen up their competitors. While all volunteers like me were to stay quiet and not comment on activity around us, I did like some of the Canada team for mocking the Austrians by rubbing each other's calves.

After one of the warmer training days, the Austrian coach signaled me to come over. He handed me the jackets of the Austrian team plus his to take to the bottom because they wanted to enjoy the sunshine. I complied but was panicking inside. I had already had trouble just getting down the side of the course which was not iced up like the center. I was remembering the first day we came up to the start. Back then the chairlift went only as far as the women's downhill start.

To get to the top of the men's downhill, we had to take a T-bar the rest of the way.

The sun was barely up because we had to get to the mountain hours before the race to set things up. Maintenance people had to carry gear up so I considered myself lucky just getting myself up there clinging to the bar in poor visibility and often over ice. One of the maintenance people behind me yelled just in time when he saw that I had slipped so far to the right I was about to collide with the T-bar tower.

So, with much trepidation, I decided to just put on all the jackets instead of trying to carry them. The coach's jacket was the largest, so I put it on last and headed down the side of the course. I was doing O.K. until I approached the steep drop we called Victoria Falls. It was here the snowcats would lose control trying to pack overnight snow from the course. Maintenance people, including some of us controllers, were asked to roll down the slope to pack it. I had even enjoyed that. But here I was now full of fear coming up to that section. Sure enough, I went down and found myself rolling out of control. I felt like a balloon with all those jackets on. I bounced around until I finally came to a stop right under the upcoming lift. With all that bulk I knew I wasn't hurt. I got up and brushed off the snow I had collected in the jackets. I looked up to see several people on the lifts watching me. I told myself I deserved this embarrassment.

After all, I had sent two of my best friends, Cash Jones and Paul Lozier, down this same course in the midst of high tension. They were both on the maintenance team in which the major duty was to cut small pine boughs and line the course with them. Because of the high speeds and sometimes low visibility, racers needed these green bough lines to orient themselves to the fall line. (Today, bright orange or blue dye colors are used.)

During the race, one of the racers had gone off course, wiping out quite a stretch of the bough markers. I relayed the report to the TD who yelled for maintenance. I immediately pointed to Cash and Paul who were standing within sight with bags of bough. Cash dashed off with a bag and was barely out of sight when the TD, to the amazement of both the starter and me, called for another racer. It seemed impossible that Cash could spread boughs that fast—let alone keep upright on the icy course carrying a bag. Fortunately, Cash has forgiven me. I am lucky he was a good skier and relieved to get a report from the ski patrolmen. He had been able to scatter enough boughs just in time before being missed by an oncoming racer.

But I was far from forgiven the next day at the top when the Austrian team arrived. I was loudly summoned by the Austrian coach. He cursed me in German. Because I had his jacket on top, it turned out some of the IOC officials on the lift line had thought it was the coach who had fallen. While I was stammering my apology, the Canadian team, led by Dave Irwin who came in eleventh, was shaking my hand and patting me on the back. In fact, Dave pulled up the downhill sign after the final race and gave it to me. I, of course, have his signature on it.

While all of us were thrilled to "work" on the downhill race, we had a competition of our own going. When the U.S. hockey team, mostly made up of college players, beat Finland and went on to face the professional Russian team, the national press went wild. So did our Capital District gang at our usual evening celebrations at the lakeside cottage bar. Tickets simply were not available for the game. Stories about those having tickets able to sell them for 100 times their value prevailed. After a few rounds of ale, someone suggested we have a contest to see who could finagle their way into the actual hockey game rather than watch it on Canadian TV at the Holiday Inn.

So the next evening, we trundled off to the hockey rink in downtown Lake Placid for the "miracle" event. A huge crowd was already there. It looked impossible to even get near the door to plead our case. It turned out that Bill Kornrumpf would be my closest competitor in gaining entry. Because his blue suit was clearly labeled "maintenance," he cleverly spotted the Zamboni used to smooth choppy ice in the arena. He decided his best chance was to follow it into the arena, hoping it didn't break down and he was called upon to repair it.

I was still feeling sick after catching what I thought must be all the foreign flus available at the international event which attracted twenty-two nations. I saw a medic at the first aid station and went over noting I was not feeling well. She took my temperature which was about 104 and said, "Come with me." We went inside the arena to the first aid facility. She gave me some Tylenol and had me lie down on a gurney. Then she left to get a sneak peek at the game now starting. I quickly jumped up and donned a doctor's smock, went through the door the nurse had taken, and soon found myself in the arena.

The noise was overwhelming and the huge crowd was on their feet yelling. Some shoving was occurring, so I decided I had better get rid of the medical outfit in case someone needed help. I dumped it in a trashcan. My blue suit sleeve identified me as a "controller" but did not say downhill.

The next thing I knew, a hockey volunteer grabbed my arm and said, "Thank goodness someone called for crowd control. Get over to Aisle 3 and clear it. People are taking each other's seats there and others are in the aisle to get the best view of the action." So naturally I did as I was told. I pointed to my identification as I asked people to move out of the aisle. Then I sat down in it to make sure it stayed clear.

I am sorry to say that at the time I did not know there were just three periods to the game, not four as in football. Moreover, I was not familiar with hockey plays. I was astounded to see the players battling it out even when they were not in play. Having done some ice skating myself, I was really impressed with the agility of the players. But I was confused when they seemed to go out of their way to bash each other up against the arena wall even after a score was made. Unlike football, there didn't seem to be penalties. Instead, the sound of clashing hockey sticks—sometimes into each other—just brought cheers.

When the U.S. team made a score, I wondered if I might lose my hearing. I was clearly in the U.S. cheering section and it seemed no one would sit down. They were constantly on their feet yelling, even when there was no action during the period change. It was during such times I would look at the Russian team members, clearly puzzled about the roar despite no action. Today, when I look back on what they now call "The Miracle on Ice," I have decided this was a case where the fans won the game. Their unrelenting, incredible support for the U.S. team had not only rallied our college athletes but had disarmed the confused professional Russians.

But most of all, I could see the ABC camera across from me. I occasionally waved hoping my friends would see me if they were at the Holiday Inn watching TV. I had also been relieved to see that when the Zamboni came into the arena during a period break, it did not contain Bill Kornrumpf.

When I left the arena, the roar of the crowd was still in my ears and I had forgotten about my temperature. Now I think about how orderly the celebrating crowd was compared to some fans today. A group had assembled and in their glee they surrounded a police car and lifted it into the air; the policemen helped them do it.

I was quite pleased to be the winner of the Hockey Game Crash and took much pleasure in the free ales at the cottage. But today as I look at my downhill sign along with other memorabilia, I have to laugh at my lack of knowledge back then.

When I took the sign to a ceremony on the lake honoring the alpine events, I met Dave Irwin again. He introduced me to the winner of the GS and slalom. I had him sign my downhill sign below Dave's signature. His name was Ingmar Stenmark. He did so amidst everyone laughing because he was known for never doing downhill races.

Vacationing Alone Has Its Benefits

Too often people are afraid to go on vacation alone because they feel they need to have someone there to help them in case of an accident. Or because their vanity doesn't allow them to be considered a third wheel among couples. Or worse, they think other people will think they have no friends and have no choice but to go alone.

When I look back on trips with friends, my memories are mostly of getting to know them better. But going alone causes you to look around, listen, and learn more. Take my one-week ski trip to Alta, Utah, as an example.

Seated beside me on the plane was a very prim, well-dressed lady in a riding outfit. She had no sooner sat down than she was on her cell phone telling the groomer for her horses in Saratoga what she wanted him to do for her horses for the next three days. She was quite specific. It was apparent that her orders were being followed without question as she never repeated herself or explained why she was asking for the chore to be done. When our flight took off, she looked at me to tell me she was going to take a nap. This told me she was not in the mood for social chit-chat. I quickly agreed it was a good thing to do, but loud cries from a kid behind us proved neither of us was going to have a restful flight. I could see she was highly agitated as she heard the doting father offer treats and toys to the kid, who screamed "No" each time. The mother, very docile, would shush him—sometimes successfully—but the father seemed intent on making the passengers on the fully-loaded plane aware of how generous he was with his son and what a good father he was.

It was finally too much for the horse lady, who turned around and said: "Quit giving your kid so many choices. That makes him a brat. When you shut up, so does he. Your baby talk is even more irritating than his whining is." She had everyone's full attention; some stifled laughs and others looked shocked.

The fury of the father, who told her to mind her own business, was picked up by the kid. He immediately began screaming at his highest pitch and kicking the back of my seat. It was then I learned how well-trained the stewardesses are. She came back and suggested to the docile mother that her son would be more comfortable with his shoes off. This immediately stopped the kicking. She also produced a lollipop, which the kid immediately started licking instead of screaming. The lesson was not lost on the passengers. There was a quiet smile of approval from everyone to the stewardess. This would not have happened had I been sitting with friends. None of them would have taken it upon themselves to confront a father on how to rear children.

When I got off the plane in Salt Lake, I hired a van to get myself and my ski gear up the mountain. Two teenage boys standing by asked if they could go with me because they were staying near my lodge. When we got to the parking lot, four more teens showed up, also with their snowboards, to join us. Having a grandson their age, I just laughed and knew I had been had.

On the way up, they began excitedly chatting. I became anonymous just like the driver. The kids were between sixteen and eighteen. They had saved all their money for the flight from Denver for the school's out week. They had chosen Snowbird because they had advertised one free trail open for snowboarders in the hopes of luring them into bigger trail tickets. Two of them had rented a room; the other four were going to sneak in after hours. All were admonishing the others not to be seen together in the lodge. They passed around a flask one of them had gotten from his father's den as they proclaimed they were going to have the best time ever. But the real clincher for the driver and me was when one kid declared: "Guys, you just gotta promise me this will be the most awesome trip ever. I'll be grounded for life when I get back. I got a DWI on the way to the airport."

When I got to the lodge, the first person I met was a woman sitting alone by the window looking out at the famous High Rustler trail. Turns out she was a *New York Times* photographer. She had spent the prior week photographing the Olympics in Salt Lake. We quickly got into a discussion about the politics because I had been one of the hundreds of volunteer workers at the Olympics at Lake Placid in 1980. At Salt Lake, she had particularly enjoyed meeting the Shea family who had the unique distinction of being the first family with three generations of Olympians. Jimmy Shea had won a gold medal at Salt Lake, his father had competed in three skiing events at the 1964 Innsbruck Games, and his grandfather, who had been killed just two weeks before the Salt Lake Olympics by a drunk driver, had won two gold medals at the 1932 Lake Placid Olympics. We discussed the tragedy of this and I had a new audience for my experience as a volunteer at the 1980 Lake Placid Olympic Games.

The small world became even more apparent when, upon learning I lived near Saratoga Springs, the photographer asked if I had heard of Sharon Springs. Just two weeks before this trip, I had been down there with friends. I told her how the turn-of-the-century watering hole was now being revitalized, particularly by two gay guys from the city who had done a great job restoring and running the old American hotel. I discussed an article I had read that was hanging on the wall with before and after photos. She asked about the photos and to her delight, I remembered nearly everyone. Turned out she was the author of the article. She was so impressed I remembered them that I did not tell her that the reason I recalled them was that I had spent at least ten minutes there waiting for a friend who had had too much of the great Cooperstown ale they served there.

We went on to discuss some of her other recent assignments. She had been in Kandahar right after it was liberated and had taken photos of the women casting off their burkas and appearing in public.

In 2001, like every other photographer in the city, she had quickly gone to the World Trade Center on September 11th. She got there just as the first tower came down. She dived under a police car not knowing if she could outrun the collapsing building. A police officer was already under the car. They formed a bond they would always share; in fact, they were now dating.

I was sorry to hear she would be leaving the next morning. But one quickly meets new people because the Snow Pine lodge is small. To make it easier for their waiters, they just set enough spots at the breakfast and dinner tables to accommodate their guests. Because the tables are for two and four, the conversations usually get personal.

I skied hard all day and laughed when a ski instructor pointed out he could tell I was from the east because we didn't stand straight up on our skis. We always seemed to be bracing ourselves for icy conditions. But conversations are pretty much over before they get started on the lifts, particularly on the new high-speed quads which generally also carry people that know each other. I miss the double chairs.

However, I will probably remember the guy from New Zealand because he not only skied so well but because he did it everywhere. He was heading to the Bugaboos for helicopter skiing. He had skied all the big areas down the western front of the Tetons starting with Targhee and on to Jackson Hole. He was now doing Park City, Snowbird, and Alta and no, he was not going to go to Deer Valley, because it was too upscale. But judging by his life of leisure and expensive clothes and gear, I questioned this rationale.

I also enjoyed meeting some locals from Salt Lake, including several who had worked on the Olympics and one Mormon who said they had decided not to recruit at the Games because several Protestant churches had said if they did then they were going to recruit, too.

One quad ride did turn out to be educational if not dismaying. Two ski bums were asking how and where to file for bankruptcy. It seemed they were able to run credit cards up to $30,000 and $40,000 before being unable to meet the minimum payments. They discussed which states were debtor-friendly and which ones would allow you to keep your car, possessions, and home. They settled on Florida as the best place to go if you went bankrupt. Their "minimum payment" fees came from tips they got working as bartenders at the very ritzy Snowbird Inn.

I had made the mistake one morning of saying out loud I hoped it would stay sunny all week. I was chastised the rest of the week by a woman for such blasphemy—the area needed more snow and it doesn't snow if the sun is shining. After apologizing for my skiing insurrection, we began talking. I found out she was head of the Rhode Island Opera Guild. Her two young guests were cellists, which explained why they had been so solicitous of her all week. She deplored the fact that fewer and fewer people were going to the opera and, as a result, our nation would become less civilized. She discussed how she was in the process of merging productions with the Connecticut Guild, which was in financial trouble. She attributed this partly to their penchant for always producing the *Nutcracker Suite* at Christmas, which everyone was tired of. She had convinced them that a joint production of Hansel and Gretel would save money and be more interesting for their audience. She asked me, condescendingly, if I was familiar with it. I guess it was being taken to task for my sunshine comment that I answered I had read the book when I was a kid. She looked through me for a while and then looked sympathetic. She explained to me I should go to the city and learn more about opera...that you didn't have to pay a fortune for a seat...there was a standing room area which she often used herself, which could be had for just $15. Moreover, if you went to a Texaco-sponsored event after the opera and answered questions correctly, you could win a free close-up seat. I laughed again at the inference of my possibly needing a reward to learn.

I enjoyed her much more when I ran into her at the hot tub before dinner that evening that overlooks the High Rustler. She showed me where she had lost a kneecap because some fool doctor thought that was the best way to cure a high school knee injury. I had noted earlier that week she skied very well and expressed my amazement she did so without a kneecap.

I also met a nursery owner who, because of my farming background, I could relate to better. We discussed how the demand for mulch was so great now it was no longer a by-product of bark from timber. People were starting to clear woods to meet the demands of making all those suburban landscapes look good. It had gotten so bad he no longer put a guarantee on shrubs because some mulch—particularly the popular red dye type—was so toxic it would eventually kill the plant.

Other people I met that week included two architects, one who had retired and had done work during the late 60s on the World Trade Center and the other still employed in Boston's big dig. The first said the Center had been designed for a hit by a 707 but not for the bigger planes that followed it with their even bigger gas tanks. He explained the steel had acted like spaghetti under the kind of heat the blazing jet fuel had produced, adding that the asbestos flying around the city now had also been ineffective as a coating for the steel beams.

The Boston architect talked mostly of the cost overruns on Boston's big dig and how difficult the political situation was as suggestions were always made in the press and not to the constructors.

There were also four salesmen at the lodge, but they always sat together because they were on vacation together. One could easily understand their reluctance to play musical chairs when one listened in on their "who has the worst customer story and wow, is it good to get away from them."

There was also a college kid from the city who had rentals and was skiing the beginner's slopes. Because this was a small lodge in the Wasatch National Forest built upon the remains of an old miner's store, most of the rooms were in the stone-walled basement. The kid was staying in the dormitory area along with the four salesmen. The next level of accommodations was four rooms without a bath and two with half-baths also in the basement area. The best rooms—of which there were only four—were doubles on the first floor with views of the entire Alta ski area.

I was staying in one of the rooms without a bath. One of the ski instructors was also staying there. It was through her I was to learn a lot more about the old days of mining. She had finished instruction and was taking a leisurely run down when I met her at a trail intersection. It is a popular spot to rest because below it, tucked into a glen area, is a large chalet with a huge outdoor hot tub. Sometimes you would see people in it.

While we were standing there chatting, a couple came out. She knew them and introduced them to me, and they invited us for lunch. It turned out the chalet was built over an old mine entrance which they had turned into a personal mining museum. After lunch we went back through the lighted tunnel. While I had been in West Virginia coal mines, I found this one to be fascinating because it had been a copper mine. The walls were adorned with mining tools. Most likely they had purchased these back with the Snow Pine Lodge, which had been a mining store. Today, the Snow Pine Lodge is a huge three-story building.

In the old days when my husband was able to ski, we used to stay at the posh Alta Lodge. He was a terrific skier. We skied Alta the way "it should be skied," he would say as we climbed accessible ridges beyond the lifts to find untracked snow and powder.

The Alta Lodge attracts well-heeled people from all over the world. One of my most lingering memories is of meeting a neat, distinguished guy who had actually gone on one of Byrd's arctic adventures. He was showing us a film of polar bears romping over the frozen tundra with the background of a sky as vivid blue as the bears were white. Then all of a sudden, a splotch of red showed up on the side of one of the polar bears. It was dismaying to see that and it didn't help when I heard he was a big game hunter, too.

So I guess meeting people from all walks of life is my cup of tea. Not only have I learned to enjoy vacationing alone, but I have also learned that going to a lodge that has prices for all pocketbooks also offers diversity in people, too.

A Cheerless Christmas

One Christmas I will never forget is the one I was returning from in 1979. For me, it had been like all other past Yule time holidays—the usual joys of seeing the family, enjoying great meals, and exchanging presents.

What made this one different was coming back on a commuter flight from Cumberland, Maryland, to Baltimore to make a connection to New York.

It was the day after Christmas. My brother had dropped me off at the airport on his way back to Ohio. I was settling down in the small lounge waiting for the 3 p.m. flight. There was only one attendant there. He was holed up in his office but assured me the plane would be there at 3 p.m. No magazines were around but there was piped music. I soon realized it was stuck on *Hark! The Herald Angels Sing*. I was told that he did not know how to shut it off and that was why he was in the office.

Even though I was still in the holiday mood, I decided to move to the entrance area where it was not as loud. It was when I got up to get a cup of coffee out of the machine beside the front door that I saw a beautiful black girl rush out of an old sedan. It was spotless and highly polished despite the snow having turned into a dirty slush. But it was the girl that held my attention. She was wearing a full-length, sleek black coat with a checkered cashmere scarf. Her red handbag matched her very high heels. Even though she was running toward the door, she was as deft on her feet as a ballet dancer. I automatically opened the door for her. It was then I saw an older woman and man start throwing packages out of the car. Some were beautifully wrapped in silver and gold with colorful bows.

I just stood there puzzled. I was amazed as I made out the words they were shouting to this classy young woman. They repeated their shouts several times of "Shame! Shame! Shame on you, Sasha! We don't want your dirty money or gifts." I was stunned. They slammed the door shut, calling her "Jezebel" as they drove off.

Sasha sailed right by me. She sat down in the chair next to the one I had been using. She was not just crying; she was sobbing. I was so confused I didn't know what to do. Should I try to calm her down or go out and get the packages scattered in the slush?

I decided I would start with the packages. I gathered them up, brought them in, and sat them down beside her. She cried even louder and pushed them out of sight. I asked if there was anything I could do for her.

After a tearful silence, she simply said, "You can have them, especially that mink coat in the checkered bag. Please get rid of it."

I saw that the labels were still attached to it. Those that were still wrapped looked just as expensive judging by the paper and bows.

"No way. It must really be expensive," I protested. "You must keep it. It would look great on you. You have the figure and style for it." Thinking about how awful I must look to her in blue jeans with a hiking bag on my back, I declared: "You have class, not me." She noticed the box next to me which had a picture of car chains on it. She turned around to look at me directly.

"So you think I have class," she said with a harsh laugh. "Well try this one on for size. Those people you saw are my family. They think I am a whore. Now what do you think?"

My amazement must have shown because a slight smile crossed her face. But I thought about it and replied, "I don't think anyone who wants to get rid of such expensive gifts makes a living that way. So no, I do not understand why they would call you that."

She did smile then. "O.K., then what do you think I am?"

"As I said, you are a classy lady with style who must have a good job. I don't see a ring."

She laughed again and, looking at my backpack, asked, "What about you? I didn't know hikers used chains."

I laughed and explained my brother's gift. I noted they were so heavy I regretted ever telling him about how I had gotten stuck skiing the weekend before I came home. Then I answered her question. "I have a good-paying job that I am heading back to. But I would be a lot happier if I could just spend the rest of my life in the outdoors doing honest work."

"Why is that?"

"I write for overpaid executives I do not respect. It's a job but when people say I do a good job, it bothers me making those assholes look good."

Again, she laughed. "You must be wondering about me and that scene outside," she said as she wiped her tear-stained face with a silk handkerchief. "They acted like assholes but they are not. That was my mother and father. I had not seen them since I ran away fifteen years ago. Life was not good then for any of us. I was hoping I could help them out by giving gifts and money. Instead, I found they have been under the influence of a harsh evangelist church. They decided I must be a prostitute to afford such gifts. They made it very clear they would have none of my dirty money or gifts."

"I am so sorry," I said, feeling every bit of it, knowing how condemning some religious people in the area were. "I feel bad that this happened to you when you had such great intentions. In fact, it makes me furious."

Not knowing what else to say, I offered her a drink from a bottle of scotch I had wrapped in bubble wrap in my backpack to keep it intact.

As she took it, I apologized for not having a glass. She laughed again, adding that she was not really as classy as I thought she looked. She took a drink and passed it back.

Feeling more friendly and anxious to be sympathetic, I remembered that Henry Louis Gates was from this area. So I said, "Say, are you related to that Harvard professor, Gates, who was from here and is becoming famous? He took a lot of heat from his family in his biography when he described a raunchy dancehall routine they did when he was young. They did not appreciate this being written about."

"No, but I do know of the family," she said as she took a second long drink. "This is pretty good scotch," she said as she looked at the bottle. "My god, it's 100 years old. I have never had scotch that old."

"Neither did I," I said, "until I was on corporate airplanes. I got caught once lifting a bottle and thought I might be fired. Instead, he laughed and gave me several bottles. So drink up."

It was after the fourth or fifth drink that we decided the gifts should be sent to the church where her parents never missed a day of worship. Sasha said the church was still having a charity event on New Year's Day where returned gifts were given to the poor. We hired a cab to take the packages to the church. We signed it: "Happy New Year—from Santa Sasha."

Then we drank to her parents, figuring they would immediately recognize the mink coat.

It was then that Sasha said, "You haven't asked what I do for a living."

So I did. She told me that when she got to Miami at fifteen she lied about her age and got a job in a cosmetics factory. Months later she decided she should cash in on her knowledge of the business.

Sasha handed me a tube of lipstick beautifully adorned with a Greek island etched with her name in the best Palmer script I had ever seen. "That tube sells for $25 in cosmetic shops on cruise lines going around the world," she said. "It cost me 75 cents at the factory plus a dollar for the label I put on it."

I must have laughed harder than she had earlier cried.

"Geez," I said, "now that is what I call an entrepreneur."

It was then the holed-up attendant came out to tell us the commuter plane was there. As it gassed up, we left the waiting room. We discovered we were the only ones on that flight to Baltimore. *Hark! The Herald Angels Sing* was still playing and both of us sang along with it.

We finished the bottle of scotch on our way to Baltimore connections. I went north and she went south. Unfortunately, because we both had enough to drink, we forgot to exchange addresses. I still have the chains. I still look for her in the Cumberland airport when I go home for the holidays. In her honor, I dress up a bit. I often wonder if her parents listen to the words when they sing *Hark! The Herald Angels Sing*, particularly that part about peace on earth and reconciling.

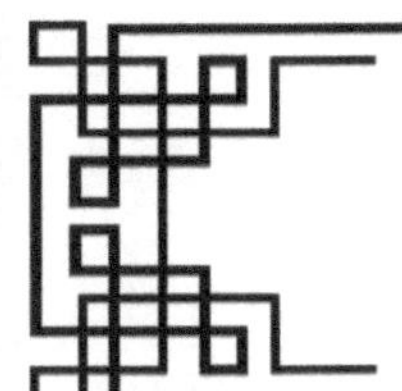

Reincarnation

Robert parked the Rolls Royce behind the seedy, rundown gas station. It was dark but the back door light was on like he said it would be. There were four cars and a pickup truck lined up beside an overflowing dumpster. Two of the cars were relatively new, but the other two, along with the pickup truck, I thought would soon find themselves in a spare parts lot. The pickup truck looked like it had partially avoided a crusher.

I was trying to hide my surprise as well as concern. *Who would have thought*, I said to myself, *that the head of the Historical Society and retired professor of an Ivy League college would be coming here to connect with his dead brother?*

Despite our less-than-civilized surroundings, Robert, who was always impeccably dressed, deftly opened the car door for me. He carried an ivory-headed cane which amused me because I seldom saw him use it. At eighty, he was physically fit with a full head of grey hair neatly parted. He was over six feet tall and still stood erect despite his age.

When he saw my concern, his blue eyes reflected uncertainty about bringing me along. So I joked about the light over the door being red as a strange welcoming for a séance. But he was in a serious mood. He explained that meant the medium was ready for everyone to come in.

Ever since I had met him as a volunteer at the historical farm owned by the society, he had been an enigma. I had donated a corn sheller to the farm and was there demonstrating its use to fourth and seventh graders. They had lined up to turn the wheel to see the machine knock off the seed into a pail with the cob shooting out the other end. Part of the program involved another volunteer taking them to the colonial granary where the kernels were stored to feed the animals and to the mill to be turned into meal for making bread.

Robert had noticed me admiring the Rolls Royce. He offered to give me a ride in it. He laughed when I told him that actually I had been in one before, a new one at that. It was when a Chivas Regal liquor dealer had come into Schenectady to a liquor store in a flashy yellow Rolls Phantom VI emblazoned with the Chivas Regal logos. I had even bought a bottle for the chance to ride in it. But I quickly added that I preferred Robert's 1938 model, which was much classier.

So off we went. It was a nice fall day in the Mohawk Valley. We headed west on Route 5 following the river. He launched into a discussion of the valley's history, starting from the time Sir William Johnson was sent by England to deal with the Indians. He gave me a tour of the fort. Farther up the road, he motioned to a historic road sign to the right. He explained that it was a memorial site to the religious leader of the Iroquois people during the peak of the fur trading with the English. Alcohol was introduced at this time. Like many Indians, he became addicted. But then, during a severe illness, he had a vision to become a prophet. He quit drinking, regained his health, and brought the Gaiwiio (the Good Word) to his people.

When I got close enough to the sign to read it, I wondered about his weird name: "Handsome Lake." Robert just smiled and said his brother's name was "Cornplanter," given to him by a relationship his mother had with a Dutch fur trader and farmer. Then he pointed below to Handsome's real name—Hadawa'ko—which meant "Shaking Snow." He told me how Handsome Lake had combined traditional Iroquois religion with Christianity which became known as the Code of Handsome Lake. "In fact," Robert said with great admiration, "Handsome Lake's visions were written down. Then President Thomas Jefferson gave his endorsement to Handsome Lake's Code in 1803. His visions were published in 1850." Then, watching me closely, he added, "I find them very helpful."

I was in total agreement; this was certainly interesting history. That I would like to learn more seemed to please him. I reminded him that I had early Dutch roots as he did and my ancestors, who had always been outnumbered in the beginning by Native Americans, learned from them. I went on to say I was not proud of how the natives were treated by the Dutch or English in later years. On top of that we had slavery to atone for and it would be good to go back to when man lived with nature, like the natives did, and learn from it.

So we became friends. As head of the society, he was an avid promoter of using the seventeenth-century Mabee farm as an educational site for city kids as well as for tourists.

He began opening up to me about his innermost feelings. He was forty years older than me and had questioned me a lot about my past. Why did I leave the farm in West Virginia? Why did I come to GE in New York? Was life not good on a farm for a girl? Were they just expected to marry another farmer? What was my religion? Why did I major in journalism? Was I always interested in what people had to say? Did I always take them at their word? Was I always so tolerant?

He would sometimes say it was good that I was open to new ideas. I think it was this last statement that made him decide to test me.

It was after a discussion about Handsome Lake and how he had seen the best of both worlds, Native American and Europeans, in his vision. It was then he told me he, too, had visions. He said he had been extremely close with his brother and had felt his presence ever since he died several years ago. He would wake up with a vision of his brother standing over him, frustrated and sad. Even when he closed his eyes, his brother would often be standing there. He tried to talk to him to no avail. He had met a medium with a Native American background who told him he could communicate with the dead. Robert had been going to his séances for the past year and now believed he was actually in contact with his brother. Intellectually, he had thought it was impossible. But there was clearly communication going on now. He was no longer waking up to see his brother hovering over him. He was at peace with their talks. Both of them seemed happy to be together again. He said he had the medium to thank for this. "Today, people would find Handsome Lake strange. The same can be said for my medium." Looking directly at me, he said it would be good to share this experience with someone he could trust—someone who would not disregard the communication but have an open mind.

"That is you," he said.

As we were about to enter the garage for the séance, I realized the visit at the Handsome Lake site had been a test. When a disheveled man in grease-stained overalls opened the door and looked at me questioningly, he turned to Robert. While Robert explained I was the girl he had told him about, I had time to survey the scene. It seemed unlikely to be the site of a séance that began with French society. There was a potbelly stove in the center of the dimly lit room. Five people were squatted around in front of it on pillows. One was nearly as well-dressed as Robert. The other two, a man and a woman, looked like they were possibly customers from this area of town known for struggling to achieve middle class. Robert sat down on a vacant pillow.

The lone woman was wearing jeans as I was. She pulled an old car seat from a pile of auto parts against the wall and offered it to me. I thanked her and sat down on it. While it made me feel conspicuous because I was at a higher level on the floor, I was more concerned about what I might be in for. But I had promised Robert I would not express any doubts about the process but just listen. He wanted my opinion after the séance as to whether I thought it was as real as he thought it was.

By this time the medium had closed the door and turned

off the outside light. He positioned himself on the floor in front of the stove. Silence filled the room for several minutes. Then he clapped two times and the dim light cast a red glow across all of us. I had no problem figuring this out because I knew of the recent introduction of turning lights on by sound as well as motion. But when his eyes rolled to the point of appearing to have no pupils and then he went into a fetal position, I was taken aback. He asked us to hold hands and began speaking in a nonstop, undefinable tongue. He reminded me of a Holy Roller religion meeting I had once attended in West Virginia where I grew up, but it was not a "Praise the Lord" trance he went into. He claimed to be in contact with people who were with the Lord as well as the devil.

Then he rose up in a squatting position and announced he was able to channel to the other side. He began with the guy next to Robert. "Your mother is coming in very clear," he told him. "It may be because your birthday is coming up," at which point the guy exclaimed that was true.

"How did you know?" he asked.

"Your mother just told me," the medium replied. "She says it is next Thursday and asks if you remember when hers was." The guy, obviously not recalling, stammered, and the medium said, "She says she didn't expect you to remember because you didn't when she was alive. But she forgives you and loves you." The guy asked the medium to tell her he was sorry for not remembering. He pleaded forgiveness for not being a better son and hoped she was happy in heaven. The medium reported she was happy there, then relayed things the mother felt her son needed to do to change his life so he could go to heaven and be with her. The guy assured his mother through the medium that he was no longer drinking and cheating on his wife. I suppressed a smile upon hearing this.

The medium then turned to the guy on the other side of Robert. He said he was now in contact with his dead wife. She had recently died. The guy teared up as he told his wife about their son and daughter and how they missed her like he did. I felt terrible for him and his tragedy but was taken aback when he declared, "Honey, I want you to know I sued that driver that killed you. He is no longer driving a garbage truck." I guess that was stark information that I didn't need to hear.

As for the gal next to me, her link to her dead husband took longer because as the medium said, he was "down below and paying for his crime." She told him the children were doing well in school and she still knew that he was innocent. She turned to me and said he had been put in jail for something he didn't do. But the medium quickly regained her attention by saying that her husband hoped she was enjoying the huge insurance policy he had left. She declared she was using it wisely. Then she assured him she was still asking the authorities to do a DNA test to show he had been wrongly accused. She would keep doing this so he could find his way to heaven.

Then the medium turned to Robert. "Your brother wants you to know he misses you," declared the medium. "He hopes you are doing well. He wants to know if your visit with the doctor went well. He thinks you should be taking a statin for your high cholesterol." Robert, looking surprised, said yes, he had just gotten a prescription. He told his brother to quit worrying about him...that he was fine but missed his big brother tremendously.

The medium, now stretching himself out on the floor, went into detail about the great life the two had growing up together. In my opinion these were things siblings commonly experienced such as fishing, swimming, and going to a one-room school. Robert was genuinely pleased when his brother reminded him they needed to always keep in touch until they were together again.

Then the medium sat up and turned to me with a direct look, which I tried to avoid. I felt my skepticism would show.

"Who would you like to talk to? Your mother or your father?"

I replied that I was at peace with both of them. I did not need to communicate with them at this time. At the same time, I wondered how he guessed they were both gone because I was not that old.

He stared at me for a minute and then said, "That's good because I am having a hard time connecting with them. Actually, the vision I am getting now is very interesting. It appears that you are one of those people who have been reincarnated."

"Really," I said with genuine interest.

"Yes, it is becoming clearer to me. A very tall image is coming up...your ancestors are different...I see a grassy plain with lots of animals like you would find in Africa."

The woman next to me asked if I had ever been to Africa. She was shushed by the medium.

"Most unusual! It is very rare to have a born-again of this type. You appear to be reaching upward. I can tell you are hungry."

As sincerely as I could reply, I noted that was often the case. I asked what I was eating.

"Leaves," he said. "Leaves." He had everyone's full attention, now on his feet, elated but speaking the strange tongue he had started the session with. Then with a roll of his eye, he clearly declared, "Your last life was as a giraffe."

I muffled a laugh.

The woman next to me saved me from commenting. "I can see it. Look at you. You have long legs, you are tall, and your ears are bigger than normal."

Again, she was shushed by the medium. He gave me a look of compassion and said, "Unfortunately I have never been able to communicate with the animal world...all I can do is see and feel what they might be doing. I can tell you that your former self is continuing to eat and her ears are on the alert for predators."

As everyone began staring at me, he closed the session, clapped to get the regular light back on, and invited me back to join the group.

When Robert and I got back into the Rolls Royce, he asked me what I thought of the whole experience. I had already been whispered to by the woman next to me that there was no charge but most people made a donation. I realized that no harm had been done. In fact, the group had left in a happy mood. Most of all, Robert seemed content. After seeing his response I did not want to cast doubt on his communication with his brother. It was obvious the medium was not living high on the hog. He was living in the front part of his old gas station. That's how Robert had met him—he used to get gas there.

So I said to Robert, "You know, being reincarnated from a giraffe is growing on me. I like the idea."

But he didn't laugh. "I knew you were different," he simply said.

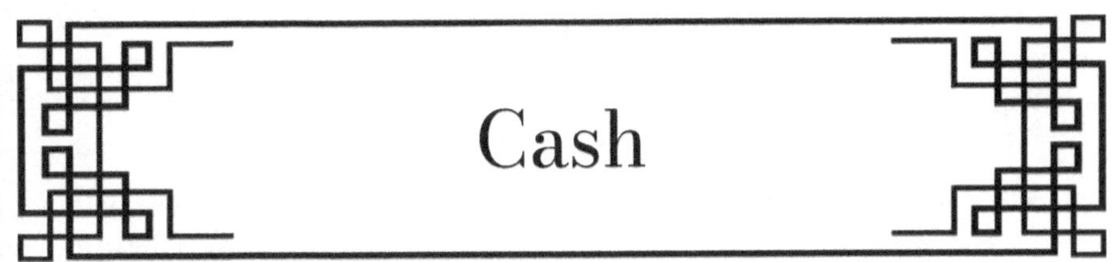

Cash

Of all my friends over the years, it must be a guy named Cash who has supported me in the best as well as the worst of times, and there have been many questionable situations when neither of us were rational in our pursuit of a good time.

We met at GE in the 60s. He was in the D.C. motor business at Schenectady. I was editing the *GE News* for some 30,000 area plant employees. He is an avid water and downhill skier with the philosophy of "you should only have a drink when you have accomplished something." It didn't take much for us to have a reason to celebrate. Just completing a day's work was enough.

I prided myself on winning the West Virginia University bladder award at a rally protesting fraternity and sorority students who had control of campus politics. For example, independent students could not sit on the 50-yard line at football games, but after a drinking contest with over 200 independents to see who could hold their booze the longest, I won the right to lead our group into the stadium to take over the 50-yard line. It also helped that I was on the student newspaper. I had the support of a journalism professor who resented the fact a lead fraternity published the yearbook.

Anyhow, I considered myself quite capable of outdrinking the young men on the GE training programs, but I made the mistake of thinking Cash, an engineer, would be an easy mark. Fortunately for me he was a considerate drinker. We always had intense discussions on everything in the news which prompted a toast if we approved of the happening.

One time that he really did me a favor was when we met in New York City at a bar near the train station. I was working at GE headquarters in Fairfield, Connecticut, and he was with GE International in the city. I don't know how many shots of scotch I had. There may have been a Jameson or two in the mix. But I do remember going to the john and being disappointed that he had not had to go. After that, I don't remember a thing until I woke up on the train going back to Connecticut.

It seems Cash, being tired of waiting for me to come out of the ladies' room, went in to find me passed out. He ordered some coffee. He was able to get me to the last train leaving for Connecticut. He told the conductor I had a Jeep at the station and to make sure I got off at Milford, which he did. I remember the conductor even made sure I had my car keys with me.

Skiing and canoeing competitions were always reasons to celebrate. We often did this at the Schenectady Wintersports Club lodge in Stowe, Vermont. On one occasion, Cash, myself, and Paul, who was well known for making his own lethal brew, drove over to New Hampshire to compete in a ski race at Cannon Mountain. I don't remember how well we did in the race but just being there was reason to toast ourselves. On the way back, one of us remembered other club members were participating in the infamous annual three-mile-long Toll Mountain Road cross-country race from the top of Stowe.

Being quite familiar with the mountain, which one could drive up in the summer, we knew a major turn not far from the top which would be quite challenging. We also remembered there was a high bank above this sharp U-turn. Soon we were at the top of the bank making snowballs to add to the challenge of our friends racing by. Most were so busy concentrating on making the turn that they did not see us. They did all they could to recover from being pelted with snow as they struggled on, dazed and confused. But one of the more adept skiers, Shields, a robotic engineer, was able to look up to see where the snowballs were coming from. He recognized us, shook his fist, and went on. And so did we. We figured he would notify the ski patrol. Shields found little humor in it because we had slowed him down in the annual contest, in which he usually came out in the top ten. Still, he did not rat us out. After our profuse apologies, he even helped us finish Paul's brew.

Cash is also great at organizing group trips for hiking and canoeing. One of these was a week-long hike on the Klondike Trail from Skagway to the Yukon River in Canada. I have to say that was a very memorable trip—perhaps because it was a sober one. We had to be judicious with our backpacks because thirty-five pounds was suggested as the maximum weight to carry over the Klondike. There was no room for alcohol even though someone asked if there was such a thing as freeze-dried ale.

Having to hoist food and items that might interest a grizzly bear up on a tree line was a new experience for me. There were times it was suggested we wear a bell to ward off bears. This didn't make sense to me. Coming from a farm, bells let you know where your animals were. I considered these dinner bills to attract bears.

At about the midway point, we had to go over the Chilkoot pass peak where the 1890s gold miners had to leave their mules. They couldn't make the climb. How those hardy miners, without the aid of lightweight, waterproof jackets, were able to do this in the winter was a question I kept asking myself. I was having trouble just getting my backpack up the mountain as it kept getting snagged by the overhanging jagged rocks. We were told they carried over fifty pounds of gear, going back down and up again until they had the supplies they needed for finding gold. I kept thinking of the mules below where some of their harnesses and other remains could be seen—including a couple of skulls that had not deteriorated. The guide told us not to pick up any of these items because the area was designated to be a "walking museum." He needn't have worried about me. There was no way I was going to add weight to my pack. I was even eating my heaviest food first.

At the top, there was a ranger station where we got water for our bottles. Then it was off over a glacier where one had to be careful to stay on the path because of the ice. I still remember dropping a water bottle and watching it slide over an ice sheet. It dropped off the glacier edge without a sound, indicating it had not yet hit anything.

Anyhow, this trip prepared me for a week-long trip through the Teton Range in Montana where we were again warned about bears as well as moose. Such scenic views made up for lack of bar conversation because one was so tired each day from roller-coaster hiking, we just wanted to inhale the view without talking. But there was one night I will not forget.

A full moon was out. We were camping just below the Grand Teton itself. I was enjoying the serenity of it all when my tent partner that night began relentlessly snoring. He could have drowned out a tugboat. I opted to pull my sleeping bag outside on the narrow trail far enough away to take in the aesthetics as well as a quiet night. About an hour later, I was being nudged by a forest ranger. He told me I had better get back in the tent if I didn't want a rattlesnake looking for warmth to come crawling into my bag. I now had rattlesnake nightmares—but at least a snoring tent mate does not bite.

The thing about hiking trips is the lasting impression they leave on you because of all the effort it takes to take it all in. One can truly enjoy a celebratory drink after such treks. I do remember a ski-lift ride at the beginning, but it was a ride on one of those bronco-busting mechanical bulls in the bar at Jackson Hole that exhilarated us most. We did it without spilling our drinks.

Being a regular tourist just doesn't cut it. Years earlier, we had been the typical tourists at Yellowstone—scenery one doesn't forget—but it was such as easy thing to do...ride in a huge snowcat with a tour guide repeating what your brochure says. Or helping the guide count down the time for Old Faithful to explode.

Our rafting trip down the Grand Canyon on the Colorado River was more like it—scenery plus excitement. We started out at Lee's Ferry in flat water after loading up our camping supplies. Adult beverages were limited to half a gallon. The guides packed all of our drinks into nets to float behind the raft which saved space as well as kept them cool. One of our more upscale members, an executive of Mary Kay cosmetics, noticed the beer Cash and I had purchased was of minimum quality. "Who drinks Safeway grocery beer?" she declared as she handed over Perrier water and a French chardonnay. Her boyfriend, Ken, merely smiled as he met his allotment with Heineken. Others had Stella Artois, Guinness, Dos Equis, and other high-end assortments of ale and wine. We didn't say anything and Ken just winked knowing how proud we had been for finding the grocery beer on sale at half-price.

The five-day trip from Lee's Ferry to Phantom Ranch at the South Rim of the Canyon was a first for all of us. Because the weather was warm, the spray from the rushing cool water released from the Glen Canyon Dam was as welcome as the sunshine bouncing off thousands of years of colorful rock layers.

We found going through Class III and IV rapids in a rubber raft was a lot easier than canoeing the upper Hudson River. No more bailing water out of an open Grumman canoe while dodging rocks. But the volume and force of the water in the Canyon was greater, so there were plenty of thrills.

At the first stop, the river had carved out a particularly intriguing cave-like entrance. We shared some of Ken's Heineken with our guide. He had a geology background and kept us in suspense telling us we would soon see the oldest rock layer known deep in the canyon. Another stop was to see the granaries carved out of the rock layers by ancient Native Americans. It was a steep climb. One can see how difficult they made it for thieves. Getting up there was not easy.

We camped out at night in wide big bend areas caused by heavy water flows to the opposite side. While all of us were environmentally minded, the first night out we were tested on just how accommodating we could be. There were two portable johns, one for pee and the other for number two. We were told to make sure neither were mixed because it was carried out. This was a new skill for me to learn. But I soon realized I was more agile than I thought. I admired Maureen's decision to hold it in rather than tolerate such conditions. I wondered how long she could do that.

But it was her concern about a nearby rattlesnake that got my full attention. We were getting into our sleeping bags. Incredibly, the eco-system guide said it was old and harmless and that he had anti-venom in case it did bite. After I pointed to a nearby bucket he could put it in, he relented and did so, much to our relief.

I had already irritated the guide by telling him I worked at the GE plant where the hydrogenerators were built for the Glen Canyon dam. While the release from this dam was providing white water for seasonal rafting, he deplored the fact the submerged canyon walls there were just as beautiful as those we were seeing. However, he did say he would like me to send him pictures of these giant generators. I told him the generators were so huge the blue-collar workers looked like dwarfs next to them. I often wondered what he did with the photos I later sent him.

It was when we got to the Little Colorado River coming into the canyon that we really had a chance to get lots of exercise. We could hike or swim in the cool, clear waters brought down from the Rocky Mountains. We wondered if we had skied on it the winter before. We still have memories of back-paddling in the peaceful Colorado River, looking up at ledges carved out over the centuries by this river so calm and cool now.

It was not too far down the canyon from this spot the guide gestured for us to look at the grey rock layer we were starting to see along the water's edge. He declared it to be the oldest known rock, called granite. Those of us from New York State who hiked the Adirondacks just laughed. It was everywhere on these mountains which geologically were still growing. Some of us had scarred knees from too much contact with it.

On the last day, he offered us two options for hiking out of the canyon. A mile-long hike nearly straight up or a five-mile walk on a wide path that the mules and tourists used to get down to the south rim. Maureen and I chose the tourist path with rest stops. The others took up the challenge of the exhausting steep hike out.

I had known Maureen was in some discomfort because she had not been pleased with the john rules and was constipated. Also, she was not big on camp food and often recalled the menus at hotels booked by Mary Kay for their top executives. Maureen was in the top echelon and was eligible for a new pink Cadillac each year.

When we were getting our gear out of the raft to leave, the guide pulled up the floating nets to reveal that the only refreshments left were some cans of grocery beer. Maureen suggested he give them to the mules after questioning the sanity of anyone bringing cheap beer on such a valuable trip.

When we met a bunch of mules coming down the trail, they had her full attention. The mules were obviously not following the rules—defecating whenever they felt like it. It was enough encouragement for Maureen to disappear behind some rocks for several minutes, coming back with the most beautiful smile on her face. She was back to her normal self. She was enjoying the scenic hike out so much she had some very helpful advice for those coming down the trail. Among these were three young Japanese women looking desperate. They asked how much farther it was because they felt they would never make it back in all the heat. They were staring at our water bottles. Obviously, they had not read the signs warning hikers to carry water. We gave them ours. It was then Maureen went into full advice mode. She noted they were wearing black when they should be wearing white which reflects the sun. She convinced them to strip down to white panties and roll their dark shirts up. They did find white panties and bras more comfortable. They were profuse in their praise for Maureen as she gave them even more hiking advice as they went back up the trail with us. Not only did Maureen buy "I climbed the Grand Canyon" T-shirts for us, but she persuaded the Japanese girls to do so even though they had not made it all the way to the bottom.

As for the secret Ken kept about who bought the Safeway beer, it was soon revealed when we packed the car to leave. Maureen noticed another $1.50 six-pack just like those from the trip. We were still living this show of "low taste" down but everyone agreed: Maureen was a great sport and made the trip much more fun.

Then there was the time Cash and I crewed for a good friend, Gary, who was a marathoner gone mad. He had entered the Great Western 100-mile Endurance Run in California. Like us, he was a working GE stiff. He had taken vacation time to do a fifty-mile run in Virginia. He was not a professional runner like so many in this noted race. His goal was to finish in thirty hours so he could win a bronze belt buckle. Those who finished in under twenty-four hours got silver buckles. Our job was to meet him at specified checkpoints to check on his needs such as water.

At sunrise, the runners started at the bottom of the Squaw Valley ski area right beside a ski lift going up to a peak some 10,000 feet high. The only one interested in taking the lift seemed to be me. Once at the top, it was a roller coaster run through the El Dorado National Forest. At the first checkpoint, Red Cross personnel were on hand to check the condition of runners, including weighing them to see if they had severe water loss. If so, they would be pulled from the race. Some of the avid veteran racers would chug down water before this checkpoint to make sure they passed the test. I already thought they should have been mentally tested when I saw them run up the ski slope rather than take the lift. Still, I was pleased to see that Gary was in fine shape after some thirty miles. He chatted with us briefly.

Cash met him at the next checkpoint. He reported he was fine even though I questioned his saying he encouraged him on because I would not wish such a race on my worst enemy. I had heard some racers were losing their toenails from jamming up against their shoes during steep descents in the forest. Moreover, they had to run through the night in this twenty-four-hour race.

The final checkpoint was just twenty-five miles or so from the finish. It was there Gary told me that if he was passed out to make sure they revived him to finish the race. At this point I was concerned about myself just hiking a few miles to get to the checkpoint. Other crew members were faster than me so in some cases I had to resort to following tracks.

When I got there, I found Gary was about to be put on a gurney by a Red Cross guy. He was protesting. I did something he has forgiven me for today. I felt so sorry for him that I gave him some chicken soup rather than water. He immediately threw up. At least the Red Cross person knew he was alive by what Gary had to say about the soup. Gary was told his leg muscles were in bad shape, causing much dysfunction in the knees. He would have to walk to the finish line. He was also told he had to have someone with him. Fortunately Cash arrived and showed what I call true friendship by saying he would do it. I watched him walk off with a very stiff-legged Gary as they calculated how much time they had left to make it there for the brass buckle win within thirty hours.

When I got to the finish line an hour or so later, they had not yet arrived. I knew they still had thirty minutes or so to show up to meet the thirty-hour goal. My attention quickly turned to several young podiatrists who were removing the shoes of some runners to attend to their callused feet. In some cases, I could see toenails in the bloody mess. It was then I decided the race was so inhumane there would be a public outcry if prisoners were punished by being forced to do this 100-mile nonstop run. Yet I knew over 100 people, including Gary, had paid to enter the race.

I was even more astounded to hear about a 1,000-mile race in Australia much like the Iditarod Race in Alaska. Those who took the least amount of time sleeping won. But as one competitor told me, the 1,000 miles were across flat land and the Australians did not do well in this endurance race. The 10,000-foot ascents and descents with temperatures that could go cold to hot in minutes were too much for them. Over half of those from Australia had not finished this race the year before.

It was about this time I spotted Gary and Cash come in with a few minutes to spare. Gary would get the bronze buckle medal. I was happy for him until I saw what a podiatrist was doing to him. He literally cut off huge calluses on both his feet. They didn't seem to bleed so I guess he knew what he was doing. Still, I remember Gary saying it took weeks to heal and he wished it had not been done.

This time we were not toasting ourselves for surviving something. Full honors went to Gary for surviving. But since then I have noticed that Gary prefers long-distance bicycle riding.

Then there was the time Cash organized a three-day hiking trip on the north end of the Presidential Range in New Hampshire. It involved staying at three Appalachian Club huts on Mt. Washington, Mt. Jefferson, and Mt. Madison. I was particularly excited because the trip started on Mt. Washington where many of us in the 60s and 70s would climb into Tuckerman's Ravine to ski the huge bowl. Mt. Washington is known for having recorded winds in the winter of 258 mph. Several hundred inches of ice and snow collect in the bowl which sometimes doesn't melt until July. One of its huge boulders is used to carve the names of skiers who died there. One of our ski club members, Ray Schlitzer, came close to it. We had finished skiing the upper part of the bowl. We were walking with our skis back to the trail leading to the Pinkham Notch Camp where we stayed. We did not realize the warm weather had melted the snow at the bottom of the bowl as we walked over the wet snowpack. Ray, being heavier, suddenly dropped through the snow. Fortunately, his long skis and pack kept him from disappearing below. We were able to pull him out by forming a line, but none of us will ever forget looking down some twenty or thirty feet and seeing rushing water.

We used to hire a bus to go there each spring and as our leader, Lee, used to say: "It is time to go. The forsythia is in bloom." Those were the days when there were no johns on the bus. This was difficult for the driver because we would bring a keg on board. This meant frequent stops with men going on the left, women on the right. I remember one unfortunate stop when we were on a hill. I was in a hurry and without looking, I found myself landing on a railroad track below.

Anyhow, the idea of a hiking trip up Mt. Washington in late July to see the bowl without snow was appealing.

When we started out on the Ammonoosac trail, the weather was great. Cash said that it was the quickest way to the top. He did not mention it was also the steepest. We were not that far from the tree line when a huge storm appeared. We were pelted with lightning and torrents of rain. When a bolt struck just ahead of us on the trail, all of us felt the ground effect. Because I was standing in water, I got the full effect. I passed out. I am told it was Cash that revived me. After eating a couple of candy bars, I was determined to be O.K. Maureen, who was holding the metal handle on her umbrella, suffered the same blisters I had on my legs. Because we were three-fourths of the way there, we decided to continue rather than go back. But the lightning and rain did not cease. When we got past the tree line, it was so foggy we could not see ahead. The trail was now over rocks. Maureen decided she was going to shelter under a rock and Ken stayed with her. Cash and the rest of us spread out to look for cairns to lead us to the Lake of the Clouds hut at the top. We always kept within earshot in doing so. We finally made it to the hut, which was filled with other hikers.

We were told by the rangers no one was to go outside until the lightning stopped even though we told them Ken and Maureen were under a rock shelf. When it did let up a little with some visibility, Cash went out and an hour later was back with them. Everyone was soaking wet. I had raised many disapproving eyebrows by well-shod hikers with my summer tennis shoes. We were the last ones there so it was top bunks for us. I saved one opposite me for Maureen. She earned further disdain from the professional hikers when she strung a line across our beds to hang her dripping clothes on.

The rest of the trip was uneventful. It was a wonderful trip going over the mountaintop trails to the other huts. Hiking above tree lines is the way to go when the skies are clear. Your views are never obstructed. It was just one great view from hut to hut.

Months later I was to discover the trip had been medically beneficial. Two years before the trip, I had gotten over a scare when one of my retinas dropped. Surgery had been performed to re-attach it. There had been many retina tears in my other eye. In fact, they just laser-sealed a few tears on the edges to preserve sight because the contact meant a loss of vision in the sealed area. I had been going to regular six-month appointments to check on deterioration. Any loose tears would have to be lasered.

After the Mt. Washington trip, I was back for another checkup. This time the retina specialist was amazed. All the tears were all nicely sealed. So he asked what I had been doing. It was during this time I had gotten married to Dick, but he dismissed that. When I told him about the lightning strike, he was very intrigued. He consulted other doctors, who looked at my charts. All were puzzled. My specialist declared I was very lucky the lighting strike had not been more lethal—that I could have been blinded. He predicted that I would have cataracts early which did happen. I only see him once a year now. He said he wishes he had the recipe for how much lightning was needed to seal retina tears.

Today, life is much more subdued. Cash and I became such good friends and we have kept it that way. Both of us are happily married to other people and there are no complications. There were times, however, when my husband was not too understanding. He had been a major athlete in skiing, including playing a major role in the 1980 Olympics. He skied the Bugaboos and went on several bicycle trips in the U.S. as well as Europe. As a pilot, he had owned and flown several helicopters and planes. When his health began to fail him, he was happy to see me enjoying myself as he had. But on one occasion he was very unhappy when some of us had used his ski lodge in Vermont. We didn't notice a neighbor's dog had found its way in without us knowing. Two weeks later the dog was found, fortunately still alive.

Then there was the time on my way to West Virginia that I stopped to join Cash in a canoe race on the Hudson River. I had not told my husband about it until he called me in West Virginia to tell me he had just read we won the race.

Somehow Cash and I always managed to get ourselves out of tough situations. I remember a time when my Renegade Jeep decided it only wanted to go backward so we backed up the hill to the ski area. Then there was the time we hit ice on the Northway. Friends behind us got a thrill watching us do a 360 and move on as if nothing had happened.

Thing is...while both of us are much older and pretty much sober (*and rational*) these days, I could not have had a better drinking partner. He was not just considerate, but he had a lot to say even though I don't remember much in the early years when I was aware of my bladder's superpowers.

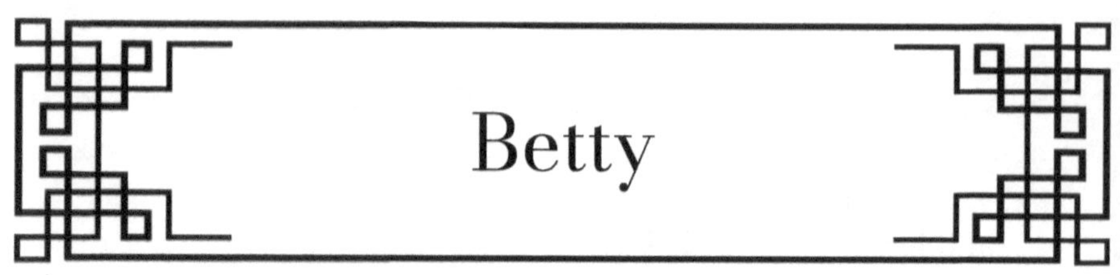

Betty

Friends come and go. Some always stay in your memory. It is not just because they make a lasting impression but often because they are a bit like yourself—trying to stay out of trouble despite good intentions.

One of these is Betty Nickerson, who married a conservative guy like I did—precise and always thinking before acting.

Betty is an artist who did it for fun or because she couldn't help herself. Once we lived in an apartment above a garage which had a terrible bathroom. The rusty metal shower was so bad you wanted to take a shower after using it. Betty was always collecting rocks or anything loose that might have a use. One weekend, she decided to tile the shower with broken bits of tile. In just one weekend, we had a wonderful floor-to-ceiling growth of colorful sunflowers covering up the grime and metal. She made good use of that green and yellow tile.

I remembered this when I was in West Virginia working with my sister Decker and her husband George on our original 1700s farmhouse. We had managed to buy it when the 1200 acre farm was bought by a corporate farmer. He recovered a lot of his investment by selling off ten-acre river lots and harvesting the timber. We were able to buy the house, horse barn, corn cribs, and granary. The French and Indian fort was also part of the ten-acre sale. However, he would not sell the nearby round barn that was on the historic register. He let the barn fall down even though he had gotten historic funds to preserve it.

Decker and George lived six hours away and it was a nine-hour drive for me. We hired out what work could more easily be done by contractors. We were able to open up two of the stone chimneys, but the third one required a liner because the stone in the two flues had fallen, blocking the airway. The contractor got the stones out and put the liner in. To do the job, he took out the facing of each fireplace, but he forgot to put the stones back. So when he poured concrete from the top to secure the liner, cement oozed out on the floor. Unfortunately, we were not there at the time and had already paid him. We were able to chip away some of the mess which was mostly on the first floor, but it was impossible for us to get the stone back into the first-floor chimney. We were able to use flat flagstone to reface the upstairs fireplace front.

Ever since we bought the place, I had become addicted to garage and estate sales to furnish it. Looking at the lower fireplace, I realized those old Dutch delft tiles I had found in the bottom of a box I had bought would be useful. Instead of using flagstone, why not be different with a tiled fireplace? Decker and George agreed. George was particularly glad I had bought something that did not require wiring or repairs. However, there were just enough tiles to cover the sides of the fireplace, not the top.

I thought of Betty and her using tiles to modernize our shower. I remembered her painting a mermaid on her kayak. Maybe she could paint on tiles. I knew of a place in Albany that made reproduction tiles for a historic place along the Hudson River.

I had pictures depicting the farm, which I gave to Betty. I decided to tell a story with the tiles as the Dutch did on their delft tiles. I would start with a feathered Native American living with nature, including wildlife such as a coon and crow. The next tile would show the French and Indian fort and our Dutch settler. Next were farm scenes including a Hampshire pig (*for our Hampshire County*), a hay wagon and horses, cows, wheat shocks, and workers at the round barn. It ended with a cornfield field scene. All that was left of the Native American scene was the coon, now a hat on the farmer. Only the crow survived and it is enjoying corn.

So over to Albany Betty and I went to discuss the project with the owner. He was intrigued but warned us we couldn't make mistakes in painting on tile. Each stroke was permanent so we had to consider it could be costly. But Betty amazed all of us by never having to redo a tile. She did not like one of the draft horses with a sagged back. But I liked it. It reminded me of one of my grandmother's horses which she refused to sell when it was old because of all it had done for her.

The next step was getting the tiles ready for the fireplace in West Virginia. Betty had mounted the reproduction delft tiles I had on boards the height of the fireplace sides. For the width across the top of the fireplace she lined up the history of the valley according to my lineup.

I was reluctant to try to mount them myself on the fire-place. When Betty said she and Bud, her husband, were going to Florida and would stop by on the way, I was thrilled. Even though it was the day before I was scheduled to fly to Florida with my mother for the wedding of my brother's daughter, we figured we could get it done. I had all the mixings ready for Betty when they arrived.

Still, my mother was nervous about the timing. Bud was just as anxious. He had a rental car he needed to return. We just had the afternoon to get the boards mounted. Bud, the precise engineer, and my skeptical mother watched while Betty and I surveyed the job. The three boards would fit with a little extra caulking, but it had to be done fast before the mortar solidified. The problem was the old fireplace was not exactly square.

Bud and my mother, standing by the doorway watching us, immediately noticed this challenge as Betty and I held the boards up to check the alignment. Both expressed many doubts about the process—with my mother even reminding me we had to leave the next day.

We decided to ignore them and proceed as fast as we could.

Betty directed me where and how much mortar to apply as she quickly used her trowel to even it up. We quickly mounted the heavy sides. Both my mother and Bud declared one side was crooked. They began instructing us to move it to the right and then left and then a little more right. Betty, knowing the limit of time it took the mortar to hold fast, announced "That's it." She took a trowel and scraped off the excess mortar that had surged out from behind the boards.

I declared it to be straight even though my mother and Bud didn't. The top was easier because Betty had already figured the right side needed to be a bit higher. When the top board went on it was square across the top. Both my mother and Bud grudgingly agreed that part was level—and maybe no one would notice one side had more caulking at the bottom.

So back to my mother's house we went, my mother relaxing. She quietly asked if Bud and Betty were leaving early in the morning. We only had four hours to get to the Pittsburgh airport. I assured her they were leaving early because Bud needed to get to Florida.

But then disaster struck when Betty was getting her bag out of the car. She mistakenly shut the trunk door with the keys inside. The trunk had automatically locked itself. I was with her when it happened. Realizing we were going to get a lot of grief over this, I quickly went to the basement and retrieved a crowbar. But in trying to open the trunk, one could see there was going to be damage. My next thought was finding someone who could pick the lock. So I suggested we make an excuse to go to town and I ran into the house to announce we would be back in a jiff before they could say anything.

Unfortunately for us, Bud went to the car and tried to get his suitcase. While this was going on I had interviewed people at a local bar. I figured they might have a customer who could pick locks. In the process I explained what had happened and not to tell my mother. There was one guy who offered to give it a try, but he needed to do something first and would call me.

There was another guy that said rental companies often had the problem of customers losing keys. If I called them, they could contact a nearby key maker with the code and have a set made.

So we quickly went home, noting we had done this in less than an hour so all would be well. We would look for the rental car's number in the car. But Bud was at the car, waiting for us, wanting to know where the keys were. We had to come clean.

In the meantime, my mother was answering the phone from the guy announcing he had the time to pick the lock after all. When my mother found out where he was calling from, she was even more irate. She did note she was glad I had sense enough not to give him directions. She had hung up on him. In trying to explain what happened, Betty, in my defense, noted that we had met some nice people who had offered to help. Mom quickly said there are no nice people at that place... that it was a bar full of drunks like the one that just called.

Bud was able to contact the car rental. Sure enough, they said they could call a nearby key maker right away. Lucky for us, the rental company found one in Cumberland, Maryland, just thirty or so miles away. If we could get there before 6 p.m., we could pick it up. Otherwise we would have to wait until tomorrow. It only took seconds for my mother to order me to leave. Bud was disgusted with both Betty and me. He wished us luck in getting there in time because he was going to take a nap.

We congratulated ourselves on getting there minutes before closing. When we got back, my mother settled down when Bud opened the trunk with the key. They would be able to leave and we would be able to catch the flight to Florida for the wedding. She had even packed my suitcase and loaded it into her car. We made it to Pittsburgh in time, where we met my brother who had come in from Ohio.

It was a wonderful wedding in a suite at the top of a condo building which the groom's father had offered for the cere- mony. While I had been to an ocean before, I knew my brother hadn't. I wanted him to enjoy it. I persuaded him during some free time we had to go swimming. We had a grand time—even when we met a small sand shark in the water. But because my brother was fair-skinned, he got a sunburn. He was bright red the next day at the wedding, perfectly matching the pink cummerbund his daughter had added to his outfit. So that resulted in another "Why can't you just try not to do so many things at one time?" reprimand from my mother. But I will say my niece thought the wedding pictures with her red-faced dad with his matching cummerbund was fine.

Back to Betty. Betty was always curious about what makes people tick—and this included religious groups. She became involved in a group that had broken away from the Catholics. They decided they were not going to take the priests' word for it but read the Bible themselves. They were trying to form a utopian village in the old Corning estate near the port of Albany. They believed in sharing assets. She stayed with the group for a while; I will always remember that old estate in a big ravine with huge old trees with branches that sometimes swept to the ground, triggering the growth of offspring. It was there I learned from Betty how to sit quietly enough to get chickadees to eat out of your hand.

The group was a religious group with good intentions, but I think all of us learned not everyone understood that when we were at the port passing out religious literature. I still recall one ship coming in from South America with bananas with a crew that did not speak English. Maybe it was because we were young, but they mistakenly thought we were offering ourselves. So we quickly dropped that conversion.

Betty was an elementary school teacher. Like me, she did not have talent for math, yet, unlike high school teachers and professors, she had to teach the whole gambit of reading, writing, and arithmetic. Once a Union College professor criticized her for how she graded his son's paper. I remember writing him and asking him to draw a picture of his son.

She decided to leave when she was offered an educational job in Italy for a year. I really missed her but kept the apartment for her return. It was beside the elegant Mohawk Club. Often its members would confuse our driveway with the one to the golf club and had to turn around. I had done a speech for a GE vice president who was giving a talk to a select group. He liked clean copy and made changes. So I had to retype it. I got there in time but I was not allowed in the all-male club. In fact, they rudely ordered me out despite my explanation.

So I sat on the steps purposely smoking a Virginia Slim "you've come a long way" cigarette until a couple of general managers from the motor departments arrived for the talk. I told them what happened and to give the VP his speech. They were upset about it and offered to sponsor me for a "glass-ceiling" membership. But it would have cost me half of my salary. I decided to put up a sign on our driveway noting "Everyone can turn around here except Mohawk Club members." That sign earned me sitting room privileges which I would occasionally use in the winter because it had a nice fireplace.

Fortunately, and it goes for me, too, we met guys who were our opposites. We have lived a much tamer life under their influence. I have fond memories of Betty always ready to do something new—even when we took our kayaks to a white-water race on the Kayderosseras Creek. We had not been on that creek before. It was the beginning of April when there was still a shimmer of ice along the shore. When we overturned in some rapids, we just looked at each other with chilly smiles. We were able to pull our overturned kayaks ashore and get a ride to a nearby restaurant to warm up. We did run the creek race the next year, but that time we knew where the obstacles were.

Then there was the time we were skiing at Stowe Vermont. Most likely we had too much of Paul Lozier's homemade wine at the top. Full of confidence, we decided to ski through the glades beside the Nosedive. We both ended up being tree huggers but were O.K. However, Betty lost a contact. In those days contacts were expensive, and we sifted through the snow where she had fallen for over an hour. When the ski patrol came by for their last sweep and we explained the situation, they just asked if we had ever found a needle in a haystack. They accompanied us to the bottom where we met some of our tailgate party friends who had reported us missing. But we were fine and in good humor.

Betty and I did some canoeing together. Our slowest time was in a New York State Canoe Regatta in the Adirondacks which was a 13.6-mile race involving a portage over a dam. It was grueling and carrying a heavy Mad River canoe over the dam was not easy. But we got some press coverage for "crossing the finish line with droopy locks hanging down the sides of their faces...a combination of the creek's dousing and honest sweat...the smiles on their faces were proof it was worth the effort." What the reporter didn't know was we had stopped at the dam to lighten our load by drinking the beer we had on board. But we were most proud of another race where we won in the women's class. We received a trophy which read "fastest women" but it didn't say what it was for. So that was one we often showed people. Another friend of ours at the time was Millie Ey. I remember a trip a group of us took to Maine to stay in a KOA camp. Millie and I had settled down in her pup tent that night after having a few drinks when a huge RV came backing into our spot and didn't see it was already taken. When the rear end clipped the top of our tent, we both rolled out in time not to be run over. Millie was game for ski racing as much as I was. We even went to a race in Waterville Valley in which the only way to the top was by a snowcat. It was a mile-long race and we were exhausted because the course included some icy ruts from the snowcat. Betty, not into ski racing as much as we were, was the better skier and could easily have taken the trophies we were getting.

That was the way it was with us then.

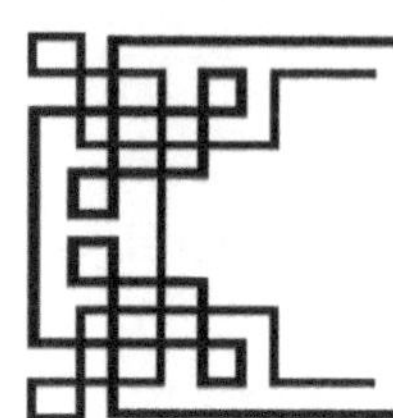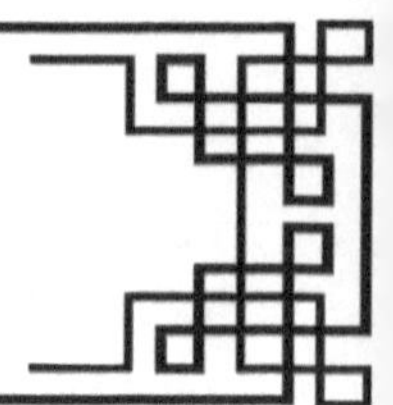

Car Problems

It was probably my father who whetted my appetite for a fancy car. He was a Ford man who could name every truck he ever owned—all of which he needed to work the farm. Growing up, I had been with him when he bought three of them, each one able to carry a ton or so more than the previous one. But what I most remember is his wistful look when he spotted the latest Thunderbird in the showroom. It was a luxury he could not afford.

The desire for a car was with me when I started my job at GE. I had been pleased to get the addresses of young men in the Manufacturing Training Program, the Creative Engineering Program, the Advertising and Sale Promotion Program, and the Marketing and Finance Programs to a party my room-mates and I were having. It turned out that some seventy-five guys showed up and left early because we were the only three women there.

Still, I remember this party best because one of them, John Munter, sold me a car for $25. Everyone laughed when I gave him a check for it. I laughed too because I knew the check was no good. But when he showed up the next morning with the car, I felt I should buy it. So I gave him my grocery money for the next week. Besides, I was already homesick; this was a cheap way to get there. Two months later, I had enough money to get home. I left at 5 p.m. after work on a Friday. Normally it would be a ten-hour drive, but it took me sixteen hours to get there and used nearly as much oil as gas. I was passed quite frequently as those behind me were anxious to get out of the cloud of smoke I left in my wake. I got home in time for lunch the next day. I was dead tired and my left leg ached. The car was missing parts of its floorboard. It had rusted out. I had to have my leg propped against the bar holding the car seat in place when I wasn't braking.

But as Munter—now a building contractor in Saratoga—laughingly reminds me, he had nothing to do with the dent in the side when it got hit by the GE train (*I always seemed to be in a rush to get my job done*).

The car, stripped of parts by my father, is still rusting away in a field ditch. My father convinced the Ford dealer that my job at GE would pay well enough for me to buy a two-year-old Ford Fairlane. It had a 420 hp engine. It was not a Thunderbird, but I was able to get a loan for it. My father was the first to drive it. He had always wanted to take those banked curves on U.S. Route 50 going over the Appalachians without braking. There was one hairpin turn so tight Greyhound buses had to stop, back up, and then proceed forward again to get around. We took that switchback at an amazing 30 mph, leaving the 10 mph marker for others to follow. The big engine easily went up to 100 mph on the straight-aways.

Maybe this is why I immediately got two tickets when I got back to New York State that Sunday night. I was north of Binghamton when I was pulled over. I had not been driving that long after transferring my West Virginia driver's license to a New York one. The Dodge never went fast enough to get me in trouble. I was unaware of New York's point system.

At that time in West Virginia, we did not have such strict traffic rules. Even when the new I-81 interstate was built from New York to Florida, the curviest part went through our eastern panhandle of West Virginia. The speed limit through this twelve-mile stretch is still 70 mph, not 65.

Anyhow, the NY trooper told me to mail my license in because they would have to mark it on the back and return it to me with a fine. About thirty miles farther up the highway, there were about ten of us caught in a radar trap and pulled aside. The trooper used a bullhorn to tell us to have our driver's licenses ready as they kept pulling more people off the road. I yelled back that I had just sent mine in and could I go, I had to get to work. The crowd, partially stunned, began to laugh.

It was then I learned about the point system. I only had two more points left for the next three years. Another speeding ticket would mean the end of my new driver's license.

The next car I bought was closer to having the glamour of a Thunderbird. It was five years old but it was a sports car, a black Triumph convertible with red leather upholstery. I particularly liked it because it was so low one could stub out their cigarettes on the highway while driving. My father liked this car, too. He had been mad when the 1958 Ford the dealer had sold me actually had a 1957 engine in it. Even though the dealer explained this often happened with the first edition of new cars, he finally agreed to forgive the last car payment on it.

It was in this TR-3 that my father and I went to see the Pittsburgh Pirates. By this time I was used to big city beltways and thruway entry and exit lanes. He chose to drive it on West Virginia's curves on Rt. 50 which were still banked. He left it to me to get us through city streets and congested, fast-moving highway traffic. While the engine did not have the power of the Ford, it more than made up for it, he declared, with its aerodynamic design and quick turning capability.

When we were coming back from the Three Rivers Stadium in Pittsburgh, I found this out big time. I saw another side to my father I never knew when he gave the finger to another sports car in the adjoining lane. I learned what road rage was then as I tried to get away from that driver. He pursued me from one lane to another until I lost him when two tractor-trailers had to wedge together for one lane. I managed to make it through the two before the two lanes ended.

The car was costly to run because foreign parts were not only hard to get and expensive, but labor was costly too. Breakdowns would result in fifty- or sixty-mile tows to a foreign car garage. I also spent many a night in motels waiting for parts to come in.

Often I could make do. When the leather top shrunk, it was difficult to get it back in all the slots. I invested in stretch cords to secure those places. Coming out of a tunnel once on the Pennsylvania turnpike, a blast of hard, driving rain ripped the cords off. I had four hours of wet driving in the middle of the night before I got home.

Soon I just gave up trying to get the top to stay on. I tried to gear my driving according to weather forecasts and punched some holes in the floorboard to let the water out.

At least the RPI engineer who bought the car knew its condition. It was as rusty underneath as the old 1948 Dodge. He only had it two weeks when the gas tank fell out. Fortunately, his father owned a garage. Today, I wonder if he still has it because it would be a classic.

My next car was a two-year-old Plymouth convertible which was the color of a swimming pool. The first problem I had with it was when I got an oil change from a new teenage employee at the dealership. I also asked that the car be winterized. Five hours into my trip to West Virginia, the engine blew. It turned out the teen had put the oil in my radiator and antifreeze in the oil pan.

A tractor-trailer driver stopped to help. In my excitement I didn't think twice about getting into his big cab to go to the next exit to find a garage. When the driver said we would be quite comfortable in the portable bed in the rear head space in the cab, I began talking about my police relatives. But he wasn't buying it. So when I saw we were coming up on the Blue Mountain tunnel where I had lost my Triumph cover years ago, I knew he would have to slow down to enter the tunnel. When he did, I bailed and actually hit the pavement running. I could see lights up ahead on the hillside and ran for them. After wandering around in a Pennsylvania shed full of snowplows, I finally found an employee who gave me a ride to a garage.

I was still in my twenties then and enjoying a ride through Lake George with the top down when I found out there were such things as off-duty cops. One passed me, flashed a badge, and pulled in front of me to get me to pull over. I was confused. He looked at my driver's license and saw that I had no room for a speeding ticket. I pleaded with him to let me go, that I would slow down even though I did not think I had been speeding. He suggested we could discuss this at a bar up the road. I got the gist of that when he put his hand on me.

My experience working at the police station when I was in high school came in handy. I knew if I could get the other half of the ticket out of his pocket, then he would have no proof of the arrest. I knew the bar he suggested had a dance floor. That might work. I agreed to go. His name was Lee Steele.

But he could hold his liquor. It looked like there was no way I was going to lift the ticket from his front shirt pocket without him noticing. He described his lodge on the lake, pointing out the view from a comfortable polar bear rug in front of the picture window was amazing. I could follow him there.

I had noticed a phone booth near the restrooms so I decided to call my good friend, Dick, the lawyer who had helped me with tickets. While Lee was getting another drink, I was lucky to get Dick on the phone. He immediately nixed my idea of trying to swipe the ticket half. He suggested we go to the Delivan bar in Lake George where he knew the bartender. I would appear to be agreeable to Lee's offer in front of the bartender. The bartender could be a witness to this entrapment. It worked. I got a signal from the bartender he had heard enough, so I got up and quickly left. For the next several years, I avoided that route because Lee had been demoted and transferred to the rural area of Chestertown. It turned out there had been other complaints about him.

However, I was to run into him at the Gore Mountain ski resort bar several years later. A bunch of us in the Capital

District were celebrating a ski race when I noticed him watching us. I was having a good time chatting with Bob Healey, who was wearing a tiger outfit he sometimes raced in. I wasn't driving, so I wasn't worried, but when I ran into Bob Healey several weeks later at a race, he told me he had been picked up for a DWI going home that day. I felt horrible about it, figuring Lee had gotten a last word in.

The Plymouth convertible was also the car my father and I drove to see the Baltimore Orioles play in the 1971 World Series. Getting World Series tickets is difficult but I was able to get tickets through a GE Vice President I interviewed. He was only able to get tickets for the seventh game should it be a reality. That meant I did not know until the evening before whether the game would be played. I drove the rest of the night to West Virginia and then in the morning we left for Baltimore. In high school, my father had achieved notoriety for his pitching skills. As a leftie, he amazingly pitched four games in a row with no hits. I have no doubt had scouts been in our rural area, he would not have become a farmer. Anyhow, when we got there, the tickets were in the black section which was no problem because my father was one of the most equal opportunity people I knew back then. He had business deals with the black hands at the stock sale which involved free sweet corn or whatever was available from the farm if they watered down his cattle for extra weight at the scales and made sure his cattle entered the auction arena after a batch of bad-looking cows. When my brother and I were cold at the winter sales, he had no problem letting us go back to the back lots to gather around a pot belly stove with the families of the black workers.

Anyhow, at the game, a group of black Baltimore Oriole fans kept my father from probably being thrown out of the stadium. When a possible home run ball came our way towards the stands, my father leaned over and nearly intercepted the fielder reaching up for the ball. Several black guys grabbed his feet and pulled him back into the stands. After hearing what brought us to the game, they even accommodated my father after the game to show him where the home run had been made the day before, making it possible for us to be there for the seventh game.

Unlike the Pittsburgh Pirates game and our fun in the TR-3, the trip back in the convertible Plymouth was uneventful although we did give a couple of his black rescuers a ride to the bus stop.

My next four cars were all brand new. They were Jeeps – the C-J, Cherokee, Wrangler and Renegade. I was glad to have four-wheel drive to get to and from ski areas on weekends.

Mostly men drove Jeeps back then and I had gotten used to strangers asking me if I was driving my boyfriend's car. When I was pulled over by a cop, they would check the registration first.

When I was transferred to GE headquarters, my red Jeep raised some eyebrows. The only other Jeeps there were three maintenance vehicles which were not allowed in the executive building. I was told it was the wrong vehicle for a corporate image if I wanted to be promoted.

My first putdown came from another woman. There were only a few of us token types there then and she saw herself in competition with me. When she saw me driving the Jeep, she pointed out I was an embarrassment to professional women. She reported me to the Vice President of Public Relations who asked me to explain why I was driving an army vehicle. I explained that I felt safer in a four-wheel drive car. Still, he suggested that image was important for career enhancement and it would be a good idea for me to realize the value of appearance. He mentioned that my female coworker was driving a nice compact.

Instead, I just started parking next to the maintenance vehicles so I wouldn't irritate anyone. This seemed to work pretty well until I started playing bridge with the private chef of the Board Chairman and two of his friends in corporate security. Each day I ran through the connecting tunnel to the executive building to meet them in the hidden security rooms behind the Board Chairman's office.

One Monday, I was late getting back from a meeting at a nearby plant. I thought I could save time by just driving into the underground garage of the executive building and taking the security elevator up from there. I forgot I had a kayak on top of the car which I had used over the weekend. I meant to take it off at my apartment. When I heard the crunch as I entered the executive building, I immediately knew what happened. Fortunately the same security men I played bridge with were able to get me unjammed—but not before I held up two limos trying to get through the entrance. One of them contained the Vice President of Public Relations. Fortunately for me, the chef had a close relationship with the Board Chairman, who had a sense of humor, and my job was saved.

After that I tried to avoid contact with the VP of PR and keep a low profile. But there were times when I could not prevent them from learning more about me. I was seeing an old boyfriend in Schenectady, Dick Weber, who would later become my husband. He was a pilot and we used to fly up to Savage Island in Lake Champlain for the weekend.

At the time GE kept a plane there for Schenectady GE executives and Dick knew the pilots. Often, I would catch a ride on a GE plane to avoid driving. Unfortunately, this time I had gotten into the executive bar on the plane. I was in no condition to buy groceries which I was supposed to. Dick had been flying a helicopter all day doing power line patrol and was dead tired. So we got a late start to go to the island because we had to take the time now to get the groceries I was supposed to get. It was nearly dark when we arrived at the island with its grass strip. The lake was so calm it reflected itself like a mirror. We thought we were landing on the strip when the water started spraying off the propeller. It would have been a perfect landing if we had pontoons. I will never forget see the strobe lights of the twin-engine Cessna still blinking as it sank in 20 or so feet of water as we swam ashore.

When the plane was lifted out of the water the next day by a barge which happened to be laying a pipe across the lake at that time, even the eggs in the grocery bags were intact. But the problem for me came when the island was surrounded by drug agents looking for dealers who often flew in from Canada. Thanks to the local sheriff who had been given a ride in a helicopter owned by Dick, we were able to explain who we were and why we were there. But the early reports to the Burlington Free Press had both our names as alleged drug dealers.

As usual, I was back at work on Monday but the Employee Relations Manager at Burlington, Vt., recognizing the unusual name and knowing I was at headquarters promptly faxed the article to the VP of PR. I was called in and asked how my weekend was when I said, "Oh, the usual." He gave me an incredulous look and handed me a fax of the newspaper article. I tried to explain what really happened, leaving out the part of going up there on the corporate jet. Fortunately, the Burlington employee relations manager called back saying it was all as mistake by the FDA investigators and that a retraction would be in the newspaper.

After that I did buy Jeeps that were not fire-engine-red. One was white and blue and the other grey with black trim.

I was to find that the blue and white Jeep became well-liked by rescue workers during a huge storm that hit the east coast in the mid 1970s. I had let myself get talked into having an operation over the Christmas holidays in Boston because we had so many projects going on at headquarters. After the operation, my surgeon went home for Christmas. Four feet of snow resulted in vital workers being unable to get to the New England Deaconess hospital. The reduced staff consolidated us into rooms. My roommate was a dying cancer patient who was suffering because there was no morphine. I had heard her confession to the priest and decided I had never met a person who had lived such a moral, clean life. When the priest chastised her for wanting him to turn off her oxygen, he declared it would be a sin to do so. I was out of it by this time because I had been bleeding internally and did not know it. When he referred to the Holy Mary, I thought he was talking about me so we got into an argument as to who the sinner was—him or the dying woman. Today, I have a young intern to thank for saving me. When I passed out from lack of blood, he actually put me on a gurney and took me outside to enter the emergency room so I could get blood there because there was no staff inside to do it. Three days later I was well enough to go back to work. But it was snowing again.

On the way back, on the Connecticut turnpike, the snow was so deep they were closing some of the ramps on and off. I was able to get around a tractor-trailer that had slipped sideways with the Jeep. Finally, I got to the Milford exit, and in getting off, a couple of officers confiscated my Jeep. They took me home and used it as an emergency vehicle for two days. They were very grateful so I asked them to write a note to the GE VP of Public Relations about how much they appreciated my donating the Jeep for public service.

I also owned two Saab Sonnets. Front-wheel drive, I was told, was nearly as good as four-wheel drive for snow and icy roads. They looked a lot like Corvettes but were half the price. I also found they were bait for cops, but I learned a very valuable lesson during one run-in. It happened around midnight. I was very tired from a long day at work and on top of that I had organized a huge retirement party for a general manager, which had gone well. I had a couple of drinks there. I volunteered to take one of the guests—who lived some thirty miles away in an area I was not familiar with—home. Thank goodness I got her home safely, but on the way back on the Northway, I was sideswiped by a tractor-trailer. The entire hood—which was one solid piece of fiberglass—was torn off. I remember sitting there dazed. The next thing I remember was being in the Saratoga police station. The officer evidently decided to scare me by telling me I had killed someone. I panicked and in my distraught condition said I would take my life, too. It ended up with me being putting in a cell with no clothes on so I could not hang myself. I nearly froze to death that night. The next morning another officer was appalled when he saw my condition. He told me I had not killed anyone, gave me my clothes, and let me make a phone call. Again, Dick the lawyer came to my rescue. No charges were made after he threatened a lawsuit.

But the experience did open my eyes to drinking and driving. After all, I could have killed somebody in that condition.

Marriage also settled me down, but still, I managed to get myself into confrontations with the police. I often swam in the Kayaderosseras Creek near Rock City Falls near our home. One afternoon I was on my way there in the last Jeep I owned in my swimsuit with the top down when I came upon a police roadblock. I was about three cars behind and I could see they were checking inspection and registrations. I was O.K. but I decided to go back and tell the people behind me what the police were doing. This infuriated one of the cops, who took my registration and said he would give it back when they were through with their checks. He told me to pull off the road, which was near where I swam. Some twenty or so minutes went by and it was hot. I decided I would go swimming and if I saw him coming I would jump back in the car. This really made him mad. He gave me a ticket for leaving the scene.

Realizing such a charge was very serious, I called Dick again. We pled not guilty before the judge. When he heard the whole story, he just looked at the cop and told him to apologize to me.

Later, when my husband became Town Supervisor of Galway, I found he was certainly not going to be one to fix tickets.

The village of Galway was being investigated by the state for having six deputies even though there were only about 500 residents. It turned out one officer decided to share his salary with the others so all could get benefits. They mostly ticketed people on their way to Sacandaga Lake. Their jurisdiction was just a little over a mile on Rt. 167. Even though I was stopped at the single stoplight there, the officer said I had exceeded the 35 mph limit as I drove out of the village. He said he had clocked me on his radar. My husband agreed that it was unlikely I could have gotten past that speed from the stoplight, but he thought it would be a good lesson for me. So I called Dick the lawyer and apprised him of the situation. When I told him that the village cops had gotten used radars donated by the state police, he decided to check that out. We went before the Town Justice of Peace who learned the radar had not been calibrated.

In the old days, a CB radio was a good way to know about radar traps ahead. My brother drove a semi and I knew the right lingo to get their assistance as to where the bears were. It was fun to use all those codes like "10-20" on those long drives to and from West Virginia. But there was one CB'er who had a lot of fun with some of us about to cross the bridge at Harrisonburg across the Susquehanna around 1 a.m.

A Roadway driver, with the handle "Flying Crate," CB'ed on the south side of the bridge he was an Eastern Airlines pilot. He had to make an emergency landing on the six-lane bridge. He told us to stop and not let others go either until he made his landing. So I and three other drivers got out to stop any oncoming traffic which might not get the message. About two minutes later, the trucker roared across the bridge announcing he had made his "landing" safely. It was a full moon that night and we all got a good laugh.

I miss the names we had for each other. Mine was given to me by my brother—"Lead Foot." My brother's was "Laughing Boy" and his two best friends were "Diesel Dan" and "Gear

Jammer." There were times when I did not answer but I sure was amused by the call from a CB'er who identified himself as "Hot Chocolate." His "Hello White Doll" included a meeting at the next rest stop.

Other technology also entered the highway cat-and-mouse game. You could buy a radar detector to find those traps before they got you. But it soon began to cost me more than the tickets because the manufacturers kept upgrading the technology, first selling new scanners to the cats and then following up with detectors for us mice. I bought five new detectors before I gave up, realizing this was a game of "cats and mice" and we mice were getting the raw deal.

Today the cats have the technology to photograph your car and your plates in those signs that flash what speed you are going. There is no plea-bargaining loophole. They can give you a printout of the speed you were going. They are not in color yet, just legible grainy black and white fax-like copies. A very nice state trooper explained all of this to me, saying that now he wouldn't have to listen to excuses from people like me anymore. The evidence goes directly to the station so any upset drivers cannot get mad at him. He is only doing a job he really does not like to do. He also warned me that the day still may come when they would replace some of them by just having the machine mail the ticket directly to you. He suggested I begin eating at toll road restaurants in case the computers analyze the time you got on versus the time you got off.

In my mature years, I also realized I would have a bigger retirement account if I had not spent all that money on tickets and rising insurance rates. While my sedate Subaru seems to attract fewer cops, none of them are police-proof. I recently contributed to the school system by going 35 mph in a 25 mph zone.

Looking back, I also realize I was my own worst enemy. When I was going after a master's degree from the State University of New York at Albany, I met a bunch of Chinese and Korean students. Five of them had transferred to New York University in Manhattan and I volunteered to drive them there with their luggage in my husband's Wagoneer. It was in the garage that day so Joan McCauley offered me her old van which was hard to start and had no windows except the one in the back. Fortunately, the Korean girl knew English well enough that even when frightened she would yell in English. With her "look out" help from the back window, I was able to get us there among many near collisions with NYC cab drivers.

When I left New York State to work at GE headquarters in Connecticut in the 1980s, I had filled up the back side of several licenses. I was able to escape a couple of tickets in Connecticut because they required you to sign the tickets, at which time I was able to quickly change a few identification and license plate numbers.

When I came back to New York, I felt I should pretend I was never there so I could have a clean slate. I took a written and driver's test. It was when I paid for it by check they ran their own check. My driving record for fifteen years came up. Because I had gone to such lengths to conceal my past, they assumed I had a criminal record. It took weeks before I was able to convince them I was just trying to start out with a clean driver's license.

Still, the cats catching us mice can be nice at times. Recently I was going at least thirty miles over the limit. I was just a half-mile from home and desperately had to go to the bathroom. When the cop pulled me over, I explained I was suffering. I declared, "O.K., give me the ticket but let me get out of the car because I do not want to mess it up."

Yes, he let me off a ticket because he said he did not want to watch me mess up the car or go in the bushes. He had run a check on my plates following me and knew that I lived up the road. He followed me to the house and had a big grin on his face when he saw me rush in.

However, I would not recommend using this as an excuse. That cat knew this mouse was telling the truth by the look of agony on my face.

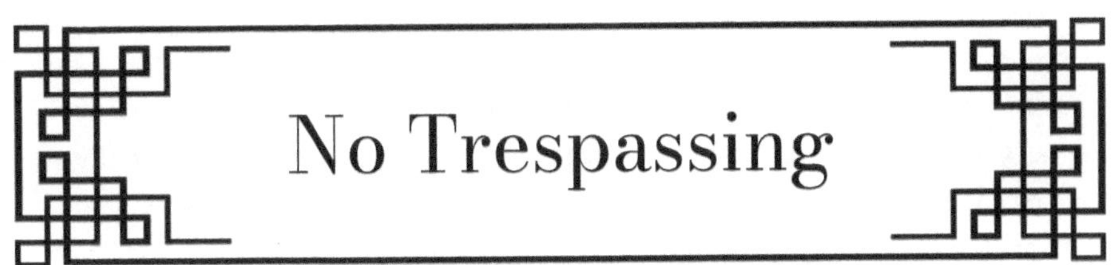

No Trespassing

They say no man is an island, although I did know one who became one.

His name was Ted Riehle. He owned the largest single island in Lake Champlain. He was not a rich man but a lucky one. As the Lieutenant Governor of Vermont in 1952, he was diagnosed with throat cancer. He decided to use his savings to buy an uninhabited island in the lake for some $5,000 where he would go to die.

There was an old A-frame on one end of the island and an abandoned cabin on the other side near the dock, so he moved in there. It had no amenities other than shelter. His water came from the lake. He supplied its outdoor john with all of the correspondence he had made to get the state to ban billboards. He was very proud of this accomplishment. He would often reread the position papers he had presented before their final use in the john.

When islands began to become valuable in the 70s as vacation homes for the upper class, property taxes started going up. Ted was in a dilemma. He realized he would need some income to preserve the island and decided to share it with a sheep herd. They only ate grass and he had plenty of it. They required little care. Besides, he liked leg of lamb—he was getting tired of fish. Most important, his new status as a farmer meant he would be paying a fourth of the commercial tax rate now hitting the islands.

His island was so big you could use one of the pasture fields as a landing strip. So one day when Dick Weber, who had been at the Sugarbush airport in Vermont trying out glider flying, heard about the island, he asked the owner—who knew

Ted—if he could make a grass landing there. He wanted to try out a Super Cub he had just bought. He met Ted and they became great friends. Dick started paying Ted to use the island on weekends as a retreat. Ted was not only living with nature but had also discarded his clothes, deeming them unnecessary when it was warm. Dick, like Ted, did not mind drinking from the lake or using the outdoor john and he was quick to take up Ted's nudity preference.

So between the rental payments and selling a sheep or two when needed, Ted was able to fix up the old cabin to make it more comfortable while Dick move moved into the A-frame. As a friend and later wife of Dick's, I found the island was a great place to get away from it all...particularly my job at GE. During the first winter, Dick even contributed an old beat-up, stripped-down VW for use on the island by driving it over the ice.

Ted had two sons on the mainland along with an ex-wife who had decided his style of island life was not for her. A visit to his doctor, who declared it was a miracle he was cured, might have caused another patient to return to a normal life— but not Ted. He loved his island life and was becoming an expert on Merino sheep. He was not about to leave what he had considered the source of his cure.

There are several islands near Ted's Savage Island—Fish Platter, Cedar, and Stave among them. We used to have parties with folks from these islands which included scavenger hunts. Two teams were set up to bring back items from the island such as a particular kind of wildflower, plant, insect, bird egg, or used nest. Our most notorious game occurred when we added the largest leaf covering for the nude men. The winner of that game went into Ted's sheep field and rounded up the infamous ram called "Penetrator." He was roped and arrived with a huge leaf as large as the one of his capturer.

For the first twenty years, Ted was able to keep his 240-acre island pristine, with only the sound of bleating sheep pleasantly disturbing the peace when he was not having parties. However, during the 80s and 90s, a lot more boats, yachts, kayaks, and canoes were traversing the lake as the population grew around the city of Burlington. Ted started finding his solitude was hard to maintain. Moreover, word was getting around that it must be a nudist island.

So if it was not someone coming ashore to illegally to have a picnic, sometimes even building a fire or using it as a restroom, it was someone with a camera.

He hated putting up "No Trespassing" signs, which he considered as offensive as billboards along the beautiful Vermont roads. But Ted realized that to legally tell someone to leave, he had to have the island posted.

But the beachcombers continued to come. Some even tore down the signs and burned them up in their campfires. Because the island was so large, it was nearly impossible to keep the trespassers off. It was a two-mile hike around the island. Ted and Dick would try to scare off the trespassers by wildly charging onto the beach nude with pitchforks. This only scared the more timid ones.

I too considered myself lucky to find such a pristine lifestyle on the island. I dutifully signed on to help them clear the beach of the most obnoxious trespassers. However, I was allowed to wear a suit because it was felt I could be an attraction instead of a distraction.

It seemed to me that the most invasive trespassers were those who came from big yachts. The canoers and kayakers might stay just long enough to take a walk on the beach; they were not carrying coolers full of food and booze and therefore did not leave trash. Ted, Dick, and I would mostly ignore them and just ask them to make sure the area was as clean as it was when they came.

But there was one particular yacht that seemed to come every weekend. Its occupants had been told time and time again it was a private island. What particularly irritated Ted was they would leave not only a lot of garbage and beer cans but they often defecated on the beach. One day they refused to leave when I told them to pack up and not leave a mess. So I decided to swim out to their yacht. They watched as I climbed aboard and began yelling at me. I happily told them I needed to go to the bathroom like they were doing on the island. I added that I had heard there were nice johns on yachts as well as a place to eat lunch. Ted liked that idea and copied it himself. He was particularly effective because of his natural appearance.

To add to Ted's "No Trespassing" warnings, I even purchased a blowup doll which Ted used as a float to go out to the yachts. From a distance, they did not know it was a rubber woman filled with air.

But the most effective warning not to trespass was when I gave Ted a T-shirt to wear over his wrinkled, sunburned body. That was all he had on. Despite his nearing eighty, he was still formidable-looking. The T-shirt read: "Trespassers will be sodomized."

Ted died several years ago in his nineties. The island is now owned by his three sons. Two have political jobs despite it being tough to win elections because their father had become notorious. They conform to society and have dressed up the island, including themselves. But they did hang that shirt on one of the "No Trespassing" signs, finding it still useful.

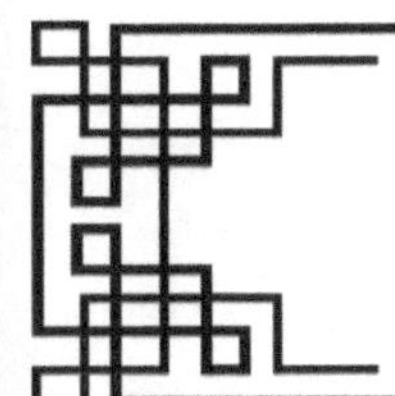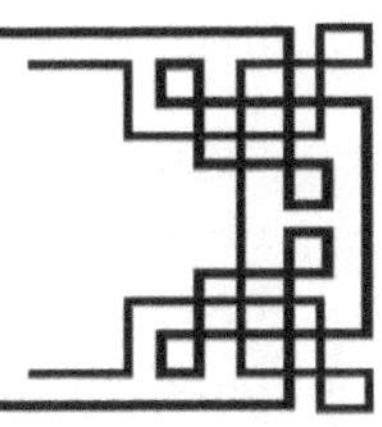

No Thanks

In the 60s and early 70s (*before EEO and my getting older*), the best way to avoid unwanted advances often took some interesting evasive actions. Some of them proved to be a lot of fun.

It was during contract negotiations with GE unions that I and four editors of department newsletters were asked to come to the Biltmore Hotel in New York City to publish a company-wide newsletter. It would be sent to some 150 plants across the U.S. by fax (*we didn't have internet then*) and the quicker the better. The union side also had their communication team reply to the company's offer.

It was felt if the company was out there first with its offer and presented it in a favorable way, the union members might decide to vote for it—or at least pressure their union leaders to accept the national contract offer.

The four editors going to the city with me were people I knew—good, supportive friends from our days of promoting the Make Schenectady Competitive campaign. This was a program that took the huge Schenectady manufacturing plant from piecework to daywork, saving the company millions of dollars. Blue-collar workers could often double their pay through piecework by finding faster, more efficient ways of producing. Daywork paid everybody the same. The campaign, which involved getting community support by hosting free information sessions at restaurants and bars, had gotten national recognition as a setback for unions. Needless to say, we communicators took advantage of these free perks.

So when all of us arrived that Sunday for companywide negotiations with the unions, the first thing we decided was to go to the bar to watch a football game after we got settled in our rooms. When I got to the bar, I looked around but figured they must still be getting situated since they were rooming together. I was about to sit at the bar when a large, burly, but well-dressed man *(even bouncers were well dressed there)* came up and told me solicitors were not allowed. Despite my protests that I was a guest there and had GE friends I was meeting, he roughly ushered me out the back door.

I found my way out of the alley. I went back into the hotel where I again approached the bar figuring my friends must be there by this time. When the bouncer saw me, he interrupted me before I could get to their table where they were watching TV. Again, he had me by my arm as I yelled to my friends. Quickly sizing up the situation, they decided it would be a good joke to say they did not know me. However, when they saw I was going to be roughly ejected, they came to my rescue.

All of us had a laugh over the incident. They decided I should skip a round in paying for our drinks since I had been so rudely ejected. In fact, they tried to get the bartender to give us all a free round, but he said I should have shown some GE identification when I came in or it would not have happened.

Still, we had a good time that evening. Between toasts and touchdowns we wondered how we were ever going to get a newsletter published as fast as management wanted. Ted had been on the Corporate Employee Relations communication team before during negotiations. He complained that lowly communicators were the last to know what was being discussed as senior vice presidents first confided in regular vice presidents. Then they met with their staff to tell them and by the time it got down to us, a day was lost. They would forget about the delay in the chain of command. Then they would complain about the slowness of getting the word out to the plants about the terrific offer the company was making to the unions. Ted, draining his glass, declared that even the secretaries typing up the negotiations from the prior day knew more than communicators.

It didn't take long for all of us to realize that if I could be mistaken for a solicitor, why not a secretary? So the next morning, I found my way to the outer room of the negotiations center where I presented my credentials. There were three secretaries from corporate headquarters, so instead I introduced myself as a proofreader, handing them the Schenectady *GE News* with my name on it.

They went out of their way to welcome me. It seemed that in a prior year one of them made a mistake in typing and actually gave the union an extra percentage in medical benefits. The clean typed copy was quickly agreed to by the union when they realized it had not been noticed by the corporation union relations staff. That typist had been fired. They were warned that it should never happen again.

They were not only pleased to have me join them, but also relieved when I told them I would take full responsibility as the final proofreader of everything they were typing. So for the next four days, I enjoyed their company and the excellent meals they were served. In fact, because of high security, their suite was just off the negotiations room and they were not let out of sight. Their meals were catered. I often stayed after negotiations work for their excellent dinners as well as making sure everyone had left the negotiation room. Then I went back to my room where I met my fellow newsletter editors. We worked on our companywide newsletter. Afterward, we adjourned to the bar for a celebration in which I was not to pay for any drinks.

When negotiations ended, we had our newsletter ready to be faxed across the country just an hour after we were told. The company negotiators were amazed at the excellent quality of the newsletter and how fast we had produced it. We were invited to their celebration of a successful four-year companywide negotiation.

Here the bar was open and a smorgasbord of gourmet food was available. It was while I was trying to figure out what that black, beady stuff was that everyone seemed to be delving into when a Corporate Relations Vice President walked up to me and said: "I hear from other communicators you are mostly responsible for the excellent communications which went out to our plants. They couldn't say enough good about you. Congratulations. We are glad to have you on our team. In fact, I would like to give you a special reward later this evening. Here's my room number."

I was so stunned I took his card. I had just taken a bite of the caviar on a cracker like I had seen others do. He didn't seem to notice I dropped the rest on the linen tablecloth as he sauntered off with a condescending smile. I couldn't believe my ears much less my tastebuds. I quickly threw a napkin over the mess and looked for my fellow communicators. I soon found them at the open bar and immediately told them their good intentions of praising me was now a major problem. They got me into this mess—now they had to figure out how to get me out.

They were as offended as I was with this turn of events. We discussed hiring someone to take my place but decided that even a professional should not have to put up with such a hypocrite. Besides, none of us wanted to come up with the money to feed his ego. Then it hit us. We had planned on enjoying the nightlife of New York before we left for Schenectady the next day. So why not stay out all night and come into the last breakfast meeting raving about the all-night entertainment in New York City? My four friends even made sure the Vice President heard them call to me that our dinner reservations in Greenwich Village were confirmed.

It was a night I will never forget. We did start at Greenwich Village, but it was at a bar, not a restaurant. I was so grateful for their help, I offered to buy the first two rounds. I also knew these guys all had wives and kids. In fact, Ted was the one who had been a negotiations communicator twice before. He told me he saved a kitty just for this once-every-four-years negotiations occasion. He had six kids. I knew one of them would be starting college soon. So when he flashed $200 in front of me, I was determined to see that he did not spend it all.

That turned out to be a tough job; he was always the first to throw out a $20 bill. But it got easier as the evening wore on. I was able to scoop up some of his bills without him noticing. Halfway through the evening we were in a place called the "Bookshelf" where the dancers gyrated on shelves across the wall behind the bar. The bartender, noticing Ted was entranced with them, told him they put the bookcases behind the bar to make the dancers less accessible to drunks. In an attempt to attract their attention, Ted was dipping his comb in my beer to slick back his hair in the style of the Fonz. It was suggested by the others—and by this time I readily agreed—that I should be drinking scotch like they were since it would kill the dandruff Ted was leaving in my drink.

When the place closed at 2 a.m., we went out to look for another bar. Again, the group came to my rescue when we saw a rough-looking gang coming down the block toward us. You could tell they immediately sized us up as tourists as they commented on the suits and ties the guys wore. I tried to hide among them but they spotted me in my dressy suit. I don't know whose idea it was, but it was one everyone quickly agreed to when it was decided the gang was more interested in me. Fred and Dick would circle around the block to see if they could find a cab or help. Ted, John, and I would cross the street to see if we could avoid them. It turned out to be a wise decision. We crossed the street again with them behind us. We began running to meet up with Fred and Dick, who came toward us yelling that the police were on their way. As luck would have it—and were we ever grateful for it—a police siren sounded several blocks away. Then it was the gang running, not us.

While we were congratulating ourselves on being so smart, Ted noticed we were standing in front of a place called the "Body Shop." Ted began laughing when he opened the door. It led up a set of stairs lined with photos of the bodies of naked women. I was reluctant to go in but they assured me they had proven to be great chaperones. So up the stairs I went with them. At the next door, a bouncer asked for $20 each. When he saw me, he told them there was no charge for women and laughed. He assured me I would not be part of their show.

So in I went. To my amazement, we entered a plush room containing a very fancy circular stage. The bouncer seated my friends in the first row. Seeing that I was going to leave and they might go with me, he told me I could sit right behind them, which I did. The first act was a comic who came out flipping a deck of cards which he began to sell after telling some raw jokes. Ted was the first to buy a set when he advertised fifty-two cards with fifty-two different positions. Next came a bevy of beauties who advertised lap dances. I was totally naive until I saw what was happening to the customers in the front row. I couldn't believe it. It was then that I retrieved a bunch of Ted's $10 bills when I saw the lap dancer reaching into his pockets. I was sitting behind him and got to his back pockets first.

My friends decided it was time to leave when it was announced the highlight of the late night performance was "Sally the Shepherd"—a huge ewe which was brought out on stage. Again, I was stunned when I saw what was going to happen. It was too much for our group. We quickly left and found a bar a safe distance away. We counted ourselves lucky the place was not raided while we were there.

When the sun began to come up, we went to the park to plan our strategy. They would have me by the arms when we came into the meeting room where breakfast had been set up. They would note how I couldn't hold my drinks and had passed out. So they just let me sleep in an all-night movie we had gone to. There was some shaking of heads and the Vice President in question looked disgusted. On the way back to Schenectady by train, we had quite a laugh and another round of drinks. Ted was even happier when I produced $120 of his money which I had confiscated—most of it from the delving hands of a lap dancer.

But avoiding advances for some women was not as easy. One of our plant-wide relations managers (*Bill, you know who you are*) was constantly hitting on his secretary/stenographer, Kathy. She was very good-looking and certainly not interested, but she needed the job and was supporting her ailing mother. When Bill called her into his office, he would make all sorts of suggestive comments while she was taking notes. When he got up to supposedly admire her shorthand, he would put his hands on her at which time she would find a way to hit the wall to signal me for help. My office was on the other side. She always told me when she was going in to take dictation. This was my cue to interrupt the session. I would rush in with an announcement such as Kathy having an emergency call from her mother. Even that did not tweak his conscience.

However, when we were having a Christmas party at the Van Dyck Restaurant in Schenectady in which spouses were invited, I inadvertently did Kathy a favor. The rumors had gone around that Bill had married for money and that his wife was also several years older. None of us had met her. I was at the bar getting a drink when this well-dressed, prim woman sitting there asked me about Kathy. She suggested that she looked like someone who was into extra office activities. I got the gist of her comment and quickly told her that, on the contrary, Kathy's good looks made her a target, particularly for our manager who was as sleazy as they come...that Kathy was as smart as she was beautiful...and that the last person in the world she would get involved with would be Bill. I told her about my efforts to save Kathy from his grasp to discover that I was talking to his wife.

After that, I did not have to interrupt Bill when Kathy was in the office. But I sure got some hard stares from him.

But undoubtedly the worst case of victimizing women

came from a marketing communication manager. Like so many other businesses which got their start in product development laboratories in Schenectady, the Gas Turbine business was on a strict budget until it started making money. Unlike its highly-profitable, well-established big steam turbine power brother, its marketing budget was small. During those lean years, its marketing communication manager, Sal, bemoaned the fact he only had a tenth of the money that his counterpart in steam turbine had to lure in customers. He used to say all his steam turbine counterpart had to do was entertain a handful of utility customers with lavish dinners, hunting trips, a safari or two, and a few showgirls. Therefore, he said he was reduced to tricking secretaries into helping him sell gas turbines.

Gas turbine markets were more diverse and international, with hundreds of potential customers, particularly in the Middle East oil fields.

I was editing the *GE News* when I first met him. As noted, I regret all those cheesecake photos I was putting on the front of the *GE News* to attract what my manager hypocritically called red-blooded blue-collar workers. But he was into it too. There were times when he had vetoed some photos saying the subject was not that pretty.

Sadly, I have to say this front-page feature became so popular that some women were volunteering for various poses, often coming up with their own reason for it. What I didn't know was that some of these women were getting calls from Sal who told them he was a professional photographer. He would like to take some really good photos of them. What he was doing was checking them out to see if they would be interested in helping him with his promotion of gas turbines.

I found this out when I was covering the arrival of some fifteen Japanese customers at the Star Dust Inn who were touring the gas turbine plant. A state-of-the-art technology program that had been put together for them had been well received. The *GE News* photographer and I celebrated our success in getting many fine photos of the customers with the displays. I had some good quotes from them on the tour as well as comments on their favorable impression of the reliability and efficiency of GE gas turbines, and we were at the bar celebrating this when one of the girls that I ran on the front page in her bathing suit came running up to me. She was in tears and asked me to take her home.

I left with her to find out Sal had been paying her for her work with customers. She had three children, was an entry-level secretary, and the pay for one night was more than she made in a week. She had even put on the kimono he had provided for her. But when her "customer" came in, she couldn't do it. Her father had been killed in World War II.

The bar manager realized what was going on and reported it to the owner. Unfortunately, another girl I had also run a cheesecake photo of was still serving customers when the police arrived. They arrested her. It was in the middle of the night I got a call from the girl I had rescued about her friend being in jail and could I help her. Feeling somewhat responsible (*and looking back, disgusted*), I decided I needed to tell A.C. Stevens, the Schenectady Works manager, about it. I felt I could trust him because he came to my rescue when the head of the YWCA locked me out.

When I first came to GE in 1960, I tried to get an apartment. I soon discovered a single woman from out of town was presumed to be in the red-light business. I went to the YW; the head woman was welcoming but her rules were strict. You had to be in the building no later than 9 p.m. Thursday nights were a problem for me as the *GE News* went to press then and often I had to work until midnight to makes changes by GE lawyers being watched by the National Labor Relations Board. The first time this happened, I was locked out. I went back to the plant and slept on the couch in A.C. Steven's outer office. He returned early and was irate when he found out why I was there. He called the YW head and reminded her of the ongoing capital improvement program GE was backing to modernize the YW. After that, I not only could come in late but I was also moved to a better room.

Remembering this, I felt he would be understanding and helpful. I went into his office when I saw his secretary was not at her desk. With some trepidation, I told him the full story. He was shocked and immediately went into action. He gave me money to bail out the girl and asked me to promise not a word of this would get out. He would fix things for everyone.

While Sal was not fired, I was assured he would not be soliciting low-paid secretaries for marketing help. As for my two white friends, he suggested I talk to them about the new Upward Mobility for minority employees, particularly black employees, as part of the 1964 Civil Right Act. Even though this would nearly double their pay and put them on a fast-track promotion path, I did have trouble convincing the one with the World War II father killed by the Japanese to participate in the program. It turned out she was also prejudiced against blacks. But with her friend enrolled, she eventually agreed to sign up for the Upward Mobility program. *(Today, I am happy to say her mathematical and organizational abilities led to a high-level managerial position in assuring product components were shipped on schedule all over the world.)*

Fortunately for Sal, the gas turbine business did pick up and his budget was increased to entertain customers legally. Years later, I asked him how the professional showgirl business was going and he gave me the finger. But there were times when sleazy guys like him came in handy for the company. I remember when an executive from the Pakistan Water and Power Authority was visiting the plant to check on a huge $82 million order for gas turbines. He was housed in an elegant hotel room in Albany. He had been there just two days when a call came in from the police that he had been picked up for soliciting a young boy in the park. They had him in jail. He was very indignant about it; he said it was a lawful practice in his country and if GE wanted his business they had better take care of him and quick. So Sal—who only hit on girls and was disgusted at the Pakistan customer—knew how to handle the situation. As he noted, there must be something to his our-culture-is-different story to the police. After all, he had assumed it was okay to get the boy's address to pick him up for dinner after he treated him to candy in the park. When he got there in the GE limo that had been provided for him, the parents, of course, had the police waiting. Obviously, the situation needed to be handled delicately or GE would lose the order. So Sal equipped the Pakistan customer with a collection of child porn films which kept him busy the rest of his stay. As he cynically told me later, you never know what it takes to keep a customer satisfied.

In fact, one had to realize Sal proved valuable in meeting some customer desires. He was quick to suggest that state-of-the-art technology seminars should be held in Amsterdam, Holland, where prostitution was legal. Girls, especially blonde ones, were of great interest to the many Saudi customers using gas turbines to pump their black gold to the ports.

We, of course, knew that Sal and his buddies would also take advantage of this free perk. When one of them gleefully told some of us he was going to have a great time making his selections for the evening, we gave him a pack of prophylactics. We asked him to use these so he would not give a disease to those selections.

Back in the 60s and 70s, secretaries were often fair game because there was little protection from harassment. I knew several secretaries who knew more about the business than their bosses did. Even other managers would recognize this by waiting for their boss to leave and then asking them for information they needed.

On the other hand, I remember one great-looking secretary to a General Manager who used her position to lure young, ambitious guys into her bed. If they wanted preferred access and treatment by her boss, they should please her.

Then there was the manager with a job opening for a secretary. He declined to hire a Certified Professional Secretary (CPS) from the Mildred Elly College. Instead, he had the gall to note he was looking for a secretary with two outstanding points. I found out about it and sent him a note that his next new boss would be an aggressive homosexual.

I remember a guy in Building 23 who used to wear a pendant chain around his neck. In the pendant he claimed to have the remains of a vasectomy. He claimed this attracted liberated women, particularly those who protested with no bras. He promoted his availability by declaring birth control pills had not been proven to be healthy for women. He also advertised he was a Planned Parenthood supporter.

When GE was one of four companies in 1972 charged by the Equal Opportunity Employment Commission for discrimination, my job and pay prospects took a leap forward. I was one of the first women from the Schenectady plant—along with a black woman from Louisville—to be hired at headquarters. We had front offices which could be seen from the Merritt Parkway. GE's attempts to show it was an EEO employer revealed it was sometimes embarrassing to make cultural change. A black Harlem Globetrotters basketball star, Willie Campbell, and I received letters from GE's prestigious Elfun Society to "join this group of company professionals, business and technical leaders." When I got to the exclusive club in Fairfield, I was asked by the host—who assumed I worked there—to collect dues from Elfun members. I thought this was funny and had a grand time fulfilling his request until my VP sponsor came in. In about ten minutes, Willie, who had been told by the host he was late for caddy duty, came in. We had a big laugh about it but not as big as Mark Russell. In those days he was a well-known piano playing pundit. When he spotted Willie and me, he wouldn't let it go. After learning our names, he quickly incorporated us in his politically-incorrect repartee, asking what we were doing there.

Yes, times have certainly changed. But even today one cannot say that GE and other company employees act as a Normal Rockwell family despite discrimination and sexual harassment laws. In fact, I know one former lecherous VP of Human Resources who learned the hard way that things were different. He was set up by a female relations lawyer who taped his overtures on one of the company planes. She earned herself a million dollars to keep it quiet.

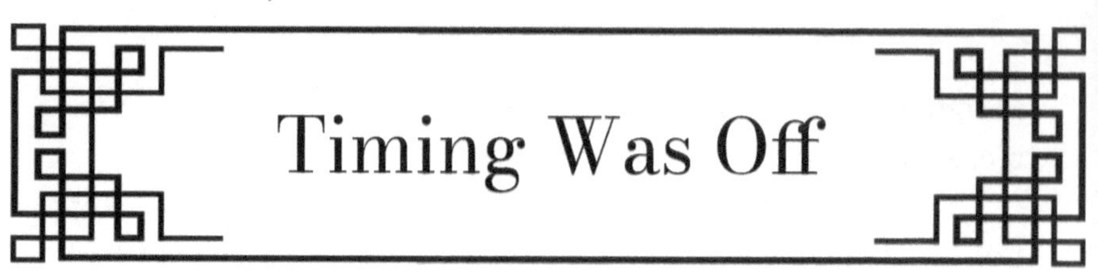

Timing Was Off

When one watches the Olympics, be it downhill skiing or swimming, it is amazing how the winner may be just a fourth or fifth of a second in front of the top ten. It reminded me of the late 1960s when a bunch of us in the Schenectady Wintersports Club decided we should broaden our scope and re-introduce the turn of the century regatta on the Mohawk River. There seemed to be plenty of reasons to do so. Some of us had competed against Bob Kennedy in the Hudson River Derby. It attracted thousands and was good for the economy up there. Most of us were spurred on by the need to clean up the river. Those of us in GE were well aware the water in the plant was not being returned in the 60s in a cleaner condition than it was received. Even the screens over the pipes bringing the water into the plant were not that effective. There were times when you would notice minnows swimming around in the toilet bowl. Today, I still have the signs written in Polish and Italian throughout the plant not to drink the river water.

The Towpath Regatta got its name from the days of the Erie Canal when mules would "tow" boats alongside the river and its canal section. Because of the regatta's connection to the historic past when the Erie Canal opened up a way to go west, we had no problem getting the press to run story after story about it. This time we were going to use the Towpath Regatta as a way to draw attention to the fact the river used to be clean. Now it was up to us to make it so again.

Because we had no money in the club to pay for the organization, we had to become dependent on volunteers. We also had to run it at no cost. We planned it as an "anything-goes" event, giving the media pictures of a couple of homemade rafts to encourage amateurs. One looked like a Rube Goldberg setup armed with two bicycles operating a paddle wheel. This GE engineer, Shield Bishop, had even installed tubes from water bottles to provide water to the bicyclers, who were busy pedaling hard to turn the rear paddle wheel.

To save costs, we decided appropriate (and cheap) awards would be different-sized bottles of the river water. They were labeled with the year of the award so winners could save their bottles to notice an improvement in their color and contents each year. The only cost to our club would be printing the labels for the bottles and I had access to the GE printing company.

Thus, free labels along with empty pill and soda bottles saved for some six months by our members enabled us to have plenty of awards. We gave them out freely to some ten different canoe, kayak, and anything-goes classes with prizes for the top three.

Our financial problem became a timing system. Because we had a lot of competitive ski racers in the club, they wanted a timing system, but renting one would be costly. There was much debate about how to arrange the start. Should we have the more competitive canoes in front with the kayaks behind them and then the anything-goes crowd? Would each group understand when it was their turn to take off at the sound of the bullhorn and what would happen if some ran ahead of the start yell? Those with a competitive nature decided we would have a mass start since the river was so wide at the start. Thus it would be fair. They suggested there would be no jamming problem because the real racers would quickly go ahead of the pack.

But what about timing at the end? It would be difficult to stretch a rope across the river to spot who was going under it first. Besides, the river was so wide that several could go under it at one time, making it difficult to see who was in what boat category.

It was then that I, still having to punch the clock at GE, thought of it and suggested we arm each competitor with a timecard. They would carry the card with them to the finish line where the lead person would then run up the bank and punch in their times. Each card would be marked with a color to indicate the race category. Moreover, it would enable all of us to be in the race and not have to be timers. The idea was quickly accepted and again GE unknowingly contributed to the event with a loan of a time clock which we mounted on a board at the top of the riverbank.

What came next no one expected. First, the media had gone all out announcing the event. When we arrived on race day, the huge parking lots at the Jumping Jacks fast-food restaurant and riverside park were overflowing. We counted 252 entries. The riverside and two bridges were jammed with spectators. Fortunately I had gotten several boxes of time-cards so we had plenty of those. After we marked the categories for each craft going into the river, we organizers got into our boats, too.

The fast-food restaurant owner, who sponsored water skiing events from his parking lot to attract customers, was thrilled to see the turnout for the clean water derby. He was more than happy to use his bullhorn to start the race. The starting line went completely across the river with the "anything goes" crowd, content not to be jostling for position among the canoes and kayaks. At the bullhorn blast, there was a tremendous churning of water which promptly sank several canoes in the family and canoe classes. They had overloaded their boat, resulting in the wake quickly swamping over their gunnels. Fortunately, they were all able to swim and had worn the required life jackets. They were picked up by the fast-food owner in his power boat which he also used to upright and tow in their air-bagged flotation canoes.

There was a huge cheer as the mass of watercrafts went under the first bridge, also loaded with spectators, with the racers well ahead. There was enough space between paddlers to keep them from colliding. But those on the right side of the river soon found out they were on the wrong side to make good time. That was where the raw sewage that could not be handled by the aging plant was coming out. Evidently the operators there had not read about the race and released their overflow. There was much gagging and yelling but those hardy competitors paddle-slugged their way through it hoping they could make time up on the riverbend ahead.

And it was the riverbend where some of the avid competitors did crash into each other trying to take the straightest line possible to win. This time it was not gagging or yelling, just cursing. But no one went over in the pileup.

Things went smoothly for several minutes until a barge appeared on the scene. The press had dutifully asked that no power boaters be on the river for two hours that day but we had forgotten about barges. However, it was slow enough that no one ran into it but those who had to turn right or left to avoid it swore their time would have been better if it had not been in their path.

When the finish line was in sight, things at first went as we expected. The competitors in long, streamlined canoes made it first and handily made it up the bank to punch in their time. However, one competitor, who was behind another, jumped out of his canoe before it reached the bank in the hopes of racing up ahead of his competitor. He quickly sank into water over his head and that was an omen of what was to come.

Soon the huge middle pack arrived and there were so many of them arriving at once there was not enough space at the bankside to accommodate them in an orderly manner. Even though this group was not considered competitive, these contestants had gotten the fever. Some were floundering in water over their heads trying to be the first to punch in. Others were ramming their canoes and kayaks into others to push them aside so they could get out. Worse, those who had been swimming ashore had dripped enough water to make the run up the bank very muddy. Soon those who did get out of their boats efficiently found themselves slipping and sliding down the bank.

Fortunately, there was also a huge crowd—mostly siblings, parents, or relatives—who came to their assistance and no one was hurt. In fact, everyone began laughing as other competitors came in to experience what had happened to them.

However, quite a few of the avid competitors did not laugh when it came time for the awards. I had forgotten the time clock did not register seconds—only minutes. Therefore, we had a lot more winners than we had counted on. When we announced each first, second, and third place, three or four or more people would show up for the award with their card with the same time stamped on it. Then there were those people who had not even been able to punch in because their card was so wet.

Again, with most of the crowd, it produced a huge laugh. But not for some of the avid competitors with the same time on their timecard, who yelled at each other: "You know that I was ahead of you." Fortunately we had plenty of bottle awards for everyone and most went away happy, asking us to run this race every year in the interest of cleaning up the river.

Amen-ing that in a loud voice was one competitor who had struggled with the sewage outflow and declared it was a fun but shitty race.

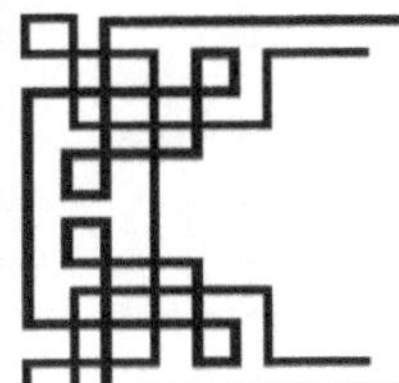

Dog Days

Unlike cats, I've had lots of problems trying to become friends with dogs. Perhaps my inability to do so goes back to my childhood when my father, a farmer, said they were of no use unless you raised sheep. He preferred cats—lots of them. Some twenty-five cats earned their keep in our three barns, two silos, and a granary which housed hay, corn, wheat, oats, and barley.

As a result, we had no mice eating into our cash crops. The cattle and horses in the barn also liked cats better than dogs. There was no snapping or biting of their heels by these barking, disruptive animals. Even the sitting hens in the chicken house liked the cats better, several of whom had a taste for black snakes which liked eggs.

Dogs became a problem for me while bike riding. Cats don't chase bikes, but dogs do. The instance I remember most happened when I was riding in a remote area on a fifty-mile trek. I was going over the top of a mountain when all of a sudden two dogs attacked me from my left side. I made the mistake of thinking I could outrun them going downhill. It was then I heard a snarl on my right and felt a piercing pain in my right lower leg. I was pulled off the bike by a hunting dog. It had been trained to not lose its prey but to clamp down and not let go. When I landed in the ditch, I could feel his teeth clamp down even harder on my leg bone. Then I heard a man yell, "Tracker, come back here, Tracker!" This only made it worse because Tracker was determined to drag me back to his owner.

Fortunately, a woman in one of those pickup trucks with oversized tires came by and immediately took action. She jumped out and hit Tracker in the head with a tire iron, causing him to release his bite. She immediately told me to get in her truck because I was bleeding. I protested that I wanted to find that dog's owner. She quickly changed my mind by telling me that Tracker's owner was even meaner than his dogs. On the way to the emergency room, she told me that Tracker had mauled a little girl once, leaving a permanent scar on her face.

I thanked her profusely at the emergency room. I was grateful she gave me her phone number in case I had a problem with Tracker's owner. It was a phone number I soon used because I was told I would have to go through a rigid two-week rabies shot program unless the dog could be found and tested in twenty-four hours. I called her and she knew the dog warden for the county but warned me that he was a hunter himself and a friend of Tracker's owner. I was told by him that yes, he did know Tracker, and was sure he did not have rabies. I explained he still had to be tested at the shelter. I waited for him to call back to tell me he had taken Tracker to the animal shelter.

When twelve hours were up and he was not answering his phone, I called the state animal control office. He forced the county dog warden to take the dog to the shelter for testing. It was closing in on twenty-four hours when an animal shelter staffer called to ask me to describe the dog. I did so, noting the name of the dog as being "Tracker," which got a quick response.

"This dog is not Tracker," he said. "We know that hunting dog. He sent in a substitute. He knows that two strikes in Saratoga County and you are out."

The shelter officer even called my rescuer to identify Tracker, which she did. Tracker was picked up by the officer. I was advised not to bike ride in that part of the county anymore because Tracker's owner was very upset with the loss of his best hunting dog.

After that, my fear of dogs escalated and maybe it is true what they say about dogs—they can spot your fear and react accordingly depending on their nature. I even became para-noid one day when I was on a bike next to a stopped car at a traffic light. A dog leaned out of the window and snapped at me.

Once, though, I did meet a dog that I liked. My neighbor, Meredith Anker, had a Burmese Mountain Dog that weighed some 140 pounds. Its name was Harley and while I am not a fan of motorcycles, the dog was built like one. Harley had a beautiful, dark brown and white shaggy coat that you just wanted to run your hands through. He would look at you with those huge, mournful eyes and nestle up to you. I was pleased to find a dog that seemed to like me.

When Meredith took the dog to a nature preserve for an open run without a leash, I used to get in the back seat with Harley. He loved to freely roam around the preserve. We used to laugh when Harley would find a deer and nearly give him-self a heart attack trying to keep up with it. Then we would feel sorry for Harley when the deer would turn around and just look at him—a spent dog, exhausted, humiliated, and no longer up for the chase.

I also accompanied Meredith on many of the walks she took Harley on at the riverside park next to her house. It was a park requiring dogs to be leashed. Occasionally, if no one was around, we would let Harley have a short run. Because he was a cold-weather mountain dog, hot summer days would see him dashing down the bank to get into the river. Then he would come back to us and repeatedly shake that shaggy coat full of water, giving us a drenching, too.

On one of those days, Meredith asked me to take Harley for a walk because she was busy, and the park was empty. I decided to let Harley have a free romp in the park. He had just come out of the water and was about to give me a drenching when he heard a car door open at a nearby entrance. I knew I was in trouble. To Harley, the sound of a door opening meant he was going to the nature preserve. It only took him a few seconds to get to the car, jump in the back seat, and worse, shake himself off. The stunned and upset owner tried to pull the still-wet Harley out but he wouldn't budge. I explained that he was used to exiting a car with a leash and that I would have to go back to Meredith's house to get it. I added that I would pay for the damages to the car.

Fortunately for me, the owner's girlfriend was charmed by Harley's good looks while I was getting the leash. I let her put the leash on him and he immediately came out of the car and gave her that mournful "Harley look." She wanted to buy him. Even if I had owned Harley, I would not have said yes.

I can still see him sitting out in a snowstorm in Meredith's yard, letting the snow pile up on him until he was no longer a dog but a snow-covered boulder. When four of us played bridge during those long winter evenings, you could count on the loving Harley to be under the table spread out like a throw rug. He would let all of us put our feet under his body to warm them up. The only problem was his bad breath—Harley was one of those dogs that ate other dog droppings.

Large dogs die sooner than small ones, usually at twelve or so. Harley made it to fourteen with some help. His arthritis got so bad that when he jumped into the river, he could no longer get up the bank. Between the two of us, Meredith and I held up his back legs while he pawed his way up the bank. Everyone loved Harley except for one of Meredith's boyfriends. He said that if he died, he wanted to come back as Harley.

Dogs can be extremely loyal to their owners. I was in the Hudson River White Water Derby race with some other 300 contestants when I discovered just how attached one dog was to his owner, Jimmy Fox. Jimmy was my partner in the couples' canoe class. He had left his yellow Labrador retriever on a leash with his friend Bob Creatura at the finish line. We had just come through the last set of some ten rapids. We could see the finish line in flat water ahead when the dog spotted Jimmy. Several thousand people were watching the race when the dog broke loose from Bob. He jumped off the bank and into the water with a huge splash. As this giant dog was surging toward us, Jimmy began yelling for him to go back. The crowd was fully aware—as Jimmy and I were—of what was going to happen if this heavy, lumbering dog tried to get in the boat with us. Despite Jimmy yelling and hitting him with the paddle to get him to go back, he kept coming. The minute he hit the gunnels, the canoe turned over. We floated through the finish line with me grabbing the paddles while Jimmy dealt with a lapping-his-face dog in water now over our heads.

We didn't win what we thought would be a second-place trophy in our class, but we were undoubtedly the most viewed competitors in the race.

There is no question that dogs have become ever more popular as pets as dog food has become a billion-dollar industry along with cat food for those who don't live in barns. Some say people choose dogs to be a reflection of themselves. Poodles can usually be seen on a leash held by tiny, well-dressed and manicured women. Drug dealers prefer pit bulls which are easier to train to scare away trespassers. Police and military men find German Shepherds to be protective and brave in the face of adversity. Afghan and Weimaraner dogs seem to be preferred by the gentry. Even though cats don't seem to have the diverse traits that dogs do, you will find some owners dress them up to look like themselves.

So you might ask if I have a dog or cat as a pet today. I am thinking about it. But first I might send 29 cents a day to UNICEF to take care of a third-world child. After all, they write interesting letters to their sponsors, something dogs and cats can't do. And if I did get a dog at this old age, I would probably get one that just lies around doing nothing. In that case, people might say I am just like my dog.

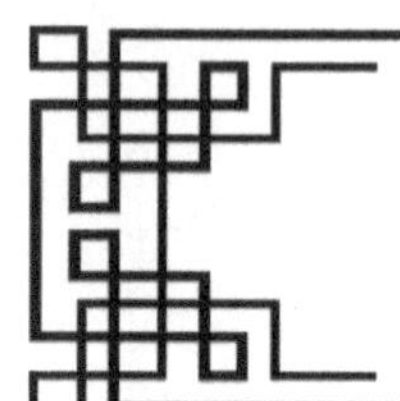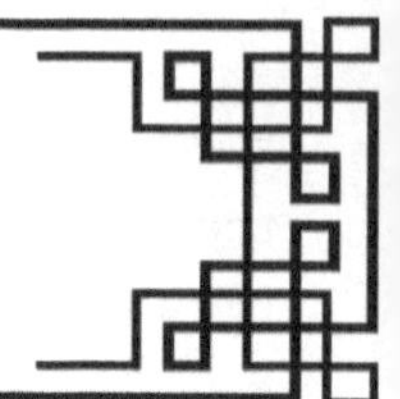

Rail Tales

When I was growing up in the 50s, the railroads still had elegant Queen City Stations across the U.S. before most people started driving or flying to get there in a hurry.

I remember the first time I saw the Queen City Hotel in Cumberland, Maryland, which was a destination in itself. It was constructed by the Baltimore and Ohio Railroad Company. The huge Victorian Italianate-style building had 174 rooms, a ballroom, a huge dining room that could seat 400, along with an outdoor garden with a huge fountain in it. I was just eleven years old when I first saw it. My two older sisters got on the train to go to Nashville to see Minnie Pearl. Being born on a farm, I was mesmerized by a building not just covering an acre itself but taller than our silo.

It was torn down in 1972 to make room for a post office. Today, a small box-style Amtrak station is near the site.

When I was in my teens, I got to experience an elegant ride to Washington, D.C., to see our capitol. It was the train ride that I remember the most. I still have the silver-plated B&O creamer which my mother thinks I returned.

Traveling by train began to deteriorate in the 60s. When I took the train to Schenectady, New York, to start my first job, it was depressing. Dining cars were replaced with fast-food service counters. The stations are just as grim. While sitting in the Pennsylvania Station waiting to make the connection from New York to Schenectady, I was harassed by a guy who finally set sail when a passing ensign saw what was happening and came to my rescue.

Economists give many reasons for the demise of rail traffic such as the growing interstate highway systems and a booming airline business that can move people and freight faster.

Others will tell you that rail traffic does not get the heavy financial government support given to the highway and airport systems. In fact, rail systems in the U.S. today are some of the poorest in the world, only capable of supporting speeds a third of that in Japan and even Africa.

I found this out recently when I booked a trip from Seattle to Boston. I no sooner got to the railroad station in Seattle than I was told we would be taking a bus to Spokane—a rail derailment would take several days to repair. After leaving Spokane, I questioned why we had to stop in the middle of nowhere every hour or so. I learned that with just one set of tracks, we had to wait on a side set of tracks for a scheduled freight train to come through before proceeding. Unfortunately, this did not happen with a view of Glacier Park but mostly in the middle of woods or cornfields. Once you get a late start, the fast-food bar attendant said, the worse it is because you are off schedule the whole way. Thus, we got into Chicago eight hours late. However, they held up the train going east so we were able to get on it—to hear passengers along the eastern route getting on complain about the delay. When we got to Albany, New York, we were again told we had to board buses to Boston because a flood had washed out the tracks near Springfield, Massachusetts. We found out that it had taken them nearly two months to repair this section.

Still, I liked that one can walk around the train, enjoy a visit to the club car for scenic viewing, and even book a sleeping unit for those long trips. Once, when I had the time, I took a one-way trip to Salt Lake City to go skiing. It was on time. Going the southwestern route out of Denver was a scenic joy. Because the railroads in the east are old, you mostly look at abandoned factory buildings or town dumps. But the trip from Denver to Salt Lake through the Rockies was a time you did not want to be sleeping. Before and after going through seventeen tunnels and numerous bridges, you get an up-close look at rivers winding their way through mountain valleys surrounded by high peaks.

I was happy enough just watching the scenery roll. But during happy hour, I was even more pleased to find out that a canned Amtrak Margaretta cost only $2. So when I arrived at the elegant Alta Lodge with twenty cans of Amtrak Margarettas, I was a hit at the outdoor hot tub looking up at the famed High Rustler trail.

A year later, I made this same trip west when an old friend, Shields Bishop, who was afraid of flying, asked me if I would go with him on the train to visit friends we both knew in Idaho. Shields was over eighty and did not feel comfortable making the trip himself. He was also very frugal and did not want to rent a Pullman sleeper for the two-day trip. At the time, Amtrak had suspended its service directly west from Schenectady and required you to go to New York City to make the connection west. So I packed my air mattress and sleeping bag after noticing on an earlier trip people used them in the scenic car.

While we were waiting, I bought the *New York Times* to while away the time while Shields took a nap beside me. On the other side was a big, burly guy who kept looking over my shoulder to read the paper, too. He distracted me enough that he was able to slowly move my bag, a large purple duffle, over to his side of the bench. Then when it was announced the train was ready to load passengers, he jumped up and ran with my bag. I yelled, waking Shields up. A lady sitting across from us immediately told me that she had been wondering why a big guy like him would be using a purple bag that matched my sweater. A savvy New Yorker, she said, he would most likely go to the men's room and search it for valuables and leave it there and there were security officers at the exits to stop thieves. Even though the announcer said the train was loading, Shields ran off to the men's room to see if he could find the bag. When he immediately came back with it, I was not just amazed but astonished. Shields was half the size of that guy and at least three times as old. He explained that all he had done was notice the purple bag in the open bottom of the stall, gone into the next one, and slid it under the partition to his side. Then he ran like hell with it.

Even my camera was still in the duffel. My old and tired companion had saved the day—or rather, the ten days that we would be gone. So I was more than happy to give him the first turn using the air mattress and sleeping bag. It fit nicely in the well of the scenic railcar when we went through the Rockies out of Denver. It was a delight to lay there and look down through the well of the glass car. It was bow-shaped to give you a "down and sideways" view of the passing cliffs with rivers below.

The challenge was to get to the scenic car early to stake your claim for a bed site in the glass wells. Because it was also the hospitality car, one was expected to patronize the bar. So while he was sleeping, I often partook in adult refreshments.

We had just gone through one of the tunnels when a group of handsome black guys in dreadlocks and black suits came to the bar. They began taking over the viewing seats. I had tried to save one of these while getting Shields set up in the sleeping bag and air mattress in the well bed. When I came back to the seat I had put my coat on, though, it was on the floor.

There were about eight of them and each stared me down as I picked up my coat. They were obviously enjoying themselves, waiting to see what I would do. I had already run into them at the bar where they had been blowing smoke in the faces of some older white passengers to see what they would do. At that time, I had commented that picking on old people was not nice, so I figured my seat predicament was payback for that comment. I explained my coat had been on that seat and that I was traveling with someone who could not afford a sleeping car. One of them picked up my West Virginia accent and began teasing me about being a southern belle. It didn't take us long to get into a discussion about the Civil War. It resulted in us finally agreeing that none of us had been in it and therefore could not be held responsible for such an awful war.

I was then given the seat I had marked. Perhaps it was the drinks as well as the discussion because they wanted to know all about my hometown changing hands fifty-two times during the Civil War. I had ancestors on both sides; I told them some had even called the horror "an unpleasant war." We became friends and they insisted on buying me a drink to make it more pleasant for me. I soon found out this band of beautiful dreadlocked black men were part of Madonna's major act in which she pirouetted and danced in her sparse all-white costume as they cavorted in black around her. They also asked me if I had seen Madonna's private rail car on the back of the train. No, she was not with them. She always flew.

When I explained that my friend, Shields, had never flown because he was afraid, they just laughed and several of them went over to inspect him. It was about this time that Shields woke up, looking up into the faces framed by dreadlocks. He yelled, jumped up, and was about to take them on when I yelled that they were friends. To the delight of Madonna's entourage, they were intrigued at his bravery, having had fun observing older passengers with their smoking and looks. So another round of drinks was purchased and toasts to Shields were made.

When we finally pulled into the Salt Lake City station, both Shields and I were in poor condition to rent a car to make the six-hour drive to Tetonia, Idaho, where our friends lived among the Mormon farmers. Unlike the posh Jackson Hole, their panoramic view of the Teton Range is one that was in the *National Geographic Magazine*. But we finally got there. The sun was just coming up over the Grand Teton when we drove in. It was so beautiful we had an outdoor breakfast to enjoy the view before we went to bed for fifteen or so hours.

While Shields did not have to come to the rescue on our

uneventful trip back, we still talk about those seventeen Rocky Mountain tunnels we went through between Salt Lake and Denver.

Hopefully one day our government will support the rail system like they do air and highway traffic. There are some small tourist trains that are giving the youth today a taste of what we old-timers once knew traveling by train was like. It is a matter of getting them to try it out. Take the tourist train from Saratoga to North Creek, New York, for example—they have a dome car with a dining room featuring round table seats covered with linen tablecloths. A little bouquet of flowers provides an even more elegant setting as you wine and dine along the scenic upper Hudson River. The conductor stops by to give you a little history of the area and the waiter has a substantial offering of cocktails and ales as well as menu with reasonable prices. To my delight, I found they give skiers who take the train a 10% discount which means that I could actually save money by not driving. No longer did I have to pump gas at nearly $4 a gallon or pollute the environment on the way to the ski area, but could sit back and enjoy the view for $34 round trip in the dome car or $24 in coach. I also did not have to schlepp my ski gear from overflowing parking lots because I never had to handle them after they put them on the train until we arrived at the front of the ski lodge via a bus which was included in the fare.

So here's to entrepreneurs like the Saratoga-North Creek Rail System. You are setting the standard for what once again could be an era of railroad elegance. When one realizes how far behind this country is in its railroad structure, it is very sad. European and Far Eastern countries have rails that can support trains traveling over 100 miles per hour and one recently went on line in South Africa that travels over 150 mph.

My enthusiasm for rail travel has been revived. Many people are tired of clogged highways, cattle-car seating, and tedious security checks at airports. Rail travel could once again be the elegant way to go. Most of all, there is so much fun to be had with rail travel.

Nothing Like a Family Reunion

There are high school and college reunions, and even reunions of retired company employees, but none compare to a family reunion in the country—particularly when these families have lived there for generations.

While my own family is one of the original settlers of the valley, there are still others who go back far enough that they have to get out their Bibles to name each generation's offspring.

Therefore, our county newspaper each summer is filled with reunions of the Parker, Decker, Pancake, Bean, Stump, Kuykendall, Shingleton, Shoemaker, Arnold, Mayhew, Dean, Kesner, Shockey, Buckley, and Haines families. Most of these events are so large they are held at the county park. Everyone brings something to eat as well as their own drinks to share. One could really call them festivals because some local women still want to be known for their cooking and baking skills. I have eaten in some fine restaurants, including several in France, but nothing tastes as good as the cuisine at these reunions. I have been to most of them, not because I am related, but at times I have been away long enough I will not be recognized. Yet, I know enough about the families that I can easily mix with no questions asked—unless I come empty-handed.

Many of these families have intermarried over the years so if you know your own history you can usually go back to the time of that connection. In fact, in our family, the reunion organizer no longer asks if the Nathaniel branch of the family will stand up, followed by the Isaac and Jacob branch and then the Matthew branch; it became embarrassing when the same people stood up for each branch.

Still, it is great to reminisce about so many good old days even though your namesake may have been buried for 250 years.

But having acquired a taste for social drinking (unlike some of my tee-totaling Dutch ancestors), I like to go to the reunions held by descendants of the English, German, Italian, and Irish in the area. Just as they changed folk ballads from the old country, so have they prepared some food West Virginia style. The English are famous for their puddings and meat pies which can be bland unless they have been spiced up with local wild pepper and ginger plants. While the Germans usually use juniper berries in their sauerkraut, the addition of elderberries and a couple of ramps added kick to this meal. Pasta is popular worldwide and you can use it as a base for almost anything including morel mushrooms, greens and what one attendee called "roadkill that has not gone bad." Even though West Virginia is famous for its ginseng root, which has become popular as an aphrodisiac, it is no longer ground up as a pasta spice because it so pricey today. But as one reunioner said, it is just as well because the valley is getting too crowded.

However, it is the Irish reunions that I like to go to best. They don't bother cooking with ales and wines in their food. This fifth generation in our valley still drinks it straight and some of their homemade stuff is just as potent as Jameson's. Soda bread, made with buckwheat flour, has an absorbing value which keeps one on their feet.

My cousin and I like reunions so much we have driven to other counties to attend some. Totally unknown, we separate and approach the crowd from different directions. We meet in the middle to loudly proclaim we have not seen each other in years—in fact, we feel like strangers we have been gone so long. We hand our food and drink contribution to those at the table and they lament how they have not seen us in years either. By this time we have figured out the name of the family having the reunion by asking one to introduce him or herself. From then on it is help yourself to all the delicious dishes that those wonderful women hope will earn them the blue-ribbon reputation in their county.

It is not only the food that has begun to attract us to family reunions; it is a way to find new relatives.

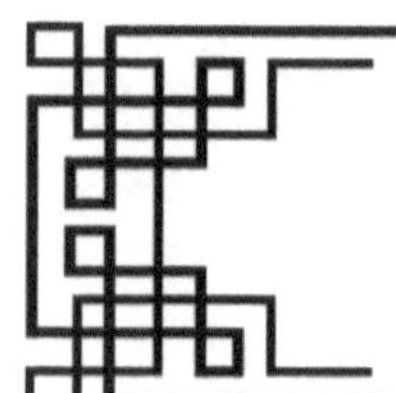 

Beyond the Call of Duty

Too often we do not hear about problems solved or acts of kindness.

My husband and I experienced both when we were going to the airport to catch a flight to see my sister whose husband had just died.

The first flight we could get was at 6 a.m. from Albany Airport to Charlottesville, Virginia. My husband, always following the advice of the professionals, declared we needed to be there two hours early as advised. So what seemed like the middle of the night at 3:45 a.m., we dutifully got up at the first beep of the alarm clock. In exactly fifteen minutes, as my husband required, we were heading south on the Northway. I was in the middle of complaining that we had rushed out of the house so fast I did not have time to go to the john. It was then that the car dashboard flashed a warning—one of our tires was losing pressure fast. We were near the exit before crossing the Mohawk River. My husband quickly pulled off, hoping the busy exit might have an overnight gas station. Instead, all we could find was a lighted bank parking lot. He drove in, deciding the lights would help while he changed the tire.

As he was getting into the trunk to find the tire, I ran to the back of the bank to relieve myself despite the fact there were lights there, too. It was so still at that early hour, I figured no one was around. At that point, I would not have cared if they were.

My husband had the car jack in hand and was about to get the spare tire out of the bin under the back floor when the quiet night was pierced by police sirens pulling into the lot behind our car.

My husband was putting his hands over his head as ordered as I ran up to see what was going on. Seeing the guns, I quickly stopped in my tracks. Having had much experience with police over traffic violations, I was not about to protest. Being fully aware of the fact we were in a bank parking lot, I then realized they might think we were robbing it.

My husband was able to convince them we were doing no such thing. He told them he did not have a gun. He had a car jack in his hand. He pointed to the right rear tire which was nearly flat. The guns were dropped as the officers realized our problem. I tried to explain why I was behind the bank. The officers were now smiling, noting the cameras banks used to catch potential robbers were not selective in what they recorded and sent to the police station. Seeing that my husband was trying to get the heavy tire out, they offered to help and had the spare tire on the car in less than ten minutes. They even wished us luck in getting to the airport in time.

When we got to the airport, we still had forty minutes to get to the gate. It took us about fifteen minutes to get through the long line for our tickets. But getting through the TSA agents was not easy. My husband, a private pilot, rarely flies commercially. He was annoyed when he had to take off his shoes and put all of his belongings in a tray for perusal. He didn't say anything about his hip replacements, so when the alarm went off, he was pulled aside. He was patted down and asked to drop his pants to make sure there were no explosives in them.

I was helping him get his shoes back on when they found the Boy Scout knife in his shaving kit—a knife he had carried for over seventy years. After an argument, they said I could go back through the security check-in area and mail it to our home address. When I got to the visitor area, I found the post office was closed. There was not enough time to go to the car and store the knife there. So I went into the ladies room and hid it under the used Kotex box.

I got back just in time to join the boarding line. Fortunately, when we changed flights in Charlottesville for Charleston, West Virginia, we did not have to go through the security check-in area.

But it became a disturbing trip for me because I had never flown over southern West Virginia. I was appalled when I saw the devastation below from mountaintop removal. I even spotted the roads I had driven on to Charleston to see my sister. I realized that at least a fifty-foot swath of trees was left on each side of the mountain roads to cleverly disguise what was happening.

Our return flight was uneventful. By this time my husband had calmed down and expected the worst. He patronized the agents by offering to undress before he went through the security monitor if they would help him take off his shoes. But his sarcastic mood turned to despair when I could not find his Boy Scout knife under the used Kotex box. A cleaning lady told me everybody does that so it is the first place to look for items which might be valuable. She suggested the knife might not have been found if I placed it under a soda machine which no one cleaned under.

But never let it be said my husband doesn't appreciate some uniformed officials. While he had little use for the TSA agents, he stopped at the police barracks on the way home to tell the captain about the two fine officers who changed our tire.

Nightlights

We were sitting around the campfire along the Dead River in Maine when I noticed lights flickering on a distant mountain ridge. We had come here for whitewater canoe races along this wild river which had been used for generations to float logs out of the wilds of Maine. We had only seen a few houses on our forty-mile drive off the main road to this remote campsite.

The lights seemed to dance up and down the ridge and then move in a circle. Occasionally one spot of light would give off a nova-like explosion and then die down. At first we thought the lights were car headlights but it was a strange pattern even for a twisty mountain road. We also knew no vehicles had gone by our campsite and that the closest town was at least twenty miles east of us. The lights flickered strangely, too, like matches on a birthday cake that somebody was trying to blow out.

Even though we were planning to go to bed early to get a good rest for a whitewater competition which involved some twenty-five miles of wild water including a portage around a dam, my curiosity got the best of me. I suggested we check out the strange lights, pointing out there was a half-moon and that there must be a road leading up to the lights. Even though I was in the race and was told to save my energy, I did get my nature-loving girlfriend, who just came along to enjoy the outdoors, to go with me.

As a professor of American literature, Helen jokingly suggested it might be John Winthrop's vision for the Massachusetts Bay Colonists to become, in the wilderness they were about inhabit, a shining light of a city on the hill for the world to emulate.

It was dark, but there was enough light coming from the moon to follow the dirt road that led into the mountains where the lights were still blinking. There were deep ruts in the road and we guessed they probably came from logging trucks. To our relief and delight on this trip, we had not seen any all-terrain vehicles which we disliked as much as we did motorcycles and dirt bikes, not just because of the noise but also because of the reputation of some of the riders.

The center of the dirt road was fairly smooth, so we were able to keep an eye on the lights ahead. After each switchback turn, we got a better view of the lights and became even more curious when one of the lights going around in a circle went out. We decided it must be a torch someone was carrying. We had already noted there were no electricity poles in the area.

When we thought we heard voices, we started to get alarmed. Why would people be up here in the middle of the night carrying torches? If they were hikers, they would have flashlights and they would not be flickering. It was when we went around a clump of low-lying bushes that we came to a dead stop. We could see several silhouettes of naked men running around a huge mound. They were carrying torches. All of a sudden, a bonfire lit up. The men were throwing things into it. There were shrieks—but it was not just human screams. Some of the shrieks sounded like animals.

Then a flash of light lit up the path about a hundred yards ahead of us. It was moving toward us. One of the torch bearers had seen us. Immediately, we were on our way back on the dirt road as fast as we could go. Even though we wore tennis shoes, I could tell that there were now three torchers following us, but by the slapping of their feet, I could tell they were barefoot. When they hit a stone in the ruts, their cursing increased.

Still, we had a long way to go and they were yelling for the others to come. I began yelling, too, calling out the names of two guys from the campsite. I even yelled for them to bring the car to us. It worked because the torches came to a standstill. But we kept running even when they were not behind us. We arrived at the campsite exhausted but safe.

The next day after the race, our friends decided we should check out this shining city on the hill before going home. On the dirt road in, we saw a sign for the town dump which we had missed during the night. When we got there, we found a charred circle of ashes. At least four dozen rat tails, blackened and partially burned by the fire, were in the ashes. We looked up and saw several live rats scurrying around the garbage. When we reported the encounter to the local sheriff, he told us there had been reports of devil cults around there.

All my literature friend could say was Winthrop never envisaged cults like this. The puritans did believe there were devils, just not people who worshipped them.

And Thank You, Too

My lifestyle is such that I no longer carry handbags for three reasons.

First, I no longer wear makeup and my hair is short so there is no need for cosmetics, combs, or brushes, plus I no longer need a notebook, checkbook, or address book because I have a cell phone and a credit card.

Second, I have begun wearing a wrap-around belt pocket because it is easily accessible for cash and a cell phone and with me in it, it is hard for a thief to grab it.

Third, I save a lot of time not digging around in a purse.

However, what really cured me of carrying a purse was my last one which was given to me when I left GE headquarters for another job. Perhaps it was the champagne, but I was disgusted that the money they had collected had gone into an expensive Gucci purse. It was the last thing I needed at a manufacturing plant and I even had the bad manners to ask if they had the receipt.

This huge purse, with the Gucci logo embossed on bright red Italian leather, could be seen coming into view before I did. I tried to sell it but could find no buyers among my friends, so I began using it.

The next-to-last time I saw it was at the ski lodge in Stowe, Vermont. There were about forty of us partying in the fireplace room when the lodge chairman rang the bell for dinner in the next room. Most everyone knew each other. I didn't give it a second thought when I left the bag on the bar where I had been telling everyone I would rather have a season ski pass than that purse.

While we were eating, someone knocked on the entry

door which came directly into the fireplace room. My best friend's daughter, who was sitting next to the dining room door, got up to answer it. She came back in to ask tentatively if there was someone there named Shirley Goodwill. While all of us knew who she was, she did not know all of her mother or father's friends.

When she went back to tell the visitor there was no one there by that name, he was gone, and when we went back to the bar after dinner, so was my purse. We looked under all the cushions and cocktail tables for it, hoping it would appear in all its red glory, to no avail. We figured he was so impressed with the Gucci label, he had not bothered with a brown bag not far from where mine had been.

I reported it to the local police and the daughter gave a description of the young man who had asked for a Shirley Goodwill. They just shook their heads and said, "He even has the nerve to ask for the same person all the time." They explained that the perpetrator had probably cased all the ski lodges in the area and knew which ones he could take a chance on someone leaving a purse behind. So far he had successfully gotten eight purses with his scam of asking for someone when he realized the room was empty and people were eating.

I gave them my contact information but I could tell that they had greater crimes to investigate when they just suggested that I carry my purse with me at all times. I tried to get the *Stowe Reporter* to run a story about what was happening, but they ignored me. I was told they did not want tourists to have a bad impression of Stowe and that the police were quietly warning all the lodges to be on the lookout. I suggested the lodge owners must be taking their attitude of not wanting to scare away tourists because there had been eight other robberies.

Before I could get my credit cards canceled, the thief did get two tanks full of gas on my card. I had over $100 in cash and a winning lottery ticket I had not cashed for $20. I had to apply for a new driver's license and registration certificate. Worse was the fact that my car keys were in the purse and the spare with the magnetic lock behind the bumper was missing, probably in a snowbank I had trouble getting out of the week before. So I had to wait on my husband to drive three hours to bring the extra set.

Cursing myself as well as the thief, every time I went up there skiing I would stop by the police department for a report on their investigation. Someone had taken a picture of me when the purse was given to me, so I gave them that for identification. I was sure there were no fools in Vermont who would carry a bright red Gucci purse.

Then in the spring, I got a call from one of the cops, all of which I knew by name now. He said they had my purse. They found it near a utility pole where it had been thrown from the interstate highway. He said the minute he saw it peeking out of a melting snow pile, he knew what it was.

He told me my driver's license and registration were still in there along with a strange note. When I got there to retrieve it, I was even madder. The thief had even taken the frames from my new glasses and left the lenses in the bag. But what really made me mad was the note. It read: "Thanks for being so stupid."

I drove back home mad and it didn't help when my husband agreed that it was stupid to leave my purse unattended. But then when the next ski season was underway, I got a call from the Stowe policeman asking if I still had that note. I did. They had a suspect and wanted to give him a handwriting test.

When I arrived, they compared the note I had with the suspect's writing. It was the same. I was told he had little money so it would take a long time to get my money back. But I said I didn't care as long as they gave him a note I had written. It said: "And thank you for being so stupid."

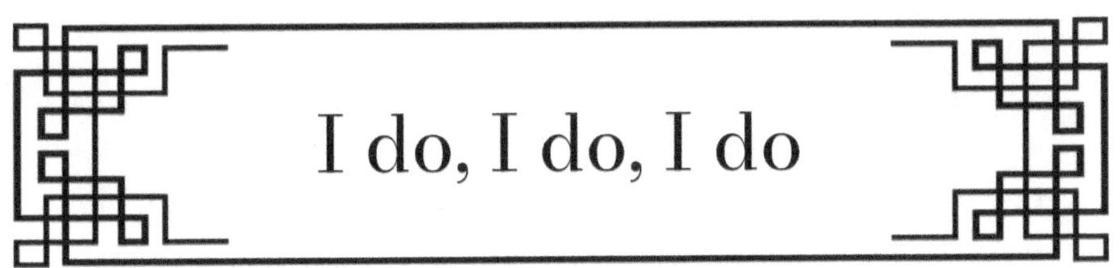

I do, I do, I do

Statistics today show if you wait a year or two, your relatives or friends with marriage-age children will be inviting you to see their dear daughter or son repeating their "I do's."

I can attest to statistics showing nearly half of marriages today end in divorce because there was a time when I averaged getting about five wedding invitations a year with three of them being repeats. In fact, I have seen one woman say her vows three times to a different guy, another one twice, and one of the guys three times.

If I get an invitation from the woman with the three-time record for a fourth wedding, I will probably step up with another gift, but this time it might be Darwin's book on "Selective Breeding." For the first two weddings, I checked off what she wanted from the list she had chosen at Bed Bath & Beyond and Macy's, a comforter and wine glasses. Evidently he was not a comfort and liked beer. I may have made a mistake at the third wedding by ignoring the gift list selection. I knew she liked gardening and gave her garden tools, one of which ended up in the back of her husband who she found cheating.

The gal that has been married twice in ten years may be prompted to marry again since she loves lavish weddings. What really bugged me was that her parents went along with it even though it meant they had to sacrifice their own middle-class lifestyle to give her the sendoff she wanted. The first wedding saw their daughter and her husband arriving from the church in a limousine and driving fifty miles for an ocean-front villa reception while her parents drove there in their twelve-year-old car.

The second wedding was more creative but just as expensive. It was held at a ski resort. This time, I knew the daughter's husband would have trouble skiing down the trail she had picked for their grand entrance to the lodge, so I gave them a complete first-aid kit. He used most everything in it at the reception.

As for the guy that got married three times in ten years, I wondered why I even went to his weddings. As a public relations director, he had a lot of photography friends and they were so active at the altar you could hardly see him and his bride saying their "I do's." By his second and third marriages, I had no problem selecting gifts for him. Fortunately, you can buy extra pages for the photography albums they sell today. I wonder what his first two wives did with their albums. Perhaps they feel his job was being too public with his relations business.

Still, their parents are my friends and I do refrain from commenting on the fact I do not get as many anniversary-celebrating invitations.

Then I think about my sister who celebrated her fifty-fifth wedding anniversary with her husband even though he was in an Alzheimer's unit at the time and is now gone. She fends for herself and has rejected several suitors looking for her nice home as well as companionship.

I remember her wedding well. It was in a small country church just two miles from our farm. As was the custom then, cameras were not allowed during the sacred ceremony. However, she did have a good friend with a new 8mm camera who must have been very unobtrusive that day filming us as we went into the church. I recalled this some forty years later when my mother died and I found the film strip in her jewelry box. Not knowing what it was, I told my sister I would send it to a lab to have it put on a VH tape. What a great surprise to see her friend had taken photos of us entering the church. There were my father and mother smiling behind my sister along with her husband's parents. And then there was me as the bridesmaid in a pink chiffon dress, fluffing it out as I went up the church steps behind them.

Then I remembered what happened to that dress. Back in those days, the rural thing to do was to tie tin cans to the car the wedding couple would be leaving in. My brother and I also marked the car windows with "Just Married" and rolled them down so they wouldn't see it. We knew that our engineer brother-in-law and my shy sister would immediately disconnect the tin cans.

I had just rolled down the final rear window when they came out of the church to leave for their honeymoon. They immediately spotted the tin cans and cut them loose. But when they abruptly took off, I did not realize the edge of my flowing chiffon bridesmaid dress got caught in the door. Unknown to them as they sped away, they disrobed me of my chiffon waist down, leaving me standing there in the silk undergarment. Everyone laughed as we saw the pink chiffon flowing along like an American flag behind their car.

When they got to their honeymoon destination at a bed and breakfast in the next county, my sister recognized the pink chiffon and called home to see if I was alright. I was. She had cleaned the windows of the car. But they did have the last laugh about my inadvertently coming up with a new way to send off the bride and groom. It was just one "I do" for them in a very happy life.

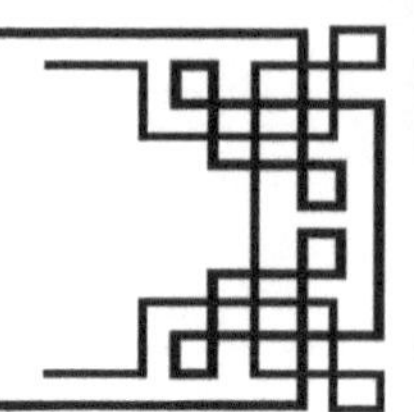

Has Anyone Seen My Robot?

Artificial Intelligence, cognitive science, systematic empirical observations, computational algorithms...words now being thrown around by my step-grandson, Nicholas, who for the first time in his life is excited about something as he seeks a degree in cognitive philosophy. As best as I can tell among all the jargon he expounds, it is a study of the mind and the more I learn about it the more it concerns me.

In his attempts to explain cognitive philosophy, he tells me about an early, very basic Turing test in which a real person and a robot were placed in a room and asked questions by a judge who was unable to identify which one was answering.

After questioning the mental capacity of this judge, I asked Nicholas if this meant there were jobs for philosophy majors in these tough economic times...that perhaps he could build robots. He gave me another lecture on how cognitive philosophy could unlock the mind. I suggested psychiatry with a quick correction from him that psychiatry was only a study of emotions, not intelligence. But he felt the expertise of both could be used by robotic engineers.

Nicholas tells me about a $3 million National Science grant awarded to the University of California where they are building a robot "whose sensors and actuators approximate the levels of complexity of human infants." Called "Project One," the group recently bought a robot with skin-like rubber that looks like Einstein. When it answers questions or tells jokes, its mouth, eyebrows, penetrating eyes, and other features reflect its emotion. A trial robot wearing a jaunty orange Harley Davidson bandanna and New Balance sneakers had already endeared itself to kids. Project One, with advanced Einstein digital cameras, will be able to visually sense what your kid is feeling by the expression on his or her face, be it anger, frustration, glee, crying fits, boredom, and so forth. It is programmed to say just the right things to rid your kid of the tears and tantrums.

Most important, the robot, with its artificial neural network, will actually learn what not to do with a troublesome child by eliminating ineffective responses and using others that work. It will even be able to remember partial responses that are acceptable against those that are not. No, the social robots will not change diapers, but they will free you of having to entertain or educate your children. They will be the perfect playmate, sharing toys and not fighting and constantly educating and solving problems for your child. More advanced robots are in the planning stages to help adults with their emotional problems, thus saving millions in psychiatry fees. These sensory-sensing robots can also be used as security guards, able to quickly identify the intent of the intruder and either calling 911 with a photo of the intruder or dealing with the situation as requested by the owner, such as using mace.

This is not the first time that artificial intelligence has boggled my mind. Twenty-five years ago when I was working at GE, the CEO was salivating over the prospect of advanced factory automation and not having to deal with factory workers who asked for raises and required lunch and restroom breaks. Numerical controlled machines were already machining parts to the precision of a Swiss watch and robotic arms reached out to drill holes in passing parts on the assembly line, only missing if the object did not arrive at the precise time.

The push to develop voice-entry robots came right after some executives attended a national computer show held in Hawaii. They had been impressed when a robot asked them their name and in a monotone voice announced their titles and then reached around in a bin and handed them special perks like a Rolex watch or a Tiffany ornament, depending on their rank. Even when one of the wives, who had used her husband's name tag to come into the show, had become enraged when the computer handed her a pass entitling her to an escort service that evening, they were still enthusiastic.

Voice-entry robots would enable CEOs to easily double their stock options by eliminating thousands of repetitive jobs in the factory. In fact, all they would really need was one inspector on each line to tell the robot what to do. The huge major appliance plant in Louisville was the place to start. They sent word down to the engineers to have a robot on the refrigerator line ready by the Kentucky Derby.

I remember the engineers trying to explain that having a robot understand humans was quite different than a robot doing the talking; that the Hawaiian robot actually read their name tag. Developing a voice entry system so the inspector could tell the robot what to do would require the robot to understand at least fifty words. A bottleneck was at the paint station—if a part was not painted properly, the robot would have to be told to lift it off the assembly line and move it to the correct bin. There were eight different bins and lines connected to the paint station.

The executives showed up in the factory after the last race and the lead engineer gave the commands. The robot did exactly as it was told. One executive interrupted the process to tell the robot it was doing a great job. It shut down and had to be restarted. Everyone laughed as the engineer explained it was not programmed for compliments. But when the inspector on the line, who had recently completed his Americanization classes at the plant, took over, the robot could not understand his broken English. It would not let anything go down the line. A New York traffic jam paled in comparison. The backup caused the automatic painting machine to belch out gallons of white paint.

I also remembered back in the 70s, the federal government

mandated all of the company's benefit booklets be written to an eighth-grade level to assure all employees understood their ERISA regulation rights. Corporate Benefits was revising the Retirement Plan booklet and were told it had to pass their computer reading test. They tried five times submitting the booklet to their reading machine and were turned down. Finally, it was suggested because I was from West Virginia (yes, stereotypes prevail) maybe I could get it approved.

I remembered how a former limo driver had been demoted to janitor after running out of gas. He told me he immediately applied for a GE pension. Then it hit us. "Pension" is a two-syllable word; "retirement" had three syllables. I changed a couple of "retirements" to sentences made up of single-syllable words like "when you leave work" or "at the end of your work days." I got it down to the seventh-grade level. In the meantime, our budget for producing the booklets had tripled. But the government's reading robot was happy.

Yes, there have been many advances in factory and office robots since my experience twenty-five years ago. I must admit how much I like my Roomba vacuum cleaner which has no bags and tells me when to dump it. It is just a little flat cylinder that eventually makes its way from room to room and if it senses a pile of dirt, it keeps circling and sucks it up until it is gone. I show it off to all of my friends while we are playing cards—even though it did embarrass me when it would not come out from under my bed for nearly twenty minutes.

Nevertheless, I fear these new self-learning humanoid robots could cause more problems than those original voice-entry, Lego-looking metal stick figures from twenty-f ive years ago.

My grandson assured me they would be more capable because once everything was understood about the human mind, the possibilities were limitless.

That night I fell into a restless sleep thinking about it all, or "being cognitive," as my grandson likes to say. I imagined what it would be like if the babysitting robot became friends with the security robot. If these new robots learn from their own experience, maybe they can learn from each other. What if the babysitting robot ran out of soothing solutions for an angry child? What if his next choice came from the security robot and he decided that macing the kid was the next option?

My dreamlike state led to an awful nightmare. My grandson's image entering the classroom to take his philosophy of the mind course kept reoccurring in my dream. There was something different about Nicholas. Then it hit me. Is it possible? Am I looking at a robot? After all, he is now getting straight As after spending years just getting by.

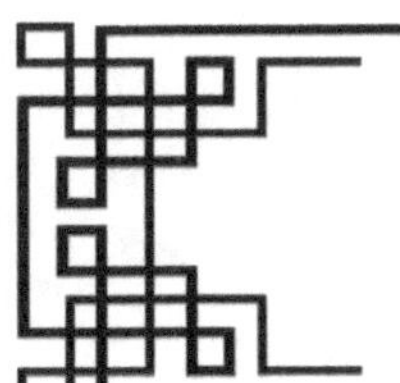

PR & Profits
at Any Cost

For the first time in forty years, I stepped back into the class-room...this time as a guest speaker. The history professor had asked me to address her class on why I did not feel Jack Welch was the most admired CEO in the world.

She knew I had written a play called *Gold Collars* which had been mentioned in a book by Thomas F. O'Boyle titled *At Any Cost: Jack Welch, General Electric, and the Pursuit of Profit.*

The history students had been studying the age of the robber barons followed by the formation of unions and McCarthyism. The question before them was analyzing statistical data from the 80s and 90s showing the rich had been getting richer while the middle class was shrinking and the poor getting poorer. The history students knew that during this time Jack Welch had been voted the most admired CEO in the world year after year. In their economics class they had learned that GE stock had outpaced the Gross National Product by a factor of 2 to 1 since 1981 when Welch became the CEO of GE. That professor had exposed them to two books written on Welch extolling his leadership abilities and financial wizardry.

I held up Thomas F. O'Boyle's book and none of them had heard of it. I asked them if they knew the writers of the books they had been reading in their economics class and several said they assumed they were business writers. I then informed them that one of the authors worked at GE's advertising firm and the other was a former speechwriter. One student did laugh and recall that one of the authors had stated how thrilled he had been riding in Welch's twin engine helicopter so that had caused him to wonder about the objectivity.

I started out by telling them why they had not heard of O'Boyle's book. Thomas F. O'Boyle was a business writer who had followed the tradition of other *Wall Street Journal* reporters who kept a watchful eye on abuses of free enterprise and business ethics. He had noticed that GE's name was often coming up for questionable pricing practices, particularly in government and international business. First there was the price fixing charge with De Beers in the artificial diamond business, then the distorted time cards on a government defense project in Philadelphia, then the sale of aircraft engines in which money changed hands but were not built.

O'Boyle's investigation led him to surmise that either Welch knew about these violations or put so much pressure on his managers that they took shortcuts to meet his demands for profits. O'Boyle began interviewing retirees and employees in various GE plants across the country for information about how the company was being run and how they felt about it. It wasn't until the manuscript was at a major printing house that the GE legal staff found out about it. Soon those who had been interviewed had to sign statements that they made comments that didn't jive with the company's public relations reports. I was one of those and did not feel threatened by GE lawyers because I had no family and very little money so what could they do to me? I had recently started receiving a pension and did check that out with my lawyer, who assured me the company would not be able to easily rescind that. But others I knew were afraid for their jobs and their families and withdrew their statements. O'Boyle himself was obviously under heavy pressure and his bravery in gathering facts took their toll. What was left of his book was not published for five years because of Welch threats, and he was able to get a new job at the *Pittsburgh Press*. Some said his leaving the *Wall Street Journal* had to do with an investment house sale Dow was making to GE Capital.

It was disappointing to see the quiet PR war set against

the book. All the major business magazines panned it as either superficial or not interesting...one even wrote off the business violations exposed in it as old "business as usual" news with no apology for the statement. It had become apparent that Welch had made corporate greed acceptable...including his own obscene salary—up to and occasionally over $150 million a year he made in salary, bonuses, and stock options.

Worse, other CEOs were jumping on the Fortune 500 list to compete for the title of richest and highest paid man in the world. It was not enough just to collect expensive toys. As MBAs, most of them had never felt the joy and satisfaction of designing, building, or manufacturing a product or service. Their only pleasure seemed to come from making money on money.

Therefore, profits came at any cost. Every rock was turned over to find cost savings, often at the expense of quality. Technology was sold to the highest bidder without regard for the competitive edge it gave American workers who developed it. Basic research was eliminated and only applied research mostly supported by government funding was allowed and then sold.

For the first ten years of Welch's reign, he made good on his promise to lay off 25,000 workers each year, which was music to the ears of Wall Street security analysts. Some companies even faked layoffs because the stock would go up on the news based on what was good for GE was good for the gold collars.

I got a quizzical look from the students about gold collars. I explained to the class that a new class had developed in GE. In the old days, the factory worker had been called blue collar, the women pink collars, and the office and technical people white collars. Starting with the Reagan administration, industrial unions soon found themselves in the no-protection zone as the airport controllers had found in their strike. Don't expect any help from the NLRB; in fact, I was at GE headquarters at the time it was announced we could start promoting programs to decertify unions.

Thus, without the balance of power a union can exert for the rights of workers, Welch was free to pursue profits at any cost and became the hero of Wall Street. He never failed to make the numbers he promised. When he took over GE it was the most diversified company in the world. He could sell a technology or business, or buy one to sell it off, to make sure the numbers were met. He became a one-man show. After getting rid of five group executives, he had an average of some 1,500 "lieutenants" working for him who would end up being most of the 15,000 GE people he boasted he had made into millionaires on GE stock. They not only walked his talk or walked the plank but so did his Board of Directors, who got paid some $250,000 for each meeting. To further assure their loyalty all they had to do to get a piece of the company's pension plan was attend four meetings a year for a minimum of five years. For life they would get $50,000 while people in plants like Schenectady where I worked who had worked forty-five and even fifty years and had retired in the 70s were struggling on pensions as low as $4,800 a year because there was no automatic cost-of-living. It was ludicrous when Welch glibly suggested they should have invested in GE stock. Their wages were so low they had little extra money, if any. Moreover, they were living in a community that saw 35,000 jobs disappear during Welch's reign as he moved them off-shore or to Mexico to take advantage of lower wages and less strict environmental regulations.

Kurt Vonnegut's first book was *Player Piano* in which he felt robots would take over manufacturing jobs. Reg Jones, CEO before Welch, had introduced a huge "Factory of the Future" investment program to automate U.S. plants to be more competitive worldwide. But Welch cancelled this and sold off businesses and technology to finance short-term GE capital to make money on money. Vonnegut did not realize that Welch also found third-world labor cheaper than robots.

The students—well aware that the company was also expending exorbitant funds to fight the PCB cleanup of the Hudson River rather than clean them up—asked if I thought PCBs were harmful and that dredging would actually cause more damage than it would prevent. We still cannot turn on the radio or TV, open mail, or even drive down the road without being exposed to GE's protests. Their best ploy had been to make the public realize they were not scientists and yet scientists were saying dredging was a mistake. One of the environmental testers GE had hired for this evidence even did business under the name of "Independent Laboratories." I, too, disclaimed any scientific knowledge but asked them to look at it like GE did—at the bottom line only. I then quoted Kurt Vonnegut who had been quoted saying that in the old days GE simply would have cleaned up the mess and gone on about their business. I then asked them what motive the EPA had for backing other environmentalists who said PCBs were harmful.

We discussed our governor's reason—even though he is a pro-business Republican governor—for supporting the EPA. Some thought he was tired of being blackmailed into giving GE tax reductions if they would stay in New York to find they continued to vacate the state. Another suggested there would be lots of jobs created to dredge the Hudson. Others commented that small business was tired of making up for the fact GE got reduced utility rates because of their size and year after year had won sizable tax concessions from cities they were doing business with their threats to leave if they didn't comply. Also, GE had gotten many grants for retraining employees and site improvements but failed to re-invest in the community. Such drastic reduction in employees and tax concessions had resulted in not just Schenectady having 80% of its downtown boarded up but that scenario was being repeated in cities across the U.S. that had once thrived with re-investments by GE. Therefore, maybe Pataki, who was from the lower Hudson region area where the fishing industry had been destroyed, knew he had public support from the silent majority.

The questions the students had were ones they asked each other as well as me. Was the middle class being destroyed by Welch and other gold collars? Would the public sector be the only middle class? How long would it be before they lost their clout? Are we heading for another robber baron age? Do we have to repeat history over again? Will we one day have a CEO like Henry Ford who decides he will have to pay the workers more because he needs them to buy his cars? Or will that day be much further into the future? How long will it take workers in undeveloped countries to keep from being exploited? Is that why big business is resisting any rules in the World Trade Organization that would include rights for workers and environmental rules? Big business talks about an equal playing field but they don't want across-the-board rules in working rights and environmental protection. What is free enterprise? Should big business get billions in tax-free grants on the premise they are building jobs while small business has to deal with the un-level playing field given them?

And then, as the class was ending, the final question we all had to consider was: What could we do about it? As a history class, they realized one could learn more about the effects of economics by studying trends. They decided that all CEOs should be forced to take a history course. Someone mentioned that they had just read that Harvard was re-instituting a history course as part of an MBA program, so maybe they were realizing the need for it.

As to the question of why everyone knew about all the books praising Welch but nothing about the one which went to the grass roots for a look, the class was in a quandary. We were victims of appearance versus reality. With today's major media controlled by big business and many of its anchors becoming billionaires themselves, we had a major problem separating appearance from reality.

Education, we decided, was the answer—perhaps a new course on Appearance versus Reality or Actions versus Reality.

Added note: Welch ended up getting the highest golden parachute of over $417 million when he retired. GE as a company will no longer exist after 2024. Recent books detailing GE's demise are *Lights Out: Pride, Delusion, and the Fall of General Electric* by Thomas Gryta and Ted Mann in 2020; *The Man Who Broke Capitalism: How Jack Welch Gutted the Heartland and Crushed the Soul of Corporate America—and How to Undo His Legacy* by David Gelles in 2022; and *Power Failure: The Rise and Fall of an American Icon* by William D. Cohan in 2023, which has two major errors. It was Reg Jones—not his successor Jack Welch—who started the Factory of the Future program and came up with the GE slogan "We Bring Good Things to Life." Ironically, Welch's activity was 180 degrees different. But Cohan was right about Welch's successor Jeff Immelt being a lot like Welch.

Righting Wrongs

Being an activist came naturally to me. I guess I have to blame or attribute it to my mother. While she was always law-abiding, there were times when she felt the government needed to be "corrected."

Maybe the feeling started when her own parents during the 20s had been sympathetic to a couple of moon-shining families. Their breadwinner dad was taken away by federal agents during prohibition. Then, there were no social services to help the destitute wives and children. So everyone pitched in to help. At the same time, people with political power were making fortunes importing liquor and building huge ocean-front homes.

My mother became active after a devastating flood in 1936. It took out a bridge across our part of the South Branch of the Potomac. It was then the Army Corps of Engineers started taking an interest in our valley.

Several Potomac River Basin studies were commissioned to determine where dams should be put on the Potomac River to provide flood control for the growing Washington, D.C. The South Branch of the Potomac was a major feeder. Our valley, surrounded by mountains and hollows, became a preferred choice.

The population of our valley was still low because it was full of small farmers. It was settled in 1740 and most of us were related. Thus, without a powerful lobby group or population, it looked like the dam project might happen. Our farms and homes would be underwater. The town clerk even started alerting everyone that some federal government employees and politicians were buying up a lot of mountain land cheap.

One of them had told her he planned to operate a marine on the lake created by the dam.

This, of course, fed into even more anti-government sentiment as the years and threats went by. But with World War II and then Korean War going on, there was not enough money to cover the cost of dam building in our valley. As my mother put it: "We provided enough sons to fight those wars, so back off on destroying our livelihoods."

The next threat to our existence came in 1967 when Stewart L. Udall was Secretary of the Interior. His promotion of the Wild and Scenic Rivers program was admirable. For us it was just a case of "not in our backyard." We would not have a backyard if it was so designated. Because our valley is narrow, a scenic river with a lot of land around it to be pristine, there would be no room left for farming.

When Udall showed up to "sell" the program, it was my mother who took him on at the meeting in the fire hall. He began by showing maps with great landscaping symbols designating picnic and boat-launching sites and scenic views. He made his mistake when he told my mother she was being selfish because such a beautiful river should be preserved and accessible to the general public. She came up with her own hand-drawn map of all the campsites already located along the river as well as the state-owned boat-launching site. She explained farmers rented out campsites at very reasonable prices. She even knew of several farmers who would let them go to the river for free if they helped them pick sweet corn or other produce for sale. Moreover, she declared, "Farmers don't allow people to trash the area like they do at public parks." She suggested Udall add some trash barrels to his colorful green maps.

Again, it ended up that another war, this one in Viet Nam, saved us from losing our livelihood in the valley. The Wild Rivers project was cancelled. We were particularly happy about it because our original farmhouse—with a French and

Indian fort still intact—was designated as suitable for a ranger's station on Udall's map. Today, it is my home.

Even though the anti-government sentiment is strong in our valley, some of us do realize the value of programs like the National Historic Register. Many valley homes have qualified for this designation, including the fort. Today, this may save our valley from being flooded or designated as public space. But we do need other protections such as zoning to prevent commercial development.

Having farmland taxed for its value as commercial use has resulted in many family farmers disappearing across the country. Fortunately, various federal and state legislation now allow reduced assessments for agricultural zoning.

But the day of reckoning came for us when inheritance taxes were based on commercial land value. The valley is not that far from Washington. Many sons of farmers like my brother ended up driving a truck as a career because all of the farm machinery had to be sold just to pay the taxes. Today, many family farmers designate one land inheritor because too many heirs can also break up a farm. Because of the high cost of nursing homes, many farmers have to turn their farms over to their heirs within a certain number of years so Medicaid will pay the monthly costs—which average about $9,000 a month now.

Having benefitted from not having to pay commercial rates, one would think farmers would support zoning that would not allow commercial development on agriculture land. But the distrust of government still prevails.

This inaction caused our valley to face another crisis in 2009 when the American Recovery and Reinvestment Act was passed totaling $831 billion. Investment in renewable energies to offset our need for fossil fuels included a mandate that all gas contain 10% ethanol. Waste-to-energy plants were high on the list because they would reduce demand for landfills. It was then we found out that our valley was targeted for a twenty-acre building which would burn waste from New England, including New York city. By burning it at temperatures over 4,000 degrees, it was stated it could handle all waste, including medical. The result would be a high-grade diesel fuel which would allow jets to meet the 10% edict for alternative fuel.

Over $300 million was allocated to fund this plant. Unfortunately, we had a farmer who was going bankrupt. He was promised several million dollars for land worth about $500,000. Even more money was promised to the railroad owner to upgrade tracks for 2,500 carloads of trash coming in each day. The fire department would get new equipment. The farmer and his family were also offered management positions after the sale.

A new company had been formed. It even got added minority status financial advantages to run this business. What they hadn't counted on was not just the anti-government sentiment among the populace, but the fact that the locals were not idiots. West Virginia probably has more retired chemists than most states. Some of them led the fight on the technical capability of such a plant. It was based on unproven Japanese technology. In fact, the only two examples of such a plant were one in Italy which had blown up and another in Germany that failed the first year.

At a public meeting, it became apparent the new company officers had no background in technology. They could not answer questions on its feasibility or safety. They even ludicrously suggested a plane could be sent from a nearby air force base to cover the twenty-acre building with foam in case it overheated.

Townspeople pointed out the plant would only be two miles from the school system. Those using the river recreationally and commercially questioned water quality. The new officers could not answer questions about air or water quality because the technology had not been proven.

Even though those who would benefit from the influx of such money were doing all they could to promote it, we were lucky our local county government consisted of only three commissioners. They were related to many of the farmers as well as townspeople. They had to weigh the economic pros against the environmental cons. All of them lived in the area so that was a plus. Thousands of new jobs were being promised in their ads. That argument was lost when it was pointed out these would be for the trash collectors in NYC and New England. It would only take a few people to run the high-tech plant. Then they argued there would be well-paying jobs of constructing the plant. Additional money was offered to the railroad and fire department.

It became obvious we needed a petition to sway the commissioners. Even though my primary residence was in New York State, I hurried home that summer to help. Because I came from a long line of farmers since the valley was settled, I volunteered to get the signatures of farmers. Like the others, I was related to the one needing to sell, but I lived in New York, so I could take the heat. The majority of the county taxpayers were farmers, so this list had a good effect on the commissioners.

When I went into a huge riverside trailer park hoping to fill up several petition sheets, I had been stunned to find out I would only get few signatures. First, I was told the plant would provide jobs, and second, their trailers along the river were above the proposed plant site so their water would still be good. I found myself arguing with one guy who said he wanted the job because it would only take a year to build. He could get unemployment after that. I added that note to my petition list.

Two things were in our favor. The federal project had listed this type of project must be approved by year-end; we needed to hold things up past this date. We had also aroused the residents to the harm this project could cost them in the long run. The commissioners waited to rule late. There was always a fear of eminent domain such as what we had when the flood project was considered. In any case, time ran out and our valley was saved.

My mother, who had died in 2001, would have certainly approved of my part in "righting this wrong." She had been aware of my activism as soon as I left home. When I went to the other end of the state to attend West Virginia University, I quickly resented the preferential treatment given to students who could afford to join sororities and fraternities. It cost more to be in a sorority or fraternity than the costs of getting a degree. So the result was a caste system with privileges.

Fortunately, we had a journalism professor, Paul Atkins, who made us see the bigger picture. Independents could not run for student government offices so we needed to sit on the University President's lawn until we were allowed to run candidates. As Atkins pointed out, we could win because independents actually outnumbered affiliated students four to one. However, many students intent on getting degrees did not care—particularly agriculture and forestry students. But those students on the GI bill from the Korean War did, so we got a lot of support there.

As journalism students, we had our own press, the *Daily Athenaeum*, to point out the unfairness of the system. One of the sororities made the mistake of thinking I would take the money I needed. All I had to do was not run for student legislature. They soon regretted putting that in writing. Ironically it was this sorority that a great aunt of mine had been a member of when farming had been profitable.

We even crashed the Panhellenic Homecoming float parade with our own wagon loaded with a beer keg, which was particularly popular with the Korean War vets. We called ourselves "Beatniks" back then as we "righted wrongs" through sit-downs. Again, it was Professor Atkins who was especially pleased when the School of Journalism was designated as the publisher of the annual Mountaineer yearbook, not the most powerful fraternity on campus.

When I got a job at GE after graduation in 1960, I was to find that I would be in a fight for equality my entire career. Atkins had gotten me a summer job at the *Wheeling News-Register* between my junior and senior year. I was about to take a permanent job there for $70 a week when the *GE News* editor in Schenectady offered me $90 a week. Even though my sister Decker, who had graduated four years before me, had been a big help and I had lots of student jobs, I still had a bank loan of over $1,500. So I took the job.

When I got there, the editor's boss, Hal Reed, decided that since I was from the backward state of West Virginia, I probably didn't need it. He lowered it to $80 a week. He told me I was lucky to have a professional job. Then I was informed I would have to punch a clock like the secretaries because they would be offended if they saw another woman not having to check in and out. I was soon to find out many secretaries were making more than I was.

When I replaced the assistant editor and then the editor, I was taken off the clock. Being on the clock meant you were paid for overtime. I had racked up so much time doing three jobs, I nearly doubled my salary. Still I never reached the editor's pay. During 1964-65 when Schenectady GE was battling the unions in a "Make Schenectady Campaign" to lower factory wages by getting rid of piecework and paying everyone the same, I wrote and edited the weekly *GE News*. It had a circulation of 45,000 area employees and retirees. I was ordered to take my name off as editor. I was told "factory workers would not read it if they knew a woman was writing it."

That got resolved when I remembered my father's advice to look for a manager who had a daughter my age. He turned out to be the plant's head lawyer, Emil Peters. He had to approve the *GE News* each week because the National Labor

Relations Board was watching GE closely to assure fair communications with employees. I noticed a photo of his daughter graduating from college.

The lawyer first came to my aid when I got caught with a
fake in-plant pass. Because I was so low-paid, I was not eligible for in-plant parking. Extra hours were spent getting rides
or hiking around the 300-acre plant to get stories. Getting a
final approval on the *GE News* on a Thursday night often went
into midnight. The final deadline was 3 a.m. to make delivery on Friday morning. The printer was several miles away.
It amused the linotype operators that the state of New York
required women who had to work past midnight to be accompanied. So the company had to pay a "sitter" to go with me
who got more pay.

The typesetters decided it was dangerous for me to walk
through the dark parking lots into the plant at night. They
duplicated a pass I "borrowed." Peters just shook his head
when I told him the head of security was going to have me
fired. He agreed it was ridiculous for me to cover the news in
the huge plant on foot and it was not a good idea to hitch
rides with battery truck operators. So when I said I knew two
guards on the morning and night shift who would be grateful
for hot coffee in the winter and milkshakes in the summer,
he just laughed. I continued to use the pass when they were
there. My next problem was where to park. Because Peters'
office building was nearby, he just looked the other way when
I showed up with a fake "reserved plate" for M. Kuykendall. I
put it beside his and the Vice President of the Steam Turbine
Division.

Peters also did me a huge favor when I complained they
would not let me have my name on the paper as editor because
my bosses were afraid the blue collars would not read it. He
quickly notified my bosses that not having a nameplate on a
publication that had a U.S. mailing (10,000 in this case) was
a violation of the law. Then he told me to run the nameplate

with my full name on it. He would make sure I was not fired. Sure enough, they tried to get me to use my initials instead, but he pointed out past editors had their full name on the *GE News*. So I told them they had to deal with the lawyer. They backed down.

Peters also proved useful when I showed him I had paid for a speeding ticket in Pennsylvania and they had sent me another. He called the governor. I often wondered what happened to that trooper or judge.

But driving in the plant finally got resolved when I left the *GE News* for a job as a newsletter editor for the newly-formed Medium Motor and Generator Department. It had a circulation of around 4,000. People couldn't believe I had taken a lesser job. But what they didn't know was it paid more. Its new general manager, Bob Smith, was only a high school graduate who started out as an electrician. He had gotten to this position in an era when "proven capabilities" got you ahead as well as college degrees. He had been impressed when I did interviews with ten other general managers about the state of their industrial and power generation businesses. He checked the salaries of other department newsletter editors and matched it—which was $4,000 more than what I had been paid working three jobs.

It turned out to be my best job for a future career as a speechwriter. Smith was brilliant at technology and manufacturing but weak in communicating his business strategies and challenges. He soon had me sitting in on all of his meetings with his manufacturing, engineering, finance, and marketing staff. I became well informed first-hand about the business and was able to write speeches and business reports for him.

At the time, he had resisted hiring a costly employee relations unit which was required in all departments. Instead, he farmed out the hiring and compensation work to the small motor and generator department to save money. He fended off the plant-wide employee relations manager by pretending to be hiring a manager. Part of this delay was assigning me to fix up an office for what would be my boss. I enjoyed reporting this "progress" to the plant manager who had so long underpaid me. In fact, I did such a good job finding fancy furniture for this office at such a good cost, Smith took the furniture for himself and sent his to the "new office." He got away with this for two years.

But my real joy at the time came when he solved my ongoing problem of driving legally in the plant. I told him about an old GE car I had seen in the plant dump. He immediately had interplant trucking get it running again even though it was rusty with many dents. Now I had a company car to drive back and forth. But I did get a heads-up from Peters to not to park it near the plant relations manager, who was complaining about its appearance.

Things improved discrimination-wise when GE was one of five companies charged in 1972 for across-the-board discrimination by the federal Equal Employment Office. I and a black woman landed as the new tokens at headquarters in Connecticut. Again, it was a long fight for recognition and better pay, but I was much more upset by the change in CEO philosophy. Paternalism was not the greatest for women. But profits at any cost by greedy CEOs affected everyone's jobs, particularly in the future. All of this is better described in my book *Rebuilding the GE House Jack Welch Blew Down.*

But my fights for equal pay pale compared to Helen Quirini, a motor winder, who taught me a lot about negotiations. I first met her when I had run an article on the first woman foreman and she came in the office and said I needed to see what was really going on, that the woman was a company "plant" to report on union activity. She invited me down to the motor assembly lines where I saw rows and rows of women winding motor coils and then she took me to a building next door where men were doing the same. She pointed out the men got $1 more an hour even though the women, known for being more dexterous with their hands, outproduced the men. How was this legal? She pointed out that a stator at each end of the line which weighed 50 pounds was to be picked up at the end of the shift. New York State, at the urging she said of GE, had passed a law that women should not have to lift anything heavier than 40 pounds. Lifting the stator had absolutely nothing to do with the coil winding work. But it allowed GE to pay $1 less an hour to the women.

We became friends and not long after I accompanied her to the New York State legislature building in Albany where we met a maid from Long Island who was trying to get Social Security rights for full-time maids. Helen and the maid exchanged roles to prevent direct retribution. Helen, as the maid, made her case when one of the Hampton women said they were kind to their maids and in fact, she took hers to the Caribbean and other places on vacation. Helen, as the maid, pointed out that this was done so she could take care of the kids while she had to send her own kids to a relative to keep. The maid, posing as Helen, made her point quickly by bringing barbells that were over 40 pounds each and effortlessly lifting them and challenging the legislators to try doing it, too.

Years later, I was to read Helen's testimony when she had been brought up before the McCarthy hearings as a communist. Helen had started out in the United Electrical Workers union which allowed women and blacks, unlike the International Union of Electrical Workers. GE and the IUE declared the UE union had been infiltrated by the communists. Professor Zahabi at SUNY Albany had gotten the transcripts through the Freedom of Information Act. The committee had finally decided Helen was truthful when she said all she was fighting for was equal pay. They came to this conclusion when they asked if she knew Karl Marx and she said, "No, who is he? I don't think I have ever met the gentleman.' Helen had passed away at this point but I know she would have gotten a charge out of reading the hearing testimony. I always remember Helen supporting the women who were burning bras in the 70s to raise awareness. Helen always brought this up as a good negotiation tactic with GE, noting that starting with an extreme brought a better middle settlement.

Yes, as busy as I was with GE, I had time for what I considered social obligations or righting wrongs. During the early 80s, when I was back working in Schenectady, I was living in the ballroom of an old Campbell mansion estate. It is where Tom Edison arranged for the purchase of the nearby Jones Car Work property to establish the Edison Machine Works which became GE. The estate was owned by Ed Cammarato, who had turned the many horse and carriage stables into apartments. He lived in the main house and rented big rooms such as the ballroom to me. You entered through huge double doors to face a huge fireplace and look up to a carved medallion ceiling. One corner of it was turned into a john and kitchen. I was soon to find out he was going to sell the property to Wilmorite for a mall. City and town folks were concerned because salt and other runoff would affect the huge water aquifer below.

It became a battle to save the aquifer because Wilmorite was promising lots of jobs in construction, as well as permanent retail store jobs. The town supervisor was anxious to chalk up more tax revenue. The city's newspaper, the *Schenectady Gazette*, desired ad revenue from Wilmorite's many stores.

Because of its impact on the aquifer, New York state officials mandated hearings. Some twenty-two organizations were approved to attend the hearings. It was heavily loaded with pro-Wilmorite organizations which could financially benefit. To join the environmental groups, I formed the Campbell Avenue Tenants Association by submitting a signed petition of twenty-four other renters living in those horse and carriage houses turned into apartments.

Wilmorite was not just a tough component with its promise of taxes and jobs; it also threw lots of free parties at a local bar and restaurant for its supporters. Among these was a reporter, Carl Strock, from the *Gazette*. One of my first confrontations with him at one of the hearings involved a prediction that he would be working as head of PR for Wilmorite in five years. I had already outraged the *Gazette* owners when I was placing an ad for the environmentalists. I noticed that a same-size political ad by Wilmorite was $10 cheaper. I made a copy of it when the ad person was not looking and sent it to NBC's *60 Minutes* program with information on the threat to the aquifer. When an NBC producer asked the *Gazette* about it, I was quickly summoned by one of their owners, Jack Hume, a lawyer and Strock. Having had experience with lawyers before, I challenged them to go public with my supposed theft to see who would prevail in public opinion. They angrily dismissed me. As for Strock, I said I would apologize five years later if he did not have a job with Wilmorite *(which I did five years later when he was still a columnist and we became friends because he was a good writer exposing police and other corruption).*

Obviously things were not going well with my landlord either. He did not want to lose the sale. He tried to evict me but I had a lease which I took to the attorney general. Then one day I got a notice from the post office that I had violated the law by putting fliers in mailboxes detailing concerns about polluting the aquifer. My landlord had hired a local video producer to film me at the boxes. The local post officer was disgusted. He tried to help me by declaring he was sure there was a very old law mandating U.S. flags should be on all boxes, but he didn't have to do the research when I sent him a photo of the landlord putting rent notices in boxes without postage.

Probably the only time I was scared was when I put out a notice inviting everyone to join me on a bicycle ride to carry bottles of pure water from the aquifer to the town hall. Rumor had it that the town hall supervisor had personally benefited as a supporter of Wilmorite, so we wanted to point out his lack of integrity.

Two days before the ride, I was threatened by a construction union member asking if I wanted to be responsible for anything happening to the bikers. He was calling drunk from one of the bars where Wilmorite held its parties. I told him the press would be covering the bike ride and they had cameras. We went ahead with it and no one was hurt—just yelled at. But after that I was careful about taking bike rides by myself.

Wilmorite ultimately won with its promise to build barricades to prevent runoff water to reach the aquifer. The barricades failed twice and today, with the area saturated with malls, the Wilmorite one is for sale. The only thing left of the historic mansion is the old family graveyard which they were forced to fence next to the vacant Sears store.

My biggest disappointment was the *60 Minute*'s producer telling me to let them know when the aquifer was polluted. They would carry the story.

An earlier righting of a wrong was a lot more peaceful because I had political backing to assure I would not get in any legal trouble. It occurred when I first came to Schenectady. I was living first in an apartment in the historic stockade section. The Dutch had been early settlers there trading with the Native Americans for beaver pelts. It had become such a tourist attraction that Judge Quinn and a developer decided they wanted to put a motel in the middle of the area. The best way to combat this was to get the district designated on the historic register. Because my last name was Dutch, the owner of a 1660 home, Lydia Van Shanklin, asked me to be one of her hostesses during the annual open house events. She had a brother, Clark Wemple, a lawyer who was in the state legislature. She and other owners were rightfully fearful the area would be commercialized.

A petition was needed to apply to the historic officials. The problem was the judge lived there as well as lawyers who feared his wrath. So getting signatures was a tough job. I was asked by the Stockade Association to edit a newsletter, called the *Stockade Spy*, to rally support. Even today it is an elite neighborhood, but back then I was a renter and not eligible to be a member of the association. But they were assured by Wemple that he would review anything I wrote about the assault on the Stockade to assure it was legal.

It didn't take Judge Quinn long to complain to the head of GE plant relations at GE that I should not be involved in a conflict of interest. The manager then was A.C. Stevens, a great guy despite some of the relations managers reporting to him. He had already come to my rescue by forcing the YWCA to exempt me from 9 p.m. curfews so I could work late. The fact that Stevens' ancestors were early settlers of the Rexford Mohawk River area and he had appreciation for history was in my favor. So Judge Quinn got nowhere with his complaint.

We ended up with historic protection for the Stockade. A couple of years later I was to confront this judge again, but that is another story in this book.

Those early years of activism did lead to what my conservative husband, Dick Weber, in later years called getting "too involved." But he often supported me and understood why I needed to spend a lot of time that summer keeping a trash plant out of my valley birthplace. He did have a calming effect on me. He often repeated his engineering warning of "measure twice, cut once" before I took an action. When he became a politician as Town Supervisor for eight years, I always used my maiden name in writing letters to protest what I considered unfair in society. These often involved the greedy Jack Welch for turning GE into GE Capital. His sale of technology and product businesses resulting in 150,000 U.S. layoffs—including 20,000 in Schenectady—was often a topic. I had to give up trying to correct Donald Trump's lies because he managed to tell 12,000 of them during the first half of his term. But some letters did help cause change.

The first letter to have an effect was one I wrote years ago when my mother complained the Deaf and Blind School now had a country music radio station so powerful the music overrode the narration on TV. She was a dedicated fan of *Wheel of Fortune* and *Jeopardy*, always beating us with the answers. I wrote to the head of the FCC in Washington about it, noting it was a shame educational programs in this rural area were now useless and overtaken by what she called "Wham-Wham" music. They sent two agents to our town. Max Carpenter, the head of the school, was furious when they had to lower the wattage of the music-making station. At least the agents told him it was her daughter that wrote them, so he berated me instead of her.

On the local level, another letter did help effect change. It was bad enough when a homeless woman froze to death outside of the Senior Citizens Center in Saratoga. But when the head of the center put a covered lock on the outdoor electric plug to keep them from plugging an electric blanket in, I had to write a letter. The new mayor of Saratoga, who was getting support for opening a homeless shelter, told me she had read it. She used it to garner support for a shelter.

I also found writing a complimentary letter can be rewarding. I was so impressed with a new type of berry tea, I wrote to the CEO about its great taste. I received a year's supply as an answer.

I often regret now having my late husband around to tell me to measure twice before I do something. But despite Dick and I being politically apart, we had a great marriage and I miss him. I am now looking at a doormat we had labeled, "Welcome to this bi-partisan household." It is the year 2023 and I recommend this doormat for use by the U.S. Congress.

Firsts

"So what do you do at that Memoir Writing Center?" joked my husband. "You live in the past, you become the past." He grinned. "I bet all of you just sit in an easy chair and go back to your second childhood."

I thought about it and decided it was not a bad idea to regress if reality was having a discussion with him in this mood, so I moved over to the La-Z-Boy chair he usually occupied in front of the TV set, closed my eyes, and let him think I was in regression. He could sit in my hardback rocker and amuse himself with Dave Letterman if he wanted to. Maybe that was where he got the irritating habit of repeating himself when he thought he was funny. He kept digging up the same old sarcastic bones.

I decided I would, indeed, regain my childhood. A way to do it was to search back for my earliest memories. I would categorize them as first happiness, first fear, first sadness, first school memory, first love, and so forth.

Happy thoughts first, I said to myself. I visualized myself at about age four. I was introducing my ducks, Duckie and Daddles, to two people visiting my mother on the front porch. It was probably Lucy Belle and Aunt Susan. They always sat in the porch swing and they were giving me their full attention, which I know today I always got from them. Mom was explaining how she let me bring the ducks on the porch because I agreed to clean up after them. I liked doing so because I could use the water hose at the side of the porch. Because my sister was allowed to bring her two cats into the house and even sleep with them, I had wanted to do the same with my ducks. But Mom quickly told me they had to stay outside because they could not be trained to use the sandbox or quack at the door when they wanted out. Not to be deterred, I tried to get them to back up to the cat sandbox which they over-squirted. I even tried using some of my mother's huge roasting pans. For a while I thought Daddles might solve the problem for me when he heard the shower running and walked in to relieve himself. Unfortunately for him my mother was in there. I soon found out that leading a duck to water was a lot easier than trying to get them to go to the bathroom in an orderly manner.

So I joined their world and became an outdoor kid. At first, I called them Duckie I and II, but my dad renamed the male one Daddles because, he said, Duckie wasn't enough for him. Daddles' straying testosterone often sent him in the hen house looking for more action, a noisy affair which not only interrupted the egg production but was also irritating the lone rooster. Still, my father tolerated him—or, as my mother used to muse, probably admired him. It was my job to let the ducks out of the coop in the morning so they could trundle off to the pond for their food and then close them up in the coop at night. All of our pets had to earn their keep. My brother frequently offered mice as proof of what good cats he had. While no one liked duck eggs for breakfast, Lucy Belle said they were great for baking and insisted on paying for them—money which went into Mom's egg money jar.

My first fear came when I was going to the pond to get Daddles and Duckie to pen them up for the night. It was nearly dark. I stepped on a big black snake which we called racers because they jumped in several places to get away fast. This one was about six feet long, my father said, and I had been so scared I fell on it. Evidently, I was so terrified I passed out and the snake kept biting me trying to get out from under me. I don't remember my dad freeing me from the snake but my mother would later say that I learned my lesson too well when they had earlier tried to make me afraid of snakes. I am told that not long after I had learned to walk, I came into the house with the front of my skirt bunched up, inside of which I carried a bunch of baby copperhead snakes.

My earliest sad memory came the morning I went to let Duckie and Daddles out of their coop and saw the screen front was torn open. Even at that age, I knew Daddles and Duckie were no longer in there. I remember seeing some of their feathers stuck in the screen. I knew the dreaded foxes that had plagued the hen house from time to time had found my ducks. My mother said it took me several weeks before I would even speak about it. They had tried unsuccessfully to get me to give up the two big, long yellow bills I found near the apple tree behind the barn where Daddles and Duckie had been consumed. I carried the bills with me in the pockets of my red corduroy pants. Rather than hand-me-down dresses from my sister, I was now getting pants from an older cousin. Not only would they be difficult to carry snakes in, but more useful for me as I often assisted my little brother in digging bathtub-size trenches by the house where he could play with his trucks.

While all of our Christmases growing up were pretty sparse as far as presents, we never lacked for good food as farm kids. We even had steak for breakfast with our eggs and lots of vegetables and fruit. Some of Mom's egg money was saved for a special Christmas treat—a gallon of shucked oysters brought over from Chesapeake Bay. To this day none of us can fry as deliciously as my mom did. She never shared the recipe so that has given the following generations a challenge still attempted.

The first day of going to school was also a traumatic event. For me it was getting on that big yellow school bus with older kids who I knew would tease me. There was also the fear of that two-room schoolhouse which had the first four grades in one room and the four higher grades in the other room. So I stayed overnight with my bigger cousin in the fourth grade who promised to defend me. We shared the same desk for eight years. Even when the teacher asked me that first day to give my name, he answered for me. I am told it took a week before I said anything in class, a happening that many today simply cannot believe.

Then there is the first love; there is no feeling like that one. I guess some of those hormones Daddles had surfaced in me. I was working in the produce fields under a big elm tree by the river bagging corn. He was picking corn with the older men and every time the fifth sled of corn came in for us to bag, I looked for him. He was as shy as I was. We would just stare, but I knew he liked me. He had given me a rabbit box for my birthday. My father let me keep it, but demanded that I catch rabbits in it and give them to the boy's father. What I didn't realize then was that his family was so poor the only thing he could give me was a rabbit box. His family used those to obtain meat. Later in life, I realized what a sacrifice that had been and that his father and mine had decided I could keep it but that it should be useful. I proved to be true to my first love. I probably cleaned out our 500 acres of all the rabbits it had and presented them to him and his father.

He died in Viet Nam. Like so many poor boys in our county, the service was the only way out of poverty. I went on to other loves and so did he. But his memory stays with me, even when I am jostled out of my regression with the *Dave Letterman Show* and my husband says to me, "Hey, snap out of it. Talk to me. I didn't mean what I was saying about your memoir writing center. Tell you what, tomorrow night let's go out to dinner."

Eulogies for four good friends and the toughest guy I ever knew, my husband.

Dave Atwell

"Follow me" was a ski instruction that Dave Atwell gave to skiers which we would all do well to emulate.

Not only was Dave a great ski instructor—talk to any graduate of the Burnt Hills-Ballston Lake Junior High School from his classroom or principal's office and they will tell you how cool he was.

We in the Schenectady Wintersports Club knew him best as a board member for many years as well as President. He served on the Board of Directors and as Ski School Director at Hickory Hill and taught skiing at the North Creek Ski Bowl. After retirement he volunteered at Windham Mountain in the adaptive ski program and became a weekday instructor at Gore Mountain.

As his wife Sue said, his sense of humor, intelligence, and love of history, nature, Vermont, and reading continued all his life. He passed this passion along to so many. Sue should know after forty-three years. She shares these sentiments, as do their children, Scott (*who I always thought they named after a ski pole we all just had to have back in those days*) and Heather, both talented on the ski hill as well as professionally

In recent years, I remember Dave best for helping me

out when I was struggling with my husband's granddaughter trying to teach her how to ski at Gore. We were at the top of Quicksilver and she refused to go any farther when Dave (*thank heavens*) came by. He took one look at the situation and, after telling me it was a case of "show not tell," he gave Heidi one of those smiles and said, "Follow me." To my amazement, off she went behind him, forgetting all about weight on the downhill, etc., to the bottom without stopping. And she did it in great style. Dave was right. One-size instruction does not fit all; you need to be flexible and the best way to learn to ski over ice, moguls, or packed powder was to follow someone who adjusted for it. Now I knew why he always looked so smooth on the hill, skiing effortlessly while the rest of us would-be racers were thrashing around the hill.

Just a few years ago, Mary Anderson and I ran into Dave (*not literally*) at this same trail. Mary A. is also a ski instructor, but as she said, it was quite a compliment from Dave that we had made some fine turns.

There are still quite a few SWC'ers around who remember the early years when we rented Jerry Kirchner's house in Vermont before the club owned its own lodge. Dave, Bob Creatura, and Jimmy Fox kept us well entertained with their nights out on the town sometimes accompanied by Dick Weber, Bobby Marra, and Don Petro. One entertainer that was not amused was Roc King who performed at Sister Kate's. Dave interjected his own sense of humor that often left Roc speechless and anxious for his so-called hecklers to leave.

Today Millie (Ey) Gittinger laughs about the time Dave complimented her on how hearty her cooking and baking was. She used to make some wonderful meals at Jerry's and was particularly good at blueberry pancakes. During spring skiing, the dirt road in to Jerry's would become a huge mudhole, making it even more difficult than a heavy overnight snowfall to get out. Dave came up with a solution to his spinning wheels by remembering that some of Millie's pancakes had been left in the oven over a two-week period. He filled the ruts with these, claiming the blueberries in the very hard pancakes had been quite sufficient in their role as studs to ease him on down the road.

As club president, Dave's wry sense of humor also made some otherwise distasteful projects seem fun. The best-attended work party at the club's Pattersonville ski area was one to help Ed Koch and Lee Tomlinson build an outhouse. It was billed as a party for those with "savoir faire."

Skiing was his major sport and as Bob Creatura said when he no longer showed up at the weekly winter meetings at the Elks Club, "Can you believe he skied 130 days last year and thinks they will be open longer this year? He must have been bitten by a snow snake."

If so, he and Sue (*after Dave did his thing during the week at Gore, she got off work and they spent the weekends at Whiteface*) were two happy skiers snaking through the snow with the grace dreamed about in the song *The Man on the Flying Snow Skis*. (*You can look it up on the internet... "Oh, I float through the air with the greatest of ease, you'd think me a man on a flying trapeze..."*) This was a song we used to sing on bus trips.

So here's to Dave: A guy to follow if you want to do well.

Paul Lozier

It is an honor for me to represent so many of Paul's friends going back to the 1960s when GE in the Schenectady area was booming with nearly 40,000 employees.

As you know, Paul was a metallurgical engineer at the Knolls Atomic Power Laboratory for fifty-two remarkable years. In fact, it was just five years ago, when he was seventy-one, that Lockheed Martin recognized his many contributions by awarding him the NOVA Award of Excellence. He and Terry received it at a special ceremony at the Smithsonian Institute in Washington, D.C.

The rest of us were mostly retired by sixty-two and six-ty-five—but not Paul. He could never be described as retired—at work or at play. One of my earliest memories of Paul during the heydays of the 60s was competing for an Ed Belcher Ski Community Service award. It went to the best ski club in the Capital District. There were twenty-one at that time instead of the four today. We even created new activities to win. One was Paul's idea to expand the Dry-Land Ski School program to the club's new Pattersonville ski area. Irwin Mortman, a co-worker at KAPL, recalls how he and others, including Lou Champlin, were recruited by Paul to teach the kids.

Avid is an understatement describing Paul's love of sports and the outdoors. What is special about him is the fact he not only competed but his enthusiasm and drive were contagious. It wasn't just enough he was competing in Capital District Ski Council and US Eastern Amateur Ski Association races; he had to get the rest of us involved, no matter how novice we were. I probably spent two years snowplowing through gates before I knew there was a faster way down.

His drive and organizational ability resulted in many titles and acclaims. He was a licensed Technical Delegate to the Federation International de Ski (FIS) where he was the official assigned to national and international events including the Women's Downhill at the 1980 Olympics in Lake Placid. Don Paige and Dick Weber remember him well for his by-the-book command of the rules. And, Kim, Dick tells me you did a great job on his quality control team. Those downhill racers would never have found their way down the mountain without your neatly-arranged pine boughs to keep them on course.

Paul was president of the Schenectady Wintersports Club for five years in a row before asking to be relieved. He was a member of the National Ski Patrol. Many of us remember being herded down to the local Red Cross in Schenectady to take lessons in first aid on the ski slopes. For many years he was co-chairman in the Adirondack region for canoe and kayak events and the New York State Empire Games. He volunteered his energy and expertise to the United States Luge and Bobsled Associations. The family garage—normally filled with fiberglass canoes and paddles under construction—also has a luge in it now which he was either improving, repairing, or most likely redesigning.

In 1970, after years of renting facilities at Stowe for ski club use, Paul was instrumental in forming the SWC Stowe Lodge Construction Bond plan to finance the building of a lodge on Goldbrook Road—a financial effort that led to the purchase of today's SWC lodge in Waterbury Center. He even found an architect by the name of Crozier for the project.

After setting up a new SWC division for paddling, Paul helped organize and chair the revival of the Schenectady Regatta in honor of Steinmetz on August 23, 1973, now called the Towpath Regatta. It was an amazing success. The first event attracted over 200 watercraft with about 450 competitors and a *Gazette* crowd estimate of over 10,000. Paul and his fifteen-year-old son, Kurt, won their class and their time was in the top five. The event lives on and its purpose is to promote clean water.

Paul also talked the Schenectady County Unit of the American Cancer Society into co-sponsoring a Steinmetz Triathlon involving one runner, two canoers, and a bicyclist. Also included was an Iron Man and Woman event with each doing all three events. A popular event during the 1980s, he served as co-chairman. And, yes, all the Wintersports Club members and KAPL employees found in the hallways were rounded up to conduct this event while the Cancer Society funded it. Proceeds went to the Cancer Society and SWC got more community relations goodwill, a win-win as Paul would say.

Area paddlers not only know Paul for his winning times

in the Hudson River White Water Derby, the seventy-mile Cooperstown to Bainbridge canoe race, the Dead River races in Maine, and many Adirondack lake and river events, but also for his organization of teams for these events. His annual Father's Day whitewater paddling of the upper Hudson attracted young and old. Many area residents have boats built by Paul and his family in their garage. Pete Hermann tells me he has four. One of his most famous boats was one he and Dick, an early Hudson River whitewater explorer, retrieved from a calamity near Blue Hole. It weighed around ninety pounds new. But as Paul began training at least a hundred of us in it, there were many times when Paul would have to bring it back in the garage for another patch and more fiberglass. In fact, it weighs over 200 pounds now and Paul—rightly so—gave it the name "Rock Bait."

He was also the organizer of an annual all-men's weekend regatta on Lake George attracting many GE engineers with sailboats ranging from wood-built Lightnings to Catamarans. A race was held from the south end to Black Mountain Point. Bud Elliott, now in Idaho, notes that despite the fact he and Paul were in a 500-pound Shark Cat, Paul would not back down when a sloop weighing 7,000 pounds came bearing down on them. They had the right-of-way and Paul yelled, "Starboard," but it kept coming and nearly ripped off their dual rudders. Bud attributes their win that day to Paul's taking the helm.

But never let it be said that it was all about winning. Betty Nickerson recalls a whitewater race on a cold, icy April day on the Kayaderosseras when her kayak overturned and she was stranded on an island, barely able to get the kayak ashore. Ladies had been first and when Paul came by, he sacrificed winning the race to rescue her off the island and talk her back into the kayak.

Paul's passion was not just for land and water sports. His penchant for flying began in college and resurfaced when he built and flew experimental aircraft as well as an Aeronca 7AC

Champ, the same make in which he earned his pilot's rating in Kansas. He was a member of the Aircraft Owners and Pilots Association and a member, past officer, and crew chief for the Condair Flyers. Paul was in the process of building a new experimental aircraft prior to his death. He flew many times to Oshkosh, Wisconsin, to attend the Experimental Aircraft Association's fly-in with friends and family.

Never afraid to take a risk, Paul survived many close calls which caused his friends to describe him as indestructible. In fact, he waged a long sixteen-year battle to stay with us, leaving all of us as fans and friends, admiring his indomitable strength.

As Mary Anderson put it when she heard the sad news: "I will always remember Paul as high energy, encouraging others to meet his expectations and modeling what it took to reach higher goals than we would have set for ourselves."

And in knowing Paul's wonderful family—Terry, Kurt, Kim and Kelly and their offspring, Aaron, Jared, Samantha, Allison, and Ryan—one doesn't have to go far to be reminded of Paul's attributes. They are, indeed, filling his shoes. I know he was proud of them. He often said so.

Thank you again, Terry, for the honor of being here.

And now I would like to offer a poem titled *I'll Be There* which I am sure has great meaning to Terry as well as the rest of the family.

> *When I leave you, don't weep for me.*
> *Pass the wine around and remember*
> *how my laughing pleased you.*
> *Look at one another, smiling,*
> *and don't forget about touching.*
> *Sing the songs that I loved best*
> *and dance one time all together.*
> *As for me, I'll be off, running*
> *somewhere on the beach, and I'll fly*

to the top of the tree I always meant to climb.
When you're ready, I'll be there –
waiting for you.
Take your time.

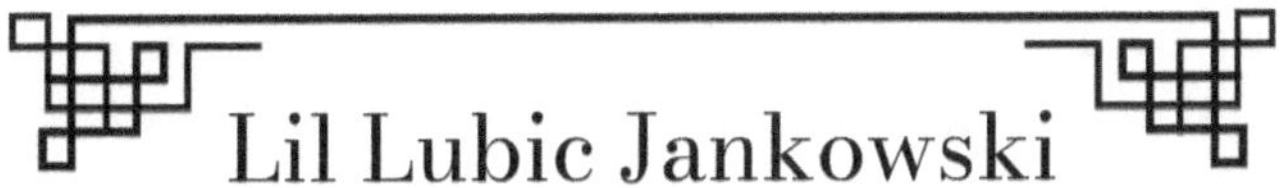

Lil Lubic Jankowski

I first met Lil in 1960 in Building 59 at GE where there were some thirty women called key punch operators—even though they were software writers using what was called Fortran and Cobol. When I heard there was someone there from West Virginia, I immediately went over to introduce myself. Even today, we West Virginians seem to automatically form a club, or, as Lil used to say, "Yes, We Wear Shoes Club."

Being on the *GE News*, I soon learned Lil had become one of the top programmers. She was often sought by an advanced steam turbine engineer to help him calculate the forces of steam on a bucket going thousands of miles an hour. She laughed about my early keypunch experience at the Newark airport when a late flight had gotten me there after the terminal facilities closed. The exit parking lot attendant using my key-punched entrance-exit card said I owed $400 instead of $40. There was no arguing about an extra hole making the mistake. So I went to the exit and was using a rope to pull the entrance gate open when a cop showed up. After seeing my proof of days in the parking lot which added up to $40, he opened the gate with his car, letting me pass by at the same time. Lil generously provided me with keypunch cards designating different amounts.

Like a lot of women at GE, Lil was not a happy camper because she was also paid half of what our male equivalents got. It didn't take her long to get a better job at RPI, marry Joe Jankowski in 1963, and later head to Vermont with him. She got a job in Burlington with IBM while Joe was on his own designing wind generators for such things as pushing oil through the Alaska oil pipelines.

Many of us, including Helen Schneider, got our start at the YWCA because it was a place where you could get a room without being asked if you were going to have visitors at night. Lil and Helen arrived there in 1959 and I was there in 1960. You had to be in your room at 9 p.m., so as soon as people could team up with roommates to share rent, they did so and got out.

Lil and I became roommates in 1962. We lived on McClellan Street across from Linton High School where Helen taught English. All of us were in the Wintersports Club learning to ski. That is where Lil met Joe, who was president of the club. Needless to say, we had some wonderful parties there because Lil was not only a great hors de'oeuvre maker, but Joe could mix some pretty potent drinks. I remember one occasion when Lil and I had decided that Manhattans were too sweet and martinis too bland, so we started drinking grasshoppers which required lots of crème de menthe. Joe had his own lethal recipe for those. By the end of the evening, we were both wearing green shirts.

While I knew Lil was sending money home to her mother, she did not talk much about her family in Wheeling. She knew I had worked on the newspaper there during my junior and senior year. I was aware of her neighborhood not being a suburban paradise. So when Joe wanted to meet her family, I understood she was reluctant. She decided she would go to Wheeling to tell them she was engaged. Joe, obviously quite fond of Lil, wanted to seal the deal. We decided we would go to Wheeling in my TR-3 before Lil changed her mind. It broke down on the way there but Joe, being the handy guy, got it fixed and we arrived there as planned. Everything went fine and we met a wonderful family. I have a picture of Lil's mother with my TR-3 which I cherish. I went on to my homeplace at the other end of the state and Joe came back with Lil. They were soon married.

Joe moved in and I moved out, but our relationship has continued over all these years with many rendezvous. They both loved hiking. I remember when they led a bunch of us to the top of Mt. Marcy in the Adirondacks where the ever-thoughtful Lil and Joe had a round of martinis and snacks in their packs.

Skiing, of course, was also their sport. When they could no longer do it, they bought a T-bar from Mt. Mansfield which was great background for a cocktail bar. Joe knew his wines and, try as I might today, I have never found a wine as good as what he ordered directly from California. Then there were those raw oysters served with unbelievable sauces. You never wanted a fried one after those. He and Lil were gourmet cooks. It was no wonder that people would organize rotating dinner parties just so they could go to their house.

Lil was a competitive chess and Scrabble player. Few were ever lucky enough to beat her. We often played Scrabble and it was nearly impossible to win even if you got all the high-scoring letters. We seldom finished a game because she would clog up the board with every two-letter word known. Finally one day I introduced a new rule: No words unless they contained five letters. What did Lil do? She played three two-letters above and under my five-letter words and won with one of her highest scores.

Both Joe and Lil were amazing people when you could get them to talk about themselves. They came from hardscrabble backgrounds and learned self-reliance at an early age. Joe came from a family farm like mine. I am still grateful he gave me a copy of his memoir. It is an excellent example of how people made do in what he titled the age of "Candle Light and Horses." I could certainly identify with this, remembering when we first got electricity.

When Lil gave me a copy of her mother's memoir, I gained a whole new appreciation for eking out a living with dignity and drive. I have met most of her sisters and brothers. All of them have been extremely successful on the West Coast as well as the East, working their way up in firms like Monsanto, Disney, Boeing, and AT&T. Several years ago, I had the privilege of going west with Lil to meet one of her sisters, Nancy, and her husband Don in Los Angeles. We drove up the coast in their new Lexus to visit another sister and brother in Seattle. We toured scenic highlights along the coastline and had some wonderful meals, too. Lil always complained when restaurants served too big of a portion, so I gained five pounds on that trip because I found what Lil couldn't eat on my plate. I guess both of us were taught to never waste food. I was also invited to several of their week-long family reunions in the famous Oglebay Park near Wheeling. In fact, a particularly memorable event for Lil was watching her daughter Mary and granddaughter Libby riding horses there.

But it is the mother's memoir that makes you realize that living the American dream is often something the second and third generation get to enjoy. Lil's mother came to Wheeling with her parents in 1921 from Croatia when she was just fourteen. It is heart-wrenching to read the struggle they endured to survive. She had to learn English and at the age of sixteen she was married to an older man who helped the family financially. Through good and bad times she always described him as a good man. They had ten children and her description of life often reminds me of how Lil would describe things. On her wedding day, she danced the polka with her husband and wrote: "He was giggly...his legs like overcooked spaghetti."

She described making many clothes from flour bags which was a "rip, wash and sew job." Then there was the excitement of getting a Maytag to replace her washboard, and her grief but pragmatism the day she had to kill and eat her pet chicken, Martha.

When Lil's father, a coal miner, died an early death of lung cancer in1954 after years of care and not being able to work, things got even tougher for the family. Even the youngest went out looking for odd jobs. Lil's mother made the decision to work at the nearby rectory for $5 a day rather than at the hospital for $6 a day because it required taking a bus and was only guaranteed three days a week.

Yet, her mother was able to take care of a huge family. I had to laugh when I read that none of them needed too much discipline. She writes: "When it was needed, I did not reach for Dr. Spock child psychology. I got it in our yard from some bush. So Mary, I am sure you are grateful this was a practice not handed down."

In fact, reading about all the jobs the kids had as soon as they were able to walk, I realized they didn't have time to do anything but keep the family fed. The older ones knew they had to take care of the younger. Frank, being the first born, probably made the greatest sacrifice. At the time their father became ill, he was eighteen in the army serving in radio communication under General Patton, sending money home. Rather than use the GI bill to go to the University of Chicago, he stayed close to home working various jobs to keep the family going and see his siblings through high school.

During this time, Lil's mother noted Lil was in the hospital which she described as "a rundown condition." She added that "she recovered enough to get a part-time job at Steubenville College which allowed her to take classes." By working a year between her freshman, sophomore, and junior years, Lil got a bachelor's degree in math.

When Lil's father died in 1954, they had $135 a month to live on from Social Security. I remember meeting Frank in the late 1900s when he was in a nursing home and was amazed at how he seemed at peace. He was very religious and rightfully pleased about how well his siblings were doing. It is no wonder his mother devoted so much time to him in her memoir.

The shortest part of the memoir is Lil's mother discussing the priests at the rectory and the cooking and cleaning she did for them. She ended that section succinctly and abruptly with five words: "Enough of Life with Reverends." I think this was Lil's favorite line because she felt that way with some of the priests at Steubenville College.

Lil often told me she had wanted to be an astronaut but soon found out that was a profession for men only. I guess we were fortunate that GE was hiring several thousand people a year in its heyday so there was room for women. So even though Lil in another life would have made a great astronaut, she has left behind some great memories for us and another generation living a good life. As Lil's mother wrote about her granddaughter Mary, "She is so much of her parents that it is hard to see whom she looks more like. You look at her, you see Joe, then blink and there is Lil. Mary likes her parents. That is very nice."

So, Mary, you have a grandmother who left quite a legacy. But as she said, you are much like your parents and that is quite a tribute.

Lil, we will greatly miss you, your wit and wisdom. You got your Cape Canaveral wish. You are up there somewhere floating around in space on Cloud Nine.

As for me and many of her friends who enjoyed all those parties Lil and Joe held, I will continue to announce, just as Lil did at every party, "It is five o'clock somewhere."

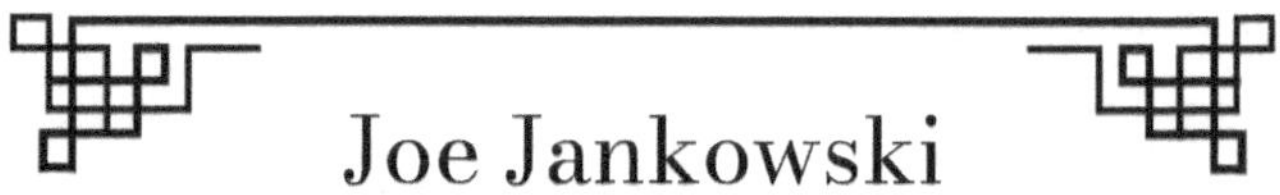

Joe Jankowski

Joe Jankowski was a jack of all trades and master of most. As a farm boy, nothing escaped his attention, be it how to plow a field in a circular pattern so you did not have to stop or go over the same ground twice or how to deliver a calf. After graduating from Burnt Hills High School in 1945, he joined the U.S. Army Air Corps and was stationed at Robins Air Force Base. He graduated from RPI in 1953 and I remember Joe saying that Tom Brokaw was right—the GI Bill was the best government program ever devised. He was one of thousands of farm boys, including his brother, Frank, who would not have been able to afford college otherwise.

Joe majored in mechanical engineering where his grades attest to his ability in that field. His first job was at Sikorsky Aircraft in Connecticut, but when an offer came from the Knolls Atomic Power Laboratory in Schenectady, he was quick to accept. Family was always first with Joe and, if I remember right, he and Frank designed and built the house on Swaggertown Road for their parents. As Irene can tell you, it is not only well-built but still an attraction for would-be Frank Lloyd Wrights looking for something different.

At KAPL, Joe quickly became a fan of Admiral Rickover because they shared the same view of safety first in designing reliable nuclear reactors for submarines. But Joe's diverse interests soon led him to another career. Joe became one of the first pioneers to go green when he left KAPL in 1978 to design load-bearing structures for wind generators. His structural work on getting the Alaska pipeline not to buckle in the ever-shifting tundra still stands today. The move to Vermont to work for North Wind Generator provided many opportunities to showcase his skills. His success in the wind power generation business found him working on international projects as far flung as Hawaii and Hong Kong. But Joe was not a nine-to-fiver. He formed his own business.

I can still see him busy at work at his bank of CAD computers in their house at Stowe designing structures for clients. Going to Vermont was also a wise decision for Lil. She had already proven her computer skills with GE and RPI, so transferring to IBM in Burlington was no problem. Daughter Mary was in on the decision too. She knew the skiing was better up there.

Joe and his brother Frank, along with some other Schenectady Wintersports Club people—including George and Shirley Kennedy, Frank's wife Pat, former *Ski Chatter* editor Diane Swanker, Joe and Martha Chernoch, Jan and Lou Champlin, Paul Berzatzky (*later Mad River Ski Instructor*) and later Lee Tomlinson at Ma Russells—were the first in the Schenectady Wintersports Club to become fans of Mount Mansfield skiing back in the 50s. For several years they rented lodges in the area which ultimately led to today's spacious SWC lodge in Waterbury Center. Joe and Lil were frequent lodge chairmen at the first formal SWC lodge rental—Jerry Kirchner's place on Goldbrook Road.

Fred Thompson reminded me that back then Joe drove a BMW diesel which was reluctant to start one very cold morning. Joe rigged up a little bonfire under the engine and within minutes he was off and at the lift right before it opened.

Joe held several Board of Director offices before becoming President of SWC for two years in the early 60s. He also supported ski racing and the Capital District Ski Council which had twenty-one ski clubs as its members. Racers today still appreciate that Joe's idea of a trophy was always something useful; winners received engraved ice buckets or silver serving trays.

I remember Joe awarding me the club's Outstanding Contributor Award, an ice bucket, right before an SWC trip to Tuckerman's Ravine. We didn't need it on the mountain but it came in handy on the bus trip to make up what was one of his favorite drinks then—Stingers, which were made with brandy and crème de menthe. One time at their house in Schenectady, he ran out of it and sent Susan Rucklehouse and I down to the Nott Street liquor store to get another bottle. We rushed out immediately to do so and in getting there spent considerable time going through our pockets to come up with the money. The owner, noting our green stained shirts, asked for our IDs which we had also left behind with our pocketbooks. We were only 30 cents short and about to leave our watch, but I must say if that happened today, I would be flattered to be turned down for being too young or green.

When you drank Joe's concoctions at Tuckerman's, you never had a hangover. He only used quality ingredients. Back then the buses did not have johns and Joe once said we would not have had to make so many stops along the road on the way to Tuckerman's if people would go easy on Paul Lozier's homemade wine. Still, he attributed Lozier's wine as the brew that gave so many of us the confidence to ski over the Headwall.

Helen Schneider can testify to Joe's good taste in cocktails. She remembers when he and Lil announced their engagement and we all ended up in the Whip at Stowe where Joe bought a round of the best drinks in the house. She was not used to a dry martini packing that much proof and found herself needing the help of Fred and Virginia Thompson to get to the lodge.

Joe was not only a connoisseur of good champagnes, wines, and hearty cocktails but he was a tremendous gourmet cook and hors d'oeuvres specialist. Even people who did not like raw oysters ate them to sample the different sauces.

Joe was also a master gardener. When he and Lil designed and built their place on a rocky hillside in Stowe, it didn't take him long to carve out a garden. While Lil was planting flowers—including Jack-in-the-pulpits and lady slippers—on the upside, Joe was downside digging out soil to raise the earliest and biggest tomatoes his Vermont neighbors had ever seen. As avid recyclers, they even used their compost as fertilizer. Their green thumbs even extended in our house where a cactus they gave Dick and I had to be cut twice even though we have a twenty-foot ceiling.

As an entrepreneur, Joe is renowned for his woodworking business which he called Chords of Wood because he did indeed make music when he created various shaped bowls, platters, and serving tools. Much of the ash, oak, and cherry wood came from trail clearing at Stowe's Spruce Peak. He was always amused and a step ahead of a well-heeled admirer who bought a bowl with the name of every town in Vermont on it for her collection. When Joe ran out of town names, he began with mountain bowl designs such as Camel's Hump. Joe sold these bowls at juried shows, earning from $200 to $500 per bowl.

Needless to say, all of us in this area were elated when Joe and Lil moved back from Vermont. We had forgotten how to party in great style and they were the instigators of our Old Timers Reunions. We started some of them at the Mabee Farm and soon we were meeting at each other's houses every couple of months. Reminding me of this were Susan and Chuck Hyson and Herb Haake who began coming over from Massachusetts for the annual events. They stayed with Joe and Lil whereas Chuck noted Joe and Lil always had the best wine and food but it was the wonderful times we had with them that we will always remember.

On a personal note, I was living with Lil, that fellow West Virginian (*obviously of great character and fortitude or, as Joe would say, "hillbillies with style"*), when they were married. Joe moved in and I moved out, but I didn't mind. I knew Joe was a helluva great guy when he and I drove to West Virginia in my TR-3 to meet Lil and her parents. Foreign cars were not big in West Virginia but when the battery went dead, Joe knew that a tractor battery would work.

I also received this personal note from Irwin Mortman who now lives in Cincinnati after retiring from GE aircraft engine. He was a big buddy of Joe's when they worked at KAPL. He had me going when he e-mailed that he has many fond memories of Joe and most important of all he was a real mensch. I didn't know what a mensch was so he sent me a three page document, most of it in Hebrew, but finally I figured it out. Originally, it was someone who was like what Mary had to say about Joe in the newspaper...generous, respectful, and compassionate. This was still true but in modern times it was also someone who was a cool guy. It is under the new interpretation that Irwin described Joe as a cool guy. He was on a European ski trip with Joe, Paul Berzatzky, and another guy they did not know that well. He wasn't sure of the year but he felt it must be right before Joe and Lil were married because even though they were having a great time skiing and living it up in the evening, Joe was always discussing "Lil, Lil, Lil" and anxious to get back. After skiing for about ten days he and Joe decided to take the train to Vienna and that Berzatzky and the other guy would follow the next day. Irwin and Joe decided they would ride second class to save money and would let the other two know when they arrived and if second class was a good way to go. The train left late at night and they were given a room assignment and a pillow. They entered the room and it was pitch black but loaded with people on shelves. The room was stifling hot and smelly and after a while they decided to take their pillows and sleep in the train hallway. Glad when the train ride was over, they found a hotel room and sent the other two a telegram, alerting them the second class accommodations were perfect. Now that is a cool guy, Mensch wrote Irwin...he shares his experience. What did Berzatzky say about it? Irwin said he got off the train and said it was a bit better than hanging on a meat hook.

Yes, we will miss this cool guy Joe who did everything well and keep on missing him, our Joe, the master of all that is good...including their daughter Mary, hubby Phil, and their three kids, Andy, Jeffrey, and Libby.

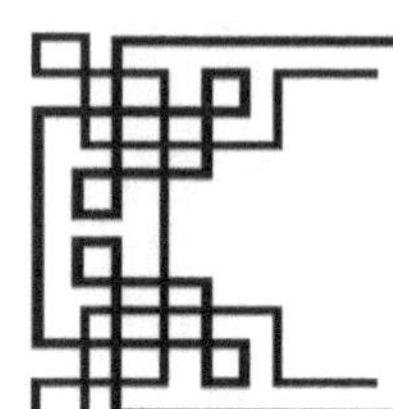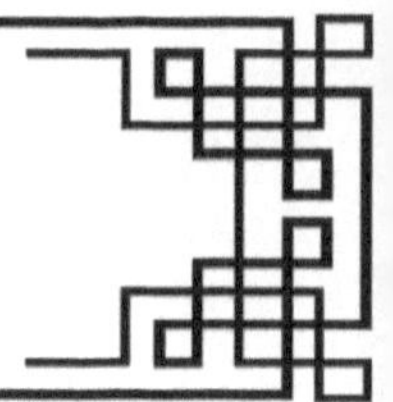

Yours Truly

If you just knew Dick Weber as a business owner and as Town Supervisor, you would agree with anchorman Tom Brokaw that he is representative of the greatest generation. He joined World War II as a marine. Thanks to the GI bill, he graduated from Cornell with a civil engineering degree. His father, who served in World War I and II, volunteered for both and got in despite being too young for the first and too old for the second. In between, he started a construction company which Dick and his father restarted when they both got out of World War II.

As his friend and wife, I was fortunate to see another admirable side—a deep love for nature and sports, and a dry sense of humor. Most of all, he never stood still.

When I met Dick, his hobbies were skiing, canoeing, biking, and flying planes and helicopters. His past adventures certainly foretold the responsible and active man he became. Back in the early 40s there were a handful of ski areas in the country. But that didn't stop the young Dick. I have a photo of him at age ten skiing down the Quarry, a deep open pit his father had used for years as a gravel source. He introduced it to other young boys who would climb up and ski down. They called it the Z Trail because it was steep and forced many abrupt jump turns. They were fans of Sweden's famed Otto Schniebs and managed to emulate him even though they were on homemade wooden skis. I was told by a longtime friend of his, Mickey Branson, that Dick was the first to schuss it.

When Dick and Mickey heard about a ski area in Vermont called Pico Peak (*it opened in 1937*), they knew about the train that went to nearby Rutland. Soon they were hopping on and hitchhiking to the area. From early forages into the Adirondack Mountains, they had learned how to avoid or con railroad conductors into letting them tuck themselves and their bikes to the back bars of the caboose for a free ride.

When they first went to Pico Peak, it was just a rope tow. But in 1940 Pico was the first ski area to install a T-bar. Just riding the T-Bar, Dick said, was a buckeroo challenge because of the icy ruts and the buckling of the overhead tow line. Snowmaking would be years away. But the tickets were cheap. Still, Dick would allow as to how their "out-of-town" budget was tight, so they would often hang around to see what color tickets were being accepted at the entrance. They saved a selection of old colored tickets in case they could be used again. Because so few people skied then, this wait often took them a couple of hours until enough tickets were sold to not raise suspicion. This area, still doing well today, produced Andrea Mead Lawrence who won the 1952 slalom in Oslo. I remember Dick introducing me to her years later at a United States Eastern Ski Association meeting.

But it was their summer and fall trips on the back of the train that ended up in Montreal, Canada, that he and Mickey talked about most in later years. Because Dick's father had built roads in the Adirondacks, including Rt. 73 that goes to Lake Placid, Dick was familiar with the territory. He had experienced outdoor living at an early age because of the construction camps his father created to cut roads through the mountains. When his father shut down the business to go to World War II, Dick was just fourteen. His trips with Mickey and other friends became more frequent with his mother allowing them to stay for days, knowing he could fend for himself.

The three trips I remember him talking about most were when he and Mickey got off the back of the train at Port Henry with their bikes to go to an old construction camp, now under the Northway at Exit 29. A wet late snow occurred, leaving about five or so inches on the route over to the North Hudson camp, some eighteen miles west of the station. It took them the rest of the day to slog through it, often pushing their bikes up the mountainous parts. He would recall the ordeal of biking through the heavy snow every time we went by it, look up the hill and say, "We called that S---t Highway."

Another trip well-remembered by Dick involved nearly a week camping in the high peaks. They started out at Elk Lake which leads to trails in the Dix Range, Panther's Gorge, Macomb, and Marcy. About halfway through, they decided to bike some fifty miles to a movie in Whitehall. They didn't remember what they saw, but they do remember being asked to leave when they began a farting contest resulting from, he joked, eating too many wild berries.

Then there are the Fulton Chain of Adirondack lakes, which years later became a well-known trek for sports people. Dick remembered his father, an avid fisherman as well as hunter, talking about how it would be possible to visit all of these lakes with very few canoe portages. So when he and Mickey were biking near First Lake, they spotted a fishing canoe rental area. Not finding anybody around, they left a note on their bikes that they would be back. Several days later, they were. The owner, seeing their age, was not terribly upset but did give them some chores to work off their rental fees.

When they were sixteen and seventeen, they were able to get some jobs "making them better paying responsible citizens," Dick would say. One of them was on Lake George which boasted three huge tourist boats. No, they were not seating passengers on the Ticonderoga or the Mohican. Their lack of experience landed them jobs pitching coal into the boiler burner of the Minne Ha-Ha to keep the steam engine going. It was a hot job below deck without a scenic view or cool breeze. It was then, both claimed, that they learned cold beer was a solution to all that heat.

This ended when Dick entered World War II a year before it ended at the age of eighteen. His father had built roads for the troops, the longest being the one through Persia to the Russian border. It enabled the Russians to come in to assist. Even though his father had fought the Germans in World War I with honors as an army foot soldier and a captain, it was felt that it was best not to have those with German heritage get directly involved in World War II. Also, he was older and had volunteered. When they realized how much road construction experience he had, they were more than happy to take advantage of those skills.

His father, like Dick in later years, was quite the photographer. His glass mount slides—not just of construction but of the countryside and natives, particularly Arabs—are amazing. Today they reside in the NYS Military Museum in Saratoga. He was prescient, too; in one of the letters he wrote home, he predicted the Russians had an arrogance about them as they drove tanks on the new road that would one day cause problems for the U.S.

Dick always downplayed his war experience because he went in near the end of the war and was in one of the Chinese Defense units for operations against Japanese forces in the area. He said they spent most of their time protecting Chiang Kai-shek. He did learn to speak some Chinese and when I asked one day to translate what he was saying, he said it was: "Take me to the British sector." Evidently all the rickshaw drivers knew the Marines liked the beer there. Even though he did not see major fighting, Tom Brokaw would give him even more credit if he knew Dick would never take a veteran's tax exemption on his property "because he never saw action and knew many who did not survive it."

One of Dick's first jobs after graduating from Cornell was an assignment by his father to check on a bridge they were building over the New York Thruway near Rotterdam. Dick did more than inspect the work site; he looked at a copy of the designs for it and checked all the dimensions called for in constructing the bridge. His father couldn't believe it when

Dick pointed out the steel undergirding spans in the design were a foot shorter than they should be. After also studying the specifications, his father immediately made a call to the state official, who apologized. Dick's father was able to cancel the order for the steel beams and get the correct size without penalty.

But the job Dick told me about on his early work on a coffer dam was not an easy one to hear. There are some twenty-five locks on the Mohawk River between the Hudson River at Albany and Lake Ontario into the St. Lawrence Seaway at the other end of the state. Coffer dams had to be built in front of locks to block the water so work could be done. This usually involved driving steel piles into the riverbed and filling forms with non-porous material. He got a call from a foreman one stormy night that the coffer dam on Lock 9 was leaking into the forty-foot-deep work area and was now covered with fifteen or sixteen feet of water.

Dick rushed out with his wetsuit and an air tank to see where the leak was and what could be done about it. He felt his way slowly down the outside of the coffer dam. It was dark. All of a sudden he felt his right leg get sucked into the hole that was leaking which jammed his whole body against the side of the dam. He knew he was in trouble. He tried to pull his leg out but the suction was too great. He knew he had about fifteen minutes of air in his tank. Getting his leg back out of the coffer maw was something he had to concentrate on. He used his engineering training to slowly edge his leg an inch or so at a time which allowed the water to fill in behind his foot, thus relieving the pressure. It took all the strength he had to keep his leg from slipping back as he inched it toward him, again and again. Each time, the strain on his leg was a little bit less as he inched it out. Finally, he was free and on his way up with a few minutes of air to spare. He swam to the bank and just collapsed in the dark. All I could say was he lived to tell about it.

At the time he was doing a lot of lock jobs, he was heavily involved in developing the Hickory Hill Ski area near North Creek. When they were putting in the poma lift with a GE motor "donated" by another investor, Dick realized the old dock keeper's hut on the huge lock at Utica Falls they were renovating would be perfect as the start house. Today it is still at Hickory Hill and the ride straddling a bouncy pad up over ruts and rocks is about as challenging as the narrow, steep trails. It became a family favorite. Just ask his son, Rick, and daughter, Kathe. In fact, when Warren Miller first got his start *(thanks to Pete Fox, who owned a ski store, and Dick, as an officer in the Schenectady Wintersport Club)*, one of his first films included scenes from Hickory Hill. It has a very young Rick and Kathe Weber skiing in it.

Dick was also involved in early canoeing of the Hudson at the time. Kayaks were rare so he went to Canada to buy a double-seated one. He laughed about the border agent not paying attention to it on top of the car. Dick was an early canoer of the upper Hudson as was his friend, Pat Cunningham, who went on to own the Hudson River Rafting Company. When the river became "too crowded" for Dick, he turned the canoe over to Paul Lozier, a friend and avid canoer. He trained many people, including me, on how to handle the Hudson River whitewater. The canoe became known as "Rock Bait" because of all the impacts with rocks in the Class 3 and 4 waters. It still exists and weighs about twice its original weight because of all the fiberglass patches.

Back in the late 70s, the Schenectady Wintersports Club sponsored the return of an early Mohawk River regatta that Dick's father had been a part of in the 1920s. By this time, Dick's father was aging but still able to get in a boat with his son, lending much needed promotion for SWC's river re-enactment. We got a kick out of it when he told reporters it was not as good as the one he had been in but his son had done a good job rowing his old Adirondack guide canoe.

When Dick's father and mother died, he was, of course, devastated. His mother was a class act. One of my favorite stories about her was the time someone gave her a fresh tomato from their garden. She put it in her purse and forgot about it. At the grocery store, she came up to the counter to pay for her purchases when the cashier spotted the tomato. His mother considered it her most embarrassing moment even though the clerk knew who she was and just laughed at her explanation. She was up to any challenge, much like her son. When Dick's father could no longer drive, she put 90,000 miles on their Lincoln in two years so he could look over old jobs.

Dick had his challenges with his father in later life, too. One time his father was to receive an award from the National YMCA for his donations of free construction work. He was on his way to receive the award when Dick got a call from the police. A lady had called them with his father's license plate number because when she was about to get out of her car on a narrow street, he drove by in his Lincoln and took the door off. Dick arrived at the local YMCA where his unaware father was about to receive his award. Dick was pleased the police were kind enough to let him accept it before arresting him. It took a long time for the authorities to take his father's license away because the judge was a very good friend of his father.

His father died on New Year's Eve. That became a time of reflection for Dick who forwent all New Year's Eve parties after that. During those years, getting construction jobs was difficult if you were a union employer. Even New York State started allowing non-union construction employers to compete for jobs. Dick spent a lot of time and money bidding on jobs he would never get with the knowledge that his bid was requested just for information on how to do the job. The final blow came when he was doing a multi-million job building the Caroga Lake dam. The bank that had loaned them money for supplies for some thirty years was taken over by a big national bank. They called in a loan of a million dollars he had in concrete at the dam site despite the fact the construction company had never failed to repay a loan. Dick was able to complete the project by selling off assets, but he went out of business after that. Every supplier he had was paid. Even the federal Small Business Association, in which the officer couldn't remember the loan, was paid back with the papers outlining the loan.

It was shortly after that Dick moved to the 224 acres he had bought years ago in Galway. He got it dirt cheap because it was filled with old cars which were not even used for parts anymore. He used his construction crews to clean them out. To save money, he even convinced the electric company to let him bury the power lines across beaver ponds and into the area where he wanted to build a house, deep in the woods. When he moved there, he was soon asked by a knowledgeable retiring Town Supervisor, Pat Bingham, who had been trying to get the town to approve building a new town hall and garage, to run for his job. Dick won and even used a spacious old landfill area of no use to farmers or anyone else to do the job. He served the terms allowed, two four-year terms. Saratoga County is composed of nineteen towns. Supervisors rotate in different positions, including Board Chairman. When Dick was head of finance, he endeared himself to the county administrators who had trouble collecting taxes from prominent people. Dick, not being political or caring about future public positions, got the list of delinquents and the county was soon flush with cash.

Dick's respect for veterans was more than evident when as Board Chairman he was asked to present medals to veterans of the Korean and Vietnam War as well as World War II. To increase public awareness, the event was held at the huge Saratoga Spring Performing Arts Center. It was to be done before the featured act that night: Henry Winkler, better known as the Fonz. A good friend of Dick's, Mike Pratt, the purchasing manager of Saratoga County—who was well aware of Dick's lack of interest in Hollywood, much less sit-coms—and I were in the front seats along with some spouses of the veterans. Dick was halfway through the solemn awarding process when the Fonz ran across the stage in his iconic white T-shirt with the hole in it. Dick immediately used his microphone to call for security to apprehend the intruder. Fortunately, security knew who Winkler was. Everyone had a laugh about it and to his credit, so did Winkler. He came back on stage, apologized to Dick, and added his congratulations to the veterans.

Pratt, of course, did not let Dick forget about it. He had often been on the end of one of Dick's jokes. During the 90s, there had been much debate about building a waste treatment plant versus opening another landfill. The county had made a deal with a paper mill to share their landfill which was, of course, much cheaper. At the time, waste to energy plants technology was still being debated. There was also pressure from other county advocates who saw such a plant needed huge volumes to be effective and wanted Saratoga to be part of it. Tempers flared. Mike, as the purchasing agent, was getting threats. One day he came in to work to find a steel bear trap under his desk. He called the sheriff (*who Dick had gotten to go in the ruse with him on*) to find the terrorist. After much "searching" for a couple of days to find the culprit, the sheriff led Mike to Dick at a bar near the jail.

Unlike many of the political supervisors, Dick did not have a lot of experience with public speaking. So when he served as Board Chairman that year, he would write his speeches at the Board meetings or have the county treasurer do it for him. Pratt began collecting his speeches, had them bound in an elaborate state binder, and gave them to each supervisor from the nineteen towns. Dick brought levity to it by showing up at the next meeting with an English wig on at which time he offered to sign the documents so carefully produced by Pratt.

Part of Dick's dry sense of humor involved a waiting period

for more effect. Another one of his best friends, Ted Riehle, who owned Savage Island in Lake Champlain, was always proud of his height. He would even stand next to every guest on the island—and they were many—to assure himself he was the tallest. One of these, Norton, was a very good friend of his and Dick's. At our house in Galway, Dick had used a white wall support post in the kitchen to measure the heights of his kids and grandkids as well as guests. Norton had accommodated him while visiting one fall at which time Dick drew the line about two inches above his head. Two years later Ted came by and noticed the wall with some fifty or so names. He wanted to be measured. He stepped away, incredulous to see that Norton's line was above his. All Dick would say was he would have to talk to Norton about it. Ted stewed for nearly a year before they were all together again and Ted learned what had happened.

Ted was also a graduate of Cornell. He prided himself on an early electrification of the huge island house he built with the installation of enough batteries, nearly filling up the basement, to power it. Guests were amazed to find all the amenities. A young *Burlington* reporter at the party asked Dick how Ted charged the batteries. Dick, quick to make construction charts, gave her an outline of Ted driving up and down the island with his tractor and wagon full of batteries being charged. When Ted got a call from the business editor asking how this was possible, Ted was furious and asked for the drawing. He was even more disturbed to see he was listed as a Cornell graduate.

But Ted gave as good as he got. He was quite an accomplished sail boater and owned a twenty-eight-foot Westsail which he took to the Caribbean during the winter. One day we were out in it with his second wife, a marriage that had shocked some relatives because she had been a babysitter for his first wife. She was thirty-five years younger than Ted. But that did not keep her from asserting herself. A sudden storm came up and she went below to read the depth meter as Ted tried to steer the boat into an island lee. He was questioning her ability to assess the depth and went below to look. All of a sudden the boat lurched on its side. Water was pouring in the portholes of the downward side where I was sitting. I just remember Dick yelling at me to block one of the portholes with my backside. Amazingly, Ted's sheep dog, which had been sitting beside me, tried to get into the other one, blocking it. While Ted was arguing with his wife, Dick took over the rudder and somehow we slid sideways into the lee with rain and thunder still hammering us. Ted, realizing we had narrowly escaped hitting a sandbar, took over.

It was after that Ted convinced Dick he should buy a sailboat because he showed potential. He took charge of finding a small one which he notified us was now in a dock across the lake from the island. He expected to see us by noon Saturday. We would recognize it because he had named it after us. When we got there that Saturday morning, Dick knew he had been had. It was embossed with huge letters: "The Merry Dick." Obviously, Ted claimed the graphic artist must not have known how to spell my name.

Ted got even greater enjoyment when he had assigned Bill Hazelett, another friend, to both him and Dick to fly over to the dock to make sure we got off okay. Bill had a Super Cub like Dick. While Dick has always excelled at every sport, sail boating was not one of them and I had even less knowledge than he did. Dick was checking off sailing directions like he used to before plane takeoffs, but we ran into a problem when I was told to unhook the main sail so it could flow free. By this time it was full of wind and no matter how hard I tried I could not get the very taut line to unhook so we could lessen the wind. We were going full speed across the lake. Circling above in his Super Cub was Hazelett yelling down instructions. Needless to say, we kept going straight ahead full speed with Hazelett continuing to shout instructions which we could no longer hear. We passed Savage Island where Ted was yelling from his deck. About two miles later we ended up in a sandbar after going under and not hitting a Grand Isle bridge. Soon Hazelett's wife, Dawn, who, unlike her husband, liked to fly their helicopter, arrived for the rescue. A marina close by dislodged the sailboat.

Dawn and Dick were great friends and often went on outings together over the Adirondacks as well as Green Mountains. Dick always admired her tolerance of her very rich husband who would often bring models to Ted's island where the rule was no one wore clothes. Hazelett, also a Cornell graduate, invented the equipment that made steel rolls. He also owned a ski binding company. I was always fascinated by him because he was a small man with a spinal disorder. But he was probably the most well-endowed man the models had ever seen. I got along fine with the models, interviewing several, although I was intimidated by their perfect bodies. I was amazed to find how many had professional lives beyond modeling. One headed the prison system in Canada and convinced me there were some inmates who could never be rehabilitated.

Anyhow, Hazelett was also part owner of the Bugaboos Ski area in the Canadian Rockies where helicopters dropped skiers off on top of peaks over 12,000 feet high for untouched powder runs. Dick went there twice and it was there he met Hans Gmoser. That friendship developed into two two-week European bike rides with Hans and his crew through the European Alps. There he became friends with Horst Eblem, who soon became our guest twice from Germany with his wife Erika. Those years were some of Dick's happiest—except maybe the time I was picking him up at the JFK airport from my GE job in Connecticut. I was late and spotted a pilot on the way in, asking him about the flight from Germany. He mistook me for a stewardess because I was wearing a similar suit and said, "Follow me." We wound down a narrow stairway behind a food counter to a gate where he said the flight would arrive. It did but there was a problem. I was in the area in which you need a passport to get out of. It took some five hours to straighten the situation out with security, making both Dick and I late for work the next day.

I probably remember Dick's skiing ability the most because that is how I first knew of him. I was gate keeping at a Capital District Race at Bromley, Vermont, when he whizzed by me with a look of determination on his face. I had seen other racers doing weight shifts in turns but he was just sailing through effortlessly with both skis level and pointed downward, a carving technique that is popular today. I was to find out years later that the council had asked him not to race so others could win, which he quickly agreed to and began setting courses.

This led to Dick becoming a member of the United States Eastern Ski Association which today is part of the US Ski Association. After learning the ropes of professional ski racing and becoming a certified FIS official, he began running ski races. One of his first Chief of Course events came in 1967 when he organized an FIS sanctioned national race for women at Bromley. Among the top ten were Cindy Nelson of Minnesota, a downhill racer who won the Olympic bronze medal in 1972, and Barbara Cochran of Vermont who won the gold medal in slalom that same year. Barbara's brother, Bob, and her two sisters, Marilyn and Lindy, were also on the U.S. Olympic team. Making Olympic headlines in 2022 was Barbara's grandson, Ryan, who took a silver medal in Super G. Dick was familiar with the Cochran family, starting with their parents, who installed the rope tow at their Richland, Vermont, home for the kids, an area now open to the public.

Dick also served as an instructor for Lynn Fox, one of Pete Fox's daughters, who showed much potential as a competitor. They traveled the race circuit. Dick often said she could have qualified for the Olympic team but chose to go to college instead. When her father died, Dick also became great friends with his son, Jimmy, who had strong skiing legs like Dick which could smoothly absorb huge moguls. I remember admiring them both coming straight down waist-high moguls on the National Trail at Stowe without a flaw.

However, I will never forget when Dick went off into the woods once, hitting a tree. He got up in excruciating pain and told me he had dislocated his shoulder. The next thing I knew he slammed himself against the tree and announced that he had gotten the shoulder back in place. In later years he did a lot of veteran's racing. While he won many, he was most proud when he came in third at Burke Mountain because the first and second place winners were former Olympians.

The 1980 Olympics in Lake Placid became a memorable event for many of us in the Capital District. Dick was asked by Sergei Lucci to be on the planning committee in 1978. Part of this involved getting some 2,000 volunteers to service all the winter sports venues. It was determined the alpine volunteers had to hone their skills by serving in selected positions for the Canada-American Race in 1978 and the World Cup race in 1979. Dick quickly offered up volunteers for the Alpine events who had helped him in local races doing course maintenance and gate keeping. I was among some lucky fifty or so people from the Capital District that happily gave up vacation time for three years to be part of it. It was a wonderful experience which I have described in another short story called *The Miracle in Placid.*

Dick's all-time favorite ski area was Alta in Utah. Every year for at least twenty years he stayed at the Alta lodge in the canyon. The lodge, with a full front view of the famed High Rustler Trail, was on a hill from which you could ski directly down to the Wildcat chairlift. He often went there with Jimmy Fox and Don Petro. My first trip west with Dick was during a ten-day tour of western ski areas with his friend from Denver, Dick Hall, and his wife, Fern. Hall was a lawyer and his wife worked for Governor Lamb of Colorado. The first area we hit was Keystone, which was owned by the city. Next came Copper and Vale and then onto Breckenridge and Arapahoe Basin. We also managed to get to Taos and Telluride, which had not been open that long and still looked like mining towns. At Steamboat Springs, we met up with Billy the Kidd from Stowe, Vermont. Dick had met him at qualifying ski races before he won the slalom in the 1964 Olympics. During those early years, athletes were not allowed to capitalize on the name. In his hometown of Stowe, people were very proud of him and a neighbor put up a sign reading "the Kidd lives next door."

Dick also liked Taos because, like his favorite ski area in the east Mad River in Vermont, it did not at the time allow snowboarders. Taos was run by a maverick, Ernie Blake, who also did not allow snowmobiles, proving his distaste by disabling one with a shotgun while we were there.

Mad River, which is still run by stockholders of which he was one (*Dick once owned a ski lodge near the area*) was particularly pleasing to him. It had a single chairlift serving three tough trails. It always had a long lift line, but to Dick it was worth it because the narrow trails would have become too crowded if served by double lifts. There were also no intersecting trails so he could schuss without obstacles. He had great respect for a guy from New Jersey, Olie, who they called the "Streaker" because he schussed the trails naked without ever falling. Some said attendance went up when it was learned he was in town.

Our years at Alta are very special to me—maybe because looking back I wonder how I survived. Dick was a powder hound and good at it. I had lots of practice on ice and rocks in the east and could manage to do a jump turn to get out of trouble, but four and five feet of fresh powder was something I thought I would never conquer—and only did to Dick's satisfaction once or twice when I managed to create a couple of good looking "S" tracks. He always gave me points for determination.

Dick particularly liked Alta because you could always find powder if you hiked and there were lots of places to do it. One was "Eddie's High Nowhere" where we had a picnic on a huge rock. I came close to getting acrophobia but my ability to do jump turns got me down a pitch that was so steep it couldn't hold much powder, which was a relief to me. Then there were the Baldy shoots he often took even though it could take over an hour to climb up to the top. But there was one time—and just one time—that I climbed up enough to take the first shoot. My jump turns saved me but after that I waited for him in the ballroom shoots below.

Just as exciting for me was flying with Dick. Over the years he had several helicopters, five or six Cessna Planes, including a twin-engine one, a Stearman, and even a hot air balloon.

We flew to West Virginia several times to visit my parents and my sister, Decker, her husband, George, and my brother, Mike, at the farm. Dick loved to land his Super Cub in a pasture field. At times he would have to fly over twice to assure he had scattered the cattle enough to land. A couple of times we went there in the helicopter. I think the happiest day my father ever had was hovering over the valley cornfields to see who had the straightest corn rows. Back then corn was checked into hills, allowing you to not only see rows in every direction but also if it was straight. Daddy took much care— even hand-planting a hill that didn't produce—so he was quite pleased to see his cornfield looking so superior.

One time with the helicopter, we got a late start because I couldn't leave GE as soon as I planned. With the sun disappearing, Dick began following a railroad into Cumberland, Maryland, where we could land at the airport. But a headwind and storm did not allow this. So when he found a clearing, we landed. He had a fold-up bike which we tried to ride to the town of Hancock, but with both of us on it, it soon folded itself up. A couple of hours later we got to an inn. The next morning the owner took us back to a road near the tracks and soon we were off. To make up for being late, I promised Dick a treat of staying at the Hilltop Hotel overlooking Harper's Ferry. President Jefferson had stayed there and later famous people like Mark Twain. I called and asked for the largest and highest room. I was amazed at how reasonable it was. When we got there, we were escorted to the top floor. When we went in there must have been fifty single beds in the entire open floor. I was told that during FDR's New Deal program, it housed WPA workers and hadn't been changed. We had a good time there and certainly a tremendous view from the thirty or so windows, but Dick never let me forget the look on my face when we opened the door.

Dick's first helicopter was a Huey and later he traded in for Bells. The cost of insurance for helicopters was about half of their price. So we often went to large events like county and state fairs and sold rides. My job was manning a sales booth with a "reduced price" sign. At one point our business was so good, Dick rented another helicopter so both he and his good friend Walt Glass could fly. I was given lots of plaudits from both of them for my selling skills. But the time I went into the horse barns at Syracuse and sold tickets to a lot of farm workers with manure on their feet, I was told to stop. Walt had been a World War II pilot noted for his raids on Berlin. He could—and wanted to—fly anything anywhere.

One of the more harrowing jobs came when Dick was hired by a New York State barge company to provide security. At the time, there was a strike by union workers and the company had hired scabs to replace them. There had been an incident of dropping a small explosion from a bridge. Many of these huge barges carried oil and were ocean-going. Walt would land on the end of barges heading from Albany down the Hudson and then on out to sea. When they came near a bridge, he would fly over the bridge to see if there was anyone suspicious on it and land back on the barge. They were approaching the Tappan Zee Bridge about sixty miles north of

New York City when the helicopter wouldn't start for his surveillance look. Walt quickly determined the part they needed and contacted Dick at his construction office. In just an hour, Dick Hyserman, his good friend and mechanic, was able to get the part to Dick, who was waiting in a rented helicopter. Dick was able to land on the barge as it was going out to sea. Barges carrying valuable freight do not stop. Walt was able to get the part in just after they went under the Verrazano Bridge. They flew back to Schenectady and were soon at Roc's, a nearby bar where they used to admonish other pilots...eight hours from bottle to throttle.

Probably the most dangerous jobs were flying high-powered power lines for Niagara Mohawk, now National Grid. Because hunters would sometimes shoot out the glass insulators at the top of the poles, Dick was hired to fly a few feet over the lines to check on their condition so they could be replaced. One line, called the "Green Giant," which went through heavy forests and over canyons, was particularly precarious. It was not just being alert to changing conditions but the knowledge there was no room to auto-rotate down safely at that minimum height. In fact, such low-flying work resulted in one of his helicopters being totally destroyed. They were asked to fly over the Saratoga Race Track to dry out the track from a heavy rain. It was well known the downdraft from helicopters was useful. They had done lots of jobs flying over orchards during frost times to push heat down on the fragile fruit. Walt had circled the track for a couple of hours to dry it out for safe horse racing when the tailbone caught a railing. He was lucky to get out of it before it was torn apart by the tailbone thrust forward and impact. So soon they were off to buy another Bell, this time in Texas.

However, there were safe jobs. Wealthy Adirondack camp owners with horses hired them to fly in hay bales. Then one of the Schenectady banks had a deal with a Wall Street bank which involved flying money down to the south end of

Manhattan. Sometimes those Adirondack camp owners would pay to just have friends brought in for a party.

Dick often donated helicopter time to non-profit projects. One of these was the making of the film, *The Adirondacks, The Land Nobody Knows.* Many of the scenes in this documentary about the need to keep the Adirondacks pristine contained aerial shots of high peaks and remote lakes.

One of his most enjoyable projects was making "Santa Claus" landings, particularly for his daughter-in-law, Abby, who taught kindergarten. One time he even had Walt with him wearing antlers. Fortunately, though, the helicopters nearly paid for themselves with jobs—risky as well as fun.

Just going to Savage Island, where we were married in a very simple ceremony because of the island rules, was lots of fun. We normally went up the Vermont side of Lake Champlain where we always checked out the wildlife center which attracted migrating birds. During one trip from the New York side of the lake, we came over a mountaintop to immediately spot Fort Ticonderoga. A huge crowd was below watching a reen-actment. When Dick saw smoke coming from a cannon, he hoped that it wasn't live ammunition because we seemed to be in direct line to it. We did notice they were scurrying around the cannon as we high-tailed out of their range.

Dick was very fond of helicopters. One of his saddest days was when he flew to Florida for a trade-up to find out that the one that served him so well was bought for a tuna-vessel. It was to be used to find porpoises which led them to huge tuna feeding areas with the porpoises often getting inadvertently caught, too. He also knew the salty sea air would mean a short life for that helicopter.

Dick had a good flying friend at the GE Research lab, Dave Fink, who went in with him on buying a Stearman. Fortunately, they were not into doing air shows with it, but they did have a lot of fun with it. I went up in it once with Dick. He was doing a four-point roll and when we were upside down, I quickly realized I had not hooked up my seatbelt. I was able to hold onto the bottom of my seat until we righted ourselves again. But I will never forget the panic and relief I felt.

Then there was the time we were flying in his Super Cub to Alaska before he put in a navigation system. In the Cub, the pilot is in front and the passenger in back. I was handing him some maps for VFR (vision) flying when one got caught in the wires that went into the wings when turning. Fortunately Dick turned again and it came back out so I could retrieve it off the wire. I gave the lame excuse that I was tired after sleeping in a small hangar near the Canadian border. We had landed there to refuel to find there was a sign on the door that they would be there the next day. He had known it would be a landing on grass, but he hadn't counted on the grass being so high. With quite a bit of maneuvering, we landed safely. It was not late in the day—so what did he do? He spotted the mower and used it to mow the field for several hours. When the owner showed up the next morning, we got the gas at half price and off we went.

But back to Dave Fink. He was well-known around the lab for building a robot to celebrate GE's 100th birthday at the request of CEO Reg Jones. But that wasn't enough fun for Dave. He decided GE should have a hot air balloon to visit plants all across the country. GE did not want the liability, though, so Dick went in with him to buy the balloon, even emblazoning it with the huge GE logo. They would rent it to GE for use. The problem was neither knew how to fly it. It had no sooner arrived than they got a GE call to fly it over the Saratoga Race Track during its famed Travers Race with record crowds. Balloons, of course, go with the wind, unless tethered. But, no, GE wanted the balloon over the track at post time.

They were not about to lose their first big sale. So Dick, well-rehearsed with wind currents as was Walt, decided on a location about a half-mile from the track that might make it possible to get the balloon over the track at post time. Dave and his pickup crew with the balloon van were to be at a nearby parking lot which would be in line with the wind direction. Walt, who was known for his skill at flying anything, knew the only control he would have over the balloon would be managing its air volume which would allow him to go up or down. So off he went. Dick and I followed him in the helicopter. The wind was steady and not changing direction. In about fifteen minutes, Walter not only made it to the track, but it was exactly at post time. Moreover, he was at the start when the bugle sounded. Walt even responded by losing some air to bring attention to it. The crowd roared and he responded with much hand waving—so much so that he missed the parking lot. Soon Walt was starting over the mountains and heading into the Adirondacks.

Dick flew ahead, looking for a spot to land. He saw a small highland pasture slightly in line with the wind direction and went back to point it out to Walt. If Walt didn't make it in that field, the last one before the mountains took over, it would mean gathering up the remains of the balloon in the trees. We were tense as we watched Walt approach the edge of the field. There was a huge, fat maple halfway in the field with nothing but other trees around it. It was then Walt released the air at the top of the tree and leaned out the basket for more leverage to fall to the right. The balloon basket teetered on the top of the tree and then slid down the bulky tree on the field side intact. Walt waved up to us that he was O.K.

So we went in search of Dave and the van crew to direct them to the field. In the meantime, what did Walt do? It is an incredible coincidence but it turned out when he went to the house at one end of the field, he found an excited group of people who were having a retirement party for a GE woman. Walt, quick on his feet, declared GE was there to help celebrate. So when we got there with Dave on the road in, he was enjoying a huge feast of fried chicken with all the salads and trimmings and a full keg of beer. We also became part of the celebration and GE never knew how they excelled at public relations that day. For several years, Dave and Dick enjoyed the extra revenue they made with the balloon.

During the Reg Jones era, the GE century balloon was popular. Dave—who now knew how to fly it—and his crew were asked to go to many GE plants across the U.S. But when Jack Welch became CEO, it was a different story. He was famous for saying you can't rest on your laurels, and he proceeded to deride the past. The first thing he did was fire Dee Logan, who had been in charge of celebrating GE's 100-year anniversary. I was at headquarters at the time and working for a vice president who had hoped to replace Jones. He defied Welch and hired the GE balloon to land, of all places, on Welch's new helipad.

That publicity stunt won some points with those group VPs still loyal to Jones, but soon they found themselves out of a job as Welch took full control of all the businesses to meet his vision of becoming a financial company. My VP, Bob Kurtz, and his staff, including me, were also out of a job. But that was O.K. The 1980 Olympics were coming and I would go there. After leaving Connecticut, I would come back to Schenectady and find another job in marketing for gas turbines.

It was not long after the Olympics—and all that bike riding Dick did around the eastern U.S. and Europe—that his right hip began giving him major trouble. He had already had the left hip replaced, a normal operation that went well. He attributed that to running, pole vaulting in high school, and football at Cornell. So this time he decided to go for the latest hip replacement technology at Brigham in Boston. The end result of this was eleven right hip operations over fifteen years. It began with a Harvard Medical study recommending strong, healthy men who wanted to get back on their feet in record time would be helped by radiation which would limit calcium buildup. Ten volunteers were needed and Dick became one of them. Well, the radiation did work. So much so that he (*and I assume others, though they wouldn't tell me*) also had to have bone marrow taken from other parts of his body to fill in what was lost. The loose prosthesis had to be packed another time. Then two staph infections resulted in a need for spacers. When he was back for the prosthesis, a pathologist came in to report the infection was not gone so it was spacer time again. We spent one winter pouring $30,000 worth of newly-released, FDA-approved antibiotics down an open port. Finally, that spring the pathologist said the infection was gone.

What did Dick do most of the time in between operations? He continued to bike ride and even bought a recumbent. During one of these times he found himself on the hood of a car. Not long after, we were back in the emergency room for a broken femur. By this time, he was referred to a surgeon who only took patients referred by other doctors. His waiting room was something out of a *Star Wars* bar. There was a huge guy with a bull fighter's jacket on who had been shot in his Texas Ranger job by a coyote bringing in illegal immigrants. The doctor not only put a new hip in him but took out three bullets which other doctors would not do for fear of possible paralysis. Then a lady so overweight that she had to come in the door sideways came in to thank him for replacing her hip. A ninety-two-year-old woman with osteoporosis wanted to have a new hip even though he told her it would only last a year or so.

Dick was, to me, the most normal. But when the surgeon showed us photos of what he had done to get Dick back on his feet, I was amazed. He had put in a cadaver bone. He had so deftly wired it in one-inch gaps that it seemed to me he had to have skinned his whole leg to do so. But then he told us his hobby was parqueting. But Dick was back on his feet and never had to go back. It worked.

He did give up biking and skiing, but this "never stand still" guy always found something to do. When his long-distance vision began to fail, he quit driving on major highways or at night. He still had good short-distance vision. A loss of hearing, which he attributed to an early construction life of jackhammering, didn't stop him either. He started reading books. In just one year, he logged some ninety books read on his Kindle. His collection of military books, starting with the original classic *On War* by Carl von Clausewitz filled our shelves along with nature books and fiction thrillers. He also stepped up his interest in photography. He had a huge collection of early Leica cameras and was early to join the digital age for close-up work.

This period of our life also settled me down. I began writing for fun and he was very supportive of it, especially when I won the George Garrett Fiction award in 2008 for *River Roots*. But when I started to watch soap operas in the afternoon, he was disgusted. His description of *Young and Restless* as "Old and Lecherous" and *Bold and Beautiful* as "Old and Timid" cured me.

Every wild fern or flower I imported to plant around the house was photographed by him in larger-than-life detail. One of his favorite projects was working with Sarah Clarkin, who ran the huge nature preserve park in Moreau dedicated to saving the rare Karner blue butterflies. Dick not only took photographs there but documented the growth of acres of lupine planting for several years. Years later Sarah would be married to his son, Rick.

Dick was always happy letting nature reign rather than be mowed down. We never had a lawn at our house on the edge of Adirondack Park. The only domestic flowers were on the deck. The surroundings were filled with trilliums, tiger lilies, lady slippers, Jack-in-the-pulpits, and every kind of fern that grew in the northeast. An architect from Saratoga designed the house to fit in with the environment. It was a large A-frame structure with a high-roofed living room braced with steel rods. From his office on the first level, Dick could look out to the stream below, knowing that he had spent a lot of his early life working on bridges, roads, and canal locks. Not only did the land cost him $11,000 because it was filled with old cars, but no one wanted wetlands either. He always laughed when my mother complimented him on a nice house but questioned why he would want to drive through a swamp to get to it. In West Virginia, wetlands were drained and used to raise crops.

His love of nature was tested over the years by beaver families clogging up the causeway across two of the ponds. They had a habit of plugging the two pipes under the causeway, which, if not cleaned out, would wash out the road to the house. His sense of humor included self-deprecation. After years of both of us cleaning out the pipes, he decided it was time to electrify the entrance with just enough power to deter them. An elaborate fixture with batteries was installed. It worked for about a week. Then he drove by to see his fixture was in disarray. He found that the $100 battery was nestled among the mud and branches clogging the pipes. It was then he jokingly said he was awarding them his engineering degree from Cornell.

His sense of humor knew no bounds at times. When he joined his buddies, mostly pilots, at the Roc's bar near the airport, he offered to buy the rounds if they succeeded in his egg challenge. He could swallow an egg whole and chew it up, shell and all. The only person that came close to matching his flawless performance was Mike Collins, who flew helicopters for New York state officials. Fortunately, Dick did not do this with his grandchildren. Instead, he taught them how to balance a spoon on their nose. His grandson, Nicholas, was quite good at it even though he attributed it to inheriting Dick's substantial nose. His granddaughter, Heidi, has probably created a generation of kids in her classroom who accomplished the skill.

This one tough guy left us on July 8, 2016. It is best just to remember his love of nature, humor, and integrity. He did not stand still when seriously ill, either. I know I will never see anyone fight for life as hard as he did despite the odds.

From the visit to the emergency room with a wait of seven hours before he passed out with a major abdominal aneurism to a midnight surgery at Albany Medical where he was resuscitated during surgery three times to setting a record of needing twenty-six pints of blood to recover to six months of dialysis with two cases of infected ports—through it all, he kept fighting. His son was able to get there the first night and his daughter flew in the next day. I know it was as hard on them as it was on me watching him quietly suffer. And in that determination to live, he continued to do it with grace and even humor.

Dick's two sisters were not your average "Cookie Cutter" kids either. His older sister, Betty, while in high school was part of the pioneering days of television, appearing in plays, then summer stock, and then a career as a *Guiding Light* TV star. Susan, his younger sister, a Cornell graduate and Kennedy scholar, was an early crusader for civil rights, starting with the 1965 Selma to Montgomery march and a "good trouble" career promoting equality in federal government positions.

Dick's genes live on with his son and daughter. They proved their love of nature at an early age. His son, Rick, was in his late teens when he hiked in Nepal and began some serious rock climbing. He became Deputy Commissioner of the Adirondack Park Agency which Dick, some forty years earlier, had served as recreation advisor for when the Forever Wild Act was passed by the New York State legislature. And I am sure Rick has left tracks on every footfall his father made in those mountains. His daughter, Kathe, who was in the Peace Corp in Africa, drove herself to Alaska right after college. One of her early trips was a six-day kayaking trip in which she never saw another human being.

So, it was a very, very sad day for us when Dick fought his last battle. But he left us with some very special memories. He lives on in a lot of people, including his four grandchildren—Nicholas, Heidi, Brandon, and Lara—and three great-grandchildren—Kylie, Brody, and Ella.

About Atmosphere Press

Founded in 2015, Atmosphere Press was built on the principles of Honesty, Transparency, Professionalism, Kindness, and Making Your Book Awesome. As an ethical and author-friendly hybrid press, we stay true to that founding mission today.

If you're a reader, enter our giveaway for a free book here:

SCAN TO ENTER
BOOK GIVEAWAY

If you're a writer, submit your manuscript for consideration here:

SCAN TO SUBMIT
MANUSCRIPT

And always feel free to visit Atmosphere Press and our authors online at atmospherepress.com. See you there soon!

About the Author

A native of West Virginia, **MARY KUYKENDALL** won the 2008 George Garrett Fiction Award for River Roots, a collection of short stories about growing up in rural America. It was published by the Texas Review Press. Mary has written over 300 short stories, fiction and non-fiction. Some have won individual awards, been published in chapbooks, small press, and magazines, and others have been read at venues such as the Chicago Book Fair, the William Faulkner Festival in New Orleans, and Soul-Making in San Francisco. Mary also self-published a book about her speechwriting career at GE, titled *Rebuilding the GE House Jack Blew Down*. She holds a bachelor's degree from West Virginia University and a master's from the State University of New York, Albany.

www.ingramcontent.com/pod-product-compliance
Lightning Source LLC
Chambersburg PA
CBHW031115160726
47991CB00004B/1388